NATIVE
HERITAGE

NATIVE HERITAGE

Personal Accounts by American Indians, 1790 to the Present

EDITED BY
ARLENE HIRSCHFELDER

*Foreword by Jeffrey L. Hamley
Director, Native American Program
Harvard University*

MACMILLAN • USA

A portion of the author's royalties will be donated to the Education/Scholarship Fund of The Wampanoag Tribe of Gay Head (Aquinnah), Massachusetts. Aquinnah, the ancestral Wampanoag name for Gay Head, means "land under the hill."

~~~~~~

MACMILLAN
A Simon & Schuster Macmillan Company
15 Columbus Circle
New York, NY 10023

Library of Congress Cataloging-in-Publication Data
Native heritage : personal accounts by American Indians, 1790 to the present / edited by Arlene Hirschfelder ; foreword by Jeffrey L. Hamley.
    p. cm.
    Includes bibliographical references and index.
    ISBN 0-02-860412-1
    1. Indians of North America.   2. Indians of North America—Biography.
I. Hirschfelder, Arlene B.
E77.N355   1995   94-42494
970.004'97—dc20   CIP

Macmillan books are available at special discounts for bulk purchases for sales promotions, premiums, fund-raising, or educational use.

10 9 8 7 6 5 4 3 2 1

Printed in the United States of America

40574

To three treasures: Dennis, Brooke, Adam

To a dream-team of editors:
Mary Ann Lynch and Laura Wood

My thanks also to publishers and authors
whose works are included here and to
Joshua McKeon,
research assistant extraordinaire.

CONTENTS

LAND AND ITS RESOURCES

LANGUAGE

NATIVE EDUCATION

TRADITIONAL STORYTELLING

TRADITIONS

FOREWORD

$\Large A$rguably, the most eloquent, powerful portrayals of Native Americans are pieces written or narrated by Natives themselves. In *Native Heritage*, authentic accounts of Native voices are brought together, some for the first time, for readers who want an informed, authentic perspective about Native Americans. This work is significant because until recent times the literature has been largely devoid of firsthand perspectives. Missing has been the voice of the people themselves. Little known, however, is the fact that many Native peoples spoke for the historical record directly through interviews, writings, autobiographies, narratives, and other means. But this record has for the most part been overlooked. *Native Heritage* succeeds in bringing to readers important materials representing a rich diversity in tribal affiliation, culture, time period, and breadth of human endeavor.

The need for accurate, authentic materials on Native Americans has never been greater. The materials in *Native Heritage* can serve as a counterpoint to the legacy of misinformation and stereotyping about Native peoples that has been generated over the years. Unfortunately, misperceptions about Native peoples are not only inaccurate, they are damaging to Native peoples, especially children. This volume is invaluable not only to anyone with an interest in history accurately told, but also to educators, like myself, who teach about Native Americans. I have found in my own teaching of graduate and undergraduate students at Harvard University and elsewhere that narrative accounts effectively represent the Native experience in a way that interpretative material, no matter how well informed, can seldom accomplish.

Underlying the need for accurate materials is the increased interest in Native Americans that has blossomed in the classroom, scholarly circles, and popular culture. As many observers have pointed out, this phenomenon was precipitated by the celebration of the quincentennial of Columbus's arrival in the Western Hemisphere. A debate, at times intense, focused on the appropriate observance of this event and the role of Native peoples in the commemoration. The debate caused many people to ponder, perhaps for the first time, the meaning of Columbus's arrival and the physical and cultural genocide of Native peoples that ensued. Accompanying the quincentennial phenomenon were newspaper editorials, scholarly articles, educational materials, books, and documentaries on Native Americans. A second "discovery" of Native peoples occurred. Although a multitude of materials in various media were produced, the impact in counteracting enduring stereotypes was negligible at times. Misperceptions about Native peoples seem especially resistant to change.

Since first contact, Native peoples have been the subject of gross stereotypes based more upon misunderstanding than informed knowledge. To give a sense of the magnitude of the misunderstanding, some of those first Europeans conjectured that the aboriginal peoples encountered might be exotic creatures of some unknown type rather than human beings. Early misperceptions formed a basis for stereotyping, racism, and cultural repression. Cultural genocide was practiced against Native peoples by European powers who came into contact with Natives, despite the fact that they little understood the people and cultures they had encountered. The historical record is quite disturbing, in fact, in instances of repression and silencing of the Native voice.

One of the greatest crimes against humankind was the deliberate and systematic destruction of Native peoples' cultural legacy by various rival colonizing powers and missionaries. The burning of Meso-American texts, the melting of cultural objects for their precious metal content, and the repression of Native languages and religions are but a few examples. Further, in more recent times the perspective of Native peoples has been dominated by the viewpoints of non-Natives. Particularly problematic has been the liberty taken by ethnologists, linguists, and other scholars to interpret the voice of Natives and to represent their oral traditions to the world. Oral tradition has always been of central importance to the cultural expression of Native peoples. It was the means by which key elements of cultural and lingual transmission occurred. Fortunately, recent contributions by leading scholars have sought to bring to the forefront the actual writings of Native peoples lost in obscurity up to this time. The hope is that more of these overlooked and uncelebrated materials will be brought to light—as this book does so well.

Despite a staggering legacy of misinformation to overcome, materials that portray Native Americans authentically are finally becoming easily accessible to general readers and educators. Arlene Hirschfelder's anthology contributes significantly to the growing body of literature portraying Native peoples accurately and sensitively and promises to become a valued resource for anyone interested in Native American studies and American history in general.

Jeffrey L. Hamley
Director, Native American Program,
Harvard University

INTRODUCTION

This anthology was created for one purpose: to share a small fraction of the rich and unique heritage of native peoples from many different regions of the United States and Canada. Herein readers are offered personal accounts of the inner mechanisms of native societies whose lifeways have worked for millennia.

All of the pieces included are narrated or written by native people and illuminate the basic experiences of Native Americans before and after contact with non-Indians. There are excerpts from autobiographies, interviews, opinion pieces, articles, oral and written history, speeches, and congressional testimony, plus curricular materials and school essays. Almost half the selections have been excerpted from as-told-to or self-written autobiographies. According to H. David Brumble III, a scholar who has written extensively about the subject, more than six hundred autobiographical narratives by Indians north of the Mexican border have been published. Since he registered that count in his 1988 work *American Indian Autobiography* many more native life stories have found their way into print. Professionally trained anthropologists, historians, and linguists as well as amateurs have collected and edited the life stories of native men and women. Unfortunately, not all of these works are easy to locate. Many exist only in out-of-print scholarly journals; others are embedded in histories or ethnographies. Some are tucked into Native American journals and newspapers with limited circulation or in almost-impossible-to-know-about pamphlets or other unlikely sources.

Native Heritage brings together for the first time a selection of these evocative personal accounts by men and women of varied tribal affiliations and from different times and places. Within each section they have been arranged in chronological order, beginning with the earliest dated piece. Although the actual published dates range from 1790 to the present, many of the pieces describe experiences and Indian ways dating from much earlier times, handed down through the oral tradition. The citations at the end of each entry tell readers where to find the entire account, as well as other writings. For instance, the excerpts by Dave Elliott ("Land and its Resources"), Peter Webster ("Language"), and John Thomas ("Native Education") come from *Children of the First People*, a volume containing the personal narratives of seven other elders who also describe their cultures, childhoods, hopes, and fears. The excerpts by Sarah Tutube ("Family") and Ruby Dunstan ("Land and its Resources") are taken from *Our Chiefs and Elders*, a book that includes the personal accounts of forty other men and women who reminisce about living in bighouses, traveling in log canoes, living off the land, speaking native languages, and celebrating potlatches. For readers wanting to find other works, the bibliography at the end of the book provides additional sources of native-authored materials.

Readers of this anthology need to be forewarned about the controversy inherent in a volume of this nature. Scholars have hotly contested the validity of some native autobiographies. They debate the merits of narrated or as-told-to autobiographies (as distinguished from those that are written) in which a recorder/editor transcribed what was spoken orally by an Indian man or woman. In his work on Indian autobiography, Brumble discusses the "absent editor" strategy where the editor creates "the fiction that the narrative is all the Indian's own . . . that the Indians speak to us without mediation" (Brumble, 1988, 75–76). Too often, in fact, the hands of the editors are heavy even though their presence appears to be absent.

While some editors may never alter or consciously control the narrative, other editors do influence the selection of content, intentionally soliciting information or insisting on the discussion of certain subjects. Some editors change chronology, even though the narrators themselves place little value on the chronological ordering of experiences. Sometimes editors even delete what to them seem unimportant details or phrases. Some scholars argue that editors who add, subtract, condense, reorder, rephrase, or stylize spoken material contaminate the Indian narrator's authentic voice.

Imperfections of these narrated cultural life histories notwithstanding, they still afford the ultimate insider's view and offer some sense of what it is to see the world through Indian eyes. Over twenty years ago, scholar Herbert Phillips affirmed the value of personal narrative:

> . . . life history is still the most cognitively rich and humanly understandable way of getting at an inner view of culture. [No other type of study] can equal the life history in demonstrating what the native himself considers to be important in his own experience and how he thinks and feels about that experience. *Current Anthropology* 14, no. 2 (1973): 200–201.

A gender imbalance exists in works narrated or written by native people: more have been written by men than by women. In 1982, Margaret B. Blackman, an anthropologist who recorded the life histories of Florence Edenshaw Davidson and Sadie Brower Neakok, wrote, "for native North America as a whole there are more than three times the number of male life histories as female life histories." She points out that the imbalance is due in part to the fact that male anthropologists (who historically outnumbered female ones) worked more closely with male members of the cultures they studied than with female members. Add to this the fact that most of the early historians, missionaries, and linguists of Indian life were also male, and, like male ethnographers, worked primarily with men in native cultures; factor in attitudes prevalent among anthropologists and other observers who found the lives of native men more interesting and significant than the lives of women; and include the reluctance of many native women to call attention to themselves—and the reasons for the disparity seem quite evident. Regrettably, this anthology reflects that imbalance even though every possible effort was made to locate selections by native women.

Native Heritage is organized into eight topical chapters. They illustrate what Ella Deloria, a Dakota anthropologist, calls in her book, *Speaking of Indians*, "a scheme of life that worked." Native American cultures survived an onslaught of government policies and wars dedicated to destroying them. What sustained them were traditional family and clan relationships; a profound identification and kinship with homelands and all the species that shared the earth; native languages perpetuating their cultural identities and spiritual values; traditional native educational practices; traditional stories in hundreds of native communities handing down histories, cultural traditions, and oral laws from elder to younger generations; shared traditions and customs that maintained each tribe's uniqueness; and religious practices that have been as necessary to native life as breathing. This anthology provides a number of brief selections for each of these culture-sustaining topics. Taken together, these narratives create a cultural mosaic of distinctive, valid, and dynamic lifeways. They also enable the reader to piece together a picture of Euro-American culture as viewed through the sharp eyes of observant native people. Their comments about cultural practices dramatically different from their own are insightful and often moving.

The last chapter, "Discrimination," includes writings by native people objecting to the numerous ways native cultures have been denied the dignity of their history and the distinctiveness of their multiple ethnicities. Sixteen native writers take aim at stereotypes and caricatures that haunt native peoples and diminish their humanity.

And finally, a point about terminology: There is probably no book about Indian people published in the last few years that has not at some point in its making debated what term to use when referring to the first peoples who lived in what is now called North America. This anthology is no different. Although the term "Native American" is now popular with some Indians and non-Indians, readers are mistaken in believing that it is the only correct term to use. Tim Giago, publisher of the Rapid City, South Dakota–based *Indian Country Today*, an important Indian advocacy newspaper, states his paper's position in his December 4, 1991, "Notes from Indian Country" editorial: "We use 'American Indian,' 'Indian,' or 'Native American,' but we prefer to use the individual tribal affiliation when possible." Indeed, following this

editorial, *Indian Country Today* received many phone calls and letters pointing out that anyone born in the Americas can refer to himself as Native
American. The term "Native American" is used most commonly in the
United States, especially in bookstores and by publishers. But keep in mind
that both collective terms, Native American and American Indian, beg the
issue. They each refer to hundreds of different cultures who prefer to be
called by their tribal names.

Over the centuries, spellings of the names of Native American nations
have varied considerably and still do. The Blackfeet in the United States
prefer this spelling to Blackfoot, more popular in Canada. The Kwagiutls in
Canada prefer that spelling to Kwakiutl, more commonly used by writers in
the United States. *Native Heritage* preserves the spelling preferred by the
native writer. Tribal names may vary as well as spellings. Ojibway (or Ojibwa
or Chippewa) are the same people as the Anishinabe, the traditional name
by which they have always known themselves. Some of the people popular-
ly called Eskimo prefer to call themselves Inuit, their name in the Inuit language. Many prefer "Yupik" or "Yupik Eskimo"—the designation of the
Eskimos of southwestern Alaska—or "Inupiat"—the indigenous people
from northwest Alaska. The people formerly called Papago have officially
declared a preference for Tohono O'odham, the name they originally called
themselves in their own language. The popular name Sioux is often used by
narrators and writers, although many of the people to whom the name refers
prefer the original Dakota or Lakota.

This anthology employs the tribal name used by the writer at the time the
piece was narrated or written. In some cases, the spelling has been changed
to conform to modern-day usage: *Sak* in place of *Sauk*, *Paiute* in place of *Piute*,
and so on. This anthology also preserves the grammar and spellings used in
the original sources, which in some cases is not "perfect" English. For a
number of native people whose excerpts appear in this volume, English is a
second language, and this fact is reflected in their writings.

Arlene Hirschfelder
March 1995

FAMILY

Navajo family in Canyon de Chelley. Navajo Reservation, Arizona. Photograph by Joseph C. Farber.
National Museum of the American Indian, Smithsonian Institution.

"With us the family was everything." Tom Johnson, a centenarian from the Pomo Tribe of northern California, further told a sociologist in 1940 that a man without a family would be poorer than a worm. For Native American peoples, this has always been true. The traditional family is large. Native people were and still are born into clans that relate them to many people, not just to their immediate or nuclear family consisting of mother, father, and siblings. Families include grandparents, aunts who are like mothers, uncles who are like fathers, cousins who are like brothers and sisters, married and adopted relatives who are like blood. Membership in a clan relates one to many people in close ways even though the biological connection barely exists. Clan members do not necessarily reside in the same place, but clan bonds were and are strong, obligating members to assist one another. Even distant clan members are considered relatives in times of crisis and ceremony, on both happy and sad occasions.*

The selections following offer a wide range of insights into traditional Indian family values. In her description of kinship—"the all-important matter"—Ella Deloria (Dakota) offers a highly accesible explanation of native social organization. Maxidiwiac (Hidatsa), Emory Sekaquaptewa (Hopi), and Paula Gunn Allen (Laguna Pueblo/Sioux) describe traditional clan organizations in their respective tribes, while Neil Buck (Apache) talks about "playing family" as a child. Vivian One Feather (Lakota) and Sarah Tutube (Tuquot) give pointers on proper terminology and the behavior required of clan members; Arthur L. McDonald (Oglala Sioux) describes the clash between traditional native family values and Judeo-Christian family values. Ed Edmo (Shoshone-Bannock) and Ardith Morrow (Chippewa) look at the ways contemporary mobility, alcoholism, and non-Indian agencies threaten traditional Indian families.

3

HIDATSA KINSHIP

~~~~~~~~~~

Maxidiwiac

Maxidiwiac, a Hidatsa woman, was born about 1839 in an earthen lodge by the mouth of the Knife River in what is now North Dakota. Interviewed between 1908 and 1918 by Gilbert L. Wilson, she tells about kinship among the Hidatsa people.

We Hidatsas do not reckon our kin as white men do. If a white man marries, his wife is called by his name, and his children also, as Tom Smith, Mary Smith. We Indians had no family names. Every Hidatsa belonged to a clan; but a child, when he was born, became a member of his mother's, not his father's clan.

An Indian calls all members of his clan his brothers and sisters. The men of his father's clan he calls his clan fathers, and the women, his clan aunts. Thus I was born a member of the *Tsistska*, or Prairie Chicken clan, because my mother was a *Tsistska*. My father was a member of the *Meedeepahdee*, or Rising Water clan. Members of the *Tsistska* clan are my brothers and sisters, but my father's clan brothers, men of the *Meedeepahdee*, are my clan fathers, and his clan sisters are my clan aunts.

These relations meant much to us Indians. Members of a clan were bound to help one another in need, and thought the gods would punish them if they did not. Thus, if my mother was in need, members of the *Tsistska* clan helped her. If she was hungry, they gave her food. If her child was naughty, my mother called in a *Meedeepahdee*, to punish him, a clan father, if the child was a boy; if a girl, a clan aunt; for parents did not punish their own children. Again, when my father died, his clan fathers and clan aunts it was who bore him to the burial scaffold and prayed his ghost not to come back to trouble the villagers.

Another clan relative is *makutsatee*, or clan cousin. I reckon as my clan-cousins all members of my tribe whose fathers are my clan fathers. Thus my mother, I have said, was a Prairie Chicken; my father, a member of the *Meedeepahdee*, or Rising Water clan. Another woman, of what clan does not matter, is also married to a *Meedeepahdee*; her children will be my clan cousins, because their father, being a *Meedeepahdee*, is my clan father.

Clan cousins had a custom that will seem strange to white people. We Indians are proud, and it makes our hearts sore if others make mock of us. In olden times if a man said to his friend, even in jest, "You are like a dog," his friend would draw his knife to fight. I think we Indians are more careful of our words than white men are.

But it is never good for a man not to know his faults, and so we let one's clan cousins tease him for any fault he had. Especially was this teasing common between young men and young women. Thus a young man might be unlucky in war. As he passed the fields where the village women hoed their corn, he would hear some mischievious girl, his clan cousin, singing a song taunting him for his ill success. Were anyone else to do this, the young man would be ready to fight; but seeing that the singer was his clan cousin, he would laugh and call out, "Sing louder cousin, sing louder, that I may hear you . . ."

Young men going out with a war party had to take much chaffing from older warriors who were clan cousins. My brother was once out with a party of fifty, many of them young men. They were fleeing from a big camp of Sioux and had ridden for two days. The second night one of the younger men, a mere lad, fell asleep as he rode his pony. An older warrior, his clan cousin, fired a gun past the lad's ear. "Young man," he cried, "you sleep so soundly that only thunder can waken you!" The rest of the party thought the warrior's words a huge joke.

From: Maxidiwiac. *Wa-Hee-Nee: An Indian Girl's Story, Told by Herself.* St. Paul, Minnesota: Webb Publishing, 1921.

PLAYING FAMILY

Neil Buck

Neil Buck, an Apache born in Arizona about 1863, was interviewed by anthropologist Grenville Goodwin in the 1930s. In his narrative, given through an interpreter, he tells about the family games he played with other children when he was young.

I can remember one time when I was a small kid and we were playing family. One girl of the *náyòdèsgìjn* clan was my mother. There were a lot of other small boys there. We made three or four little piles of dirt, calling them cans of tulibai (a drink). When we finished one can, we leveled the pile. Soon we all said we were drunk. I was my mother's only child, so I was alone. The other boys pretended to start a fight with me. They all jumped on me. The girl who was my mother hollered at the top of her lungs as a grown person would do, "The [clan] boys are fighting my son." She shouted so loud that my real mother and older sister back at camp heard her. They used to laugh afterward when they told about it. But we didn't play at having clan blood-feuds. Maybe some children did, but then, you know, not all children play in the same way.

From: Goodwin, Grenville. *Social Organization of the Western Apache*. Chicago: University of Chicago, 1942.

WITHOUT THE FAMILY
WE ARE NOTHING

Tom Johnson

Tom Johnson, a Pomo man over 100 years old living in northern California, spoke to B. W. Aginsky, a sociologist from New York University, about the importance of family to his people. In his lifetime Johnson saw the whites move into his territory, the Spanish raids, the massacres of his people by the whites, and the herding of his people into reservations.

What is a man? A man is nothing. Without his family he is of less importance than that bug crossing the trail, of less importance than the sputum or exuviae. At least they can be used to help poison a man. A man must be with his family to amount to anything with us. If he had nobody else to help him, the first trouble he got into he would be killed by his enemies because there would be no relatives to help him fight the poison of the other group. No woman would marry him because her family would not let her marry a man with no family. He would be poorer than a newborn child; he would be poorer than a worm, and the family would not consider him worth anything. He would not bring renown or glory with him. He would not bring support or other relatives with him. The family is important. If a man has a large family and a profession* and upbringing by a family that is known to produce good children, then he is somebody and every family is willing to have him marry a woman of their group. It is the family that is important. In the white ways of doing things the family is not so important. The police and soldiers take care of protecting you, the courts give you justice, the post office carries messages for you, the school teaches you. Everything is taken care of, even your children, if you die; but with us the family must do all that.

Without the family we are nothing, and in the old days before the white people came the family was given the first consideration by anyone who was about to do anything at all. That is why we got along. We had no courts, judges, schools, and the other things you have, but we got along better than

---

*Specialized occupation requiring years of training and preparation. Other specializations are deer hunter, gambler, doctor, and money manufacturer.

you. We had poison, but if we minded our own business and restrained ourselves we lived well. We were taught to leave people alone. We were taught to consider that other people had to live. We were taught that we would suffer from the devil, spirits, ghosts, or other people if we did not support one another. The family was everything, and no man ever forgot that. Each person was nothing, but as a group joined by blood the individual knew that he would get the support of all his relatives if anything happened. He also knew that if he was a bad person the headman of his family would pay another tribe to kill him so that there would be no trouble afterward and so that he would not get the family into trouble all of the time.

That is why we were good people and why we were friends with the white people when they came. But the white people were different from us. They wanted to take the world for themselves. My grandfather told me that the white people were homeless and had no families. They came by themselves and settled on our property. They had no manners. They did not know how to get along with other people. They were strangers who were rough and common and did not know how to behave. But I have seen that these people of yours are even worse. They have taken everything away from the Indians, and they take everything away from one another. They do not help one another when they are in trouble, and they do not care what happens to other people. We were not like that. We would not let a person die of starvation when we had plenty of food. We would not bury our dead with no show. We would kill another person by poisoning him if he was an enemy, but we would not treat a stranger the way they treat their own brothers and sisters. Your people are hard to understand. . . . What is wrong with you? The white people have the land. They own the courts, they own everything, but they will not give the Indians enough money to live on. It is hard to understand.

With us the family was everything. Now it is nothing. We are getting like the white people, and it is bad for the old people. We had no old peoples' homes like you. The old people were important. They were wise. Your old people must be fools.

_____

From: Aginsky, B.W. "An Indian's Soliloquy." *American Journal of Sociology*, volume 46 (1940–41): 43–44.

KINSHIP WAS THE
ALL-IMPORTANT MATTER

Ella Deloria

Ella Deloria, a Yankton Dakota woman born in 1889 on the Yankton Sioux Reservation in South Dakota, studied at Columbia University's Teachers College where she received a bachelor of science degree in 1915. At the request of Franz Boas, the preeminent American anthropologist, she translated and edited some written texts in the Sioux language in the late 1920s. Her work in assisting Boas as a research specialist in American Indian ethnology resulted in several books. Ella Deloria's in-depth knowledge of Dakota life enabled her to write about it with uncommon intelligence, clarity, and sensitivity. In Speaking of Indians, *published in 1944, she explains how the "rules" of kinship enable the Dakota people to coexist peacefully.*

All peoples who live communally must first find some way to get along together harmoniously and with a measure of decency and order. This is a universal problem. Each people, even the most primitive, has solved it in its own way. And that way, by whatever rules and controls it is achieved, is, for any people, the scheme of life that works. The Dakota people of the past found a way: it was through kinship.

Kinship was the all-important matter. Its demands and dictates for all phases of social life were relentless and exact; but, on the other hand, its privileges and honorings and rewarding prestige were not only tolerable but downright pleasant and desirable for all who conformed. By kinship all Dakota people were held together in a great relationship that was theoretically all-inclusive and coextensive with the Dakota domain. Everyone who was born a Dakota belonged in it; nobody need be left outside.

This meant that the Dakota camp-circles were no haphazard assemblages of heterogeneous individuals. Ideally, nobody living there was unattached. The most solitary member was sure to have at least one blood relative, no matter how distant, through whose marriage connections he was automatically the relative of a host of people. For, in Dakota society, everyone shared

9

affinal relatives, that is, relatives-through-marriage, with his own relatives-through-blood.

Before going further, I can safely say that the ultimate aim of Dakota life, stripped of accessories, was quite simple: One must obey kinship rules; one must be a good relative. No Dakota who has participated in that life will dispute that. In the last analysis every other consideration was secondary—property, personal ambition, glory, good times, life itself. Without that aim and the constant struggle to attain it, the people would no longer be Dakotas in truth. They would no longer even be human. To be a good Dakota, then, was to be humanized, civilized. And to be civilized was to keep the rules imposed by kinship for achieving civility, good manners, and a sense of responsibility toward every individual dealt with. Thus only was it possible to live communally with success; that is to say, with a minimum of friction and a maximum of goodwill. . . .

All peoples have their own ways of showing courtesy. The fundamental idea is the same: to be gracious and kind and to show goodwill; to abide by the rules of etiquette as practiced by the majority, so as not to appear boorish or queer. The idea is one; the methods are many. Among the Dakota it was rude to speak another's name boldly; one must employ the kinship term instead. Not "Swift Cloud," but "*My uncle*, Swift Cloud," or where there was danger of ambiguity, simply, "My uncle." Furthermore, it was improper to plunge into conversation without first using the polite term of kinship. . . . Consequently, it was of the utmost importance to know the right term for each person and not be caught unaware. Naturally it followed that the right terms of address were always the people's preoccupation.

This need of first establishing proper relationship prevailed even when one came to pray. It gave a man status with the Supernatural as well as with man. The Dakota words "to address a relative" and "to pray" are familiar everyday words. It was not until a few years ago, when I was listing and defining verb stems for linguistic students at Columbia University, that suddenly I realized that the two words are not really two; they are one. *Wacekiya* means both acts. Nor is that surprising, come to think of it, for a Dakota did not like to deal with another person without first avowing his own status, as a relative mindful of the duties incumbent on him as such, while also reminding the other of his. *Wacekiya* implies that in every meeting of two minds the kinship approach is imperative; it is the open sesame to any sincere exchange of sentiment between man and his neighbor or man and his God. Once the channel is clear between the two, a reciprocal trust and confidence are guaranteed. It is tantamount to smoking the peace pipe; in fact, to smoke ceremonially is to *wacekiya* . . . .

But the use of kinship terms of address was only the beginning, important as it was from the standpoint of etiquette. The core of the matter was that a proper mental attitude and a proper conventional behavior prescribed by kinship must accompany the speaking of each term. As you said "Uncle"— or "Father" or "Brother"—in either address or reference, you must immediately control your thinking of him; you must assume the correct mental attitude due the particular relative addressed, and you must express that attitude in its fitting outward behavior and mien, according to accepted convention. Thus, term, attitude, behavior, in the correct combinations, were what every member of society must learn and observe undeviatingly. They were standard and inexorable; they had always been. One simply was born into their rule and conformed to them invariably as a matter of course. The more correctly he could do this, whatever the personal sacrifice involved at times, the better member of the group he was, the better his standing as a Dakota, the higher his prestige as a person.

What did this exacting and unrelenting obedience to kinship demands do to the Dakotas? It made them a most kind, unselfish people, always acutely aware of those about them and innately courteous. You see, everyone who would be rated well as a relative had to *make* himself feel and act always in the same way. "How monotonous!" you might say. But it wasn't. For there was as great a variety of permissible attitudes and behaviors as there were kinds of relatives. In that way all the natural human impulses were satisfied: to be gay and irresponsible, or flippant and rude, for fun; to be excessively respectful and dignified; to enjoy being foolish, as with those called father and mother; and then to turn serious and protective as with sons and daughters. . . .

For the most part, then, everyone had his part to play and played it for the sake of honor, all kinship duties, obligations, privileges, and honorings being reciprocal. One got as well as gave. Thus kinship had everybody in a fast net of interpersonal responsibility and made everybody like it, because its rewards were pleasant. There were fewer rebels against this system than you might think, since as I have said, social standing and reputation hinged on it. Only those who kept the rules consistently and gladly, thus honoring all their fellows, were good Dakotas—meaning good citizens of society, meaning persons of integrity and reliability. And that was practically all the government there was. It was what men lived by.

From: Deloria, Ella. *Speaking of Indians*. New York: Friendship Press, 1944.

TIOSPAYES: LAKOTA RELATIVES

∿∿∿∿∿∿∿∿∿

Vivian One Feather

Vivian One Feather, Lakota, the principal curriculum writer at the Oglala Sioux Culture Center at Red Cloud Indian School in Pine Ridge, South Dakota, created a unit in 1972 entitled "Tiospayes." The follow-ing selection, from that unit, focuses on the Oglala Lakota [Sioux] of the Pine Ridge Indian Reservation in South Dakota and describes how every Lakota person is born to have many relatives.

Every Lakota person is born having many relatives. The *tiospaye* is the name given to indicate a person's relatives. There is more than just the father and mother of a child. The *tiospaye* includes grandparents, aunts, uncles, cousins, and all married and adopted relatives.

As the Lakota person grows up, his relatives will give him help. All the families of a *tiospaye* give attention to the young child growing up. Their interest in a growing person is their hope for a respectful, full-grown adult. Later in life, the young Lakota will be given responsibility to help his rela-tives when it is necessary.

During all of Lakota history, the *tiospaye* has been very important. Even though some families have left the Pine Ridge Indian Reservation, the *tiospaye* is as important as ever. Everyone should know their relatives. When a person is acquainted with his relatives, he knows where he comes from and who he is. This is why the *tiospaye* is so important.

The word in Lakota, TIOSPAYE, can be broken into two meaningful small words:

Ti—a short form of Tipi, meaning house

Ospaye—group of people separated from a larger or the main body of people

The *tiospaye* is a small group of persons who are related to each other. A long time ago, this small group traveled separately from the rest of the main body of the Lakota. Each *tiospaye* claimed its own hunting territories and kept peace with each other. One man was the headman of the group. He was the leader of the *tiospaye*.

During the summer, all the *tiospayes* would come to camp in one place. It was time for a large buffalo hunt and the Sun Dance. Allof these *tiospayes*, together, were the Oglala Sioux people. To use a more formal and older word, all the *tiospayes* would be the main body of Lakota people. . . .

Throughout their history, the Oglala Sioux people had never stayed together as a main body of people. Small groups or *tiospayes* would break away to live by themselves. Sometimes the separation was short, but usually it was a permanent break. When such a separation took place, the followers of the headmen, who left the main body of people, were mainly his own relatives. . . .

When Woope, daughter of Mahpiyate, came before the people as White Buffalo Calf Woman, she brought two very important laws: Respect Your Elders and Take Care of Your Relatives. These laws were the basis for the *tiospaye*. When wise men speak at feasts and meetings, they have always reminded the people that these laws are important to the Oglala Sioux people. . . .

There are older, mature persons who are well respected throughout their life. They are usually listened to, their advice on serious matters is important, and they are willing to help out their relatives. When anything disrupts the *tiospaye*, it is these persons who help things return to normal. The feasts, memorial dinners, and pow-wows are put on by these people. With the help of all the relatives, the *tiospaye* continues to exist.

It is proper to say another relative's name correctly. It is not proper to call a relative wrongly. So, the correct *Wowahecon* must be used. In using the correct *Wowahecon* word, a speaking person will show his relationship to another person. The listening person will understand the relationship between himself and the speaker. In the *tiospaye*, each person has a particular relationship to each member of the group. He has a definite place.

After a person is born, he is taught the proper *Wowahecon*. As the child grow, he first learns the proper names for his closest relatives. This includes his father, mother, grandparents, aunts, and uncles.

After the child is grown-up, he will marry and accept other people as his married relatives. He must address these married relatives in a certain way. There are also certain manners he must learn about his in-laws.

At last, he is a part of the whole society and will have a relationship to young and old people. These persons will be addressed in a certain way, also. By this process, each person becomes related to many people and learns a correct word to identify other people.

From: One Feather, Vivian. *Tiospaye.* A Curriculum Materials Resource Unit. Pine Ridge, S.D.: Oglala Sioux Culture Center, Red Cloud Indian School and Spearfish, S.D., Black Hills State College, 1972.

HOPI CLANS

Emory Sekaquaptewa

Emory Sekaquaptewa, a member of the Hopi tribe of northern Arizona, was born and raised in a small Hopi village and has taught at the University of Arizona. In this excerpt from an essay published in 1972, he explains the traditional Hopi clan system, or extended family units, and its functions.

Under the Hopi system, the female is the progenitor of the clan, and all offspring belong to the mother's clan. Clan leadership and offices are inherited by men, although female members do have important ceremonial functions. Since the transfer of clan office is restricted to the clan membership, the line of transfer is from brother to brother, or from a maternal uncle to his nephew. This relationship also exists outside of the natural family, because the kinship terms "brother" and "sister" are extended to persons who are, by the rule, members of the clan. For instance, "brothers" include male offspring of female members of the clan who are in Anglo terms cousins to each other by one or more degrees, with a loose requirement that such offspring be of the same generation. This extension means, further, that a man's "nephews" include not only his natural sister's (or sisters') sons, but also the male children of all of his clan children.

Each clan recognizes a female head or matriarch, who is usually the eldest woman—but not necessarily so, since a younger woman may be designated as head by virtue of the exercise of clan discretion—and her home becomes the clan home. In the case of the ruling clan, this home is referred to as *Kii-kyam*, which means "their home" and suggests literal possession of the village. The female head of this home who, in Hopi terms, is either a sister or "niece" to the *kikmongwi* [office of chief], takes her place beside him as *goh-aya* (keeper of the fire). In other words, she maintains the spiritual home fires, and it is this house which serves a great many of the *kikmongwi's* functions of office, as well as the place where his ceremonial paraphernalia is kept. This is the house that the *kikmongwi* calls "home," rather than the house where he, his wife, and children live. Ceremonially, the *kikmongwi*, as is true of other married men, is a stranger in the house of his wife and children, since he is not a member of their clan. Furthermore, his teaching of clan knowledge and practices takes place in his clan home, and in the homes of his female clan relatives, where members gather from time to time. It should be noted that these gatherings are generally informal and casual, hardly ever of a formal nature except when a ceremony is conducted.

From: Sekaquaptewa, Emory. "Preserving the Good Things of Hopi Life," In *Plural Society in the Southwest*. Edited by Edward H. Spicer and Raymond H. Thompson. New York: Weatherhead Foundation, 1972.

TRADITIONAL INDIAN
FAMILY VALUES

Arthur L. McDonald

Arthur L. McDonald, a member of the Oglala Sioux tribe in South Dakota, is well published in academic circles. In an article, published in 1978 when he was a faculty member at the California School of Professional Psychology, Dr. McDonald addressed the question, "Why do Indian students drop out of college?" According to McDonald, who based his analysis on interviews with Indian students, some dropped out because of the clash between their traditional Indian (extended) family value system and the Judeo-Christian (nuclear) family values present in the institution.

In the Judeo-Christian culture, the family carries with it rather clear-cut definitions and expectations of responsibility. When a child becomes an adult in the white world he is on his own. He is expected to be independent and legally responsible. If one's brother participates in socially unacceptable behavior, shame is brought to the family name. This seems to miss the point. There is little shame or concern about the fact that the behavior was detrimental to the community. Rather, a great deal of emphasis is placed upon the reputation of the family. At the same time, misfortune occurring to outlying members of the family such as grandparents, uncles and aunts, or cousins, while unfortunate, is not considered the responsibility of the family. The basic principle seems to be: "You take care of yours and I'll take care of mine," with *mine* being defined as the immediate nuclear family.

In the traditional Indian value system, the family is much extended in terms of caring and responsibility. Aunts are often considered to be mothers, uncles are called fathers, and cousins are brothers and sisters of the immediate family. Clan members are considered "relatives." The philosophical generalizations must be understood between the two systems before any of the rest of the values can truly make sense. In the Western European tradition the greatest good has been the development and perpetuation of the self. Although some lip service is paid by Christian doctrines to praying for others, primarily the ultimate objective is personal salvation. Day-to-day behavior is geared toward this objective in terms of economics, religious values, education, status needs and family relationships. This produces an extremely competitive, consumptive, exploitative interaction with the environment and with other people.

The traditional Indian culture by contrast has as the ultimate good the survival of the tribe. The individual is expendable in the sense that one does what is good for other people at the sacrifice of individual goals and objectives. This is seen in a variety of behaviors, such as the "giveaway" ceremony. Those that have share what they have with others as a point of honor. . . . In Indian culture, people give away their material possessions in an act of sharing. The more you share, the more honor, prestige, and status you enjoy. Indians do not collect material things for status symbols as found in white culture. . . . it is often difficult for people living in an academic environment to understand the tremendous sense of responsibility a student may have towards apparently distant relatives. In Indian culture, if one is asked to help, he simply cannot refuse. Thus, a student who receives a phone call telling him he is needed at home will go. The threat of receiving an "F" for a course is of little relative importance. If he is needed, he is needed. The fact that administrative officials do not understand what is real and true to the Indian community is very bewildering to the Indian student.

A final consideration that is difficult for the white community to understand involves most of the philosophical, sociological, psychological and religious values previously discussed. In the rural white community, the fact that a son or daughter has left the farm to pursue a college education is pointed out with great pride. The family will make great sacrifices to get their children into higher education. In small communities everyone points with civic pride to those who have "gone on and amounted to something." In the more traditional reservation culture, if a child makes the decision to leave the reservation and go to the university and get a white man's education, the community is not enthusiastic. In other words, it is a clear-cut decision that the person has made to reject the old traditional ways and go the white man's road. It is generally assumed that the person is lost to the traditional community. Many Indian students who have completed their degrees find it extremely difficult to return to their reservation to work. . . . There is mistrust toward an Indian who has obtained an education, and the educated Indian must face a rather continuous attack by family as well as others for having that education.

From: McDonald, Arthur L. "Why Do Indian Students Drop Out of College?" In *The Schooling of Native America*. Edited by Thomas Thompson. Washington, D.C.: American Association of Colleges for Teacher Education in collaboration with the Teacher Corps, U.S. Office of Education, 1978.

FAMILY IS A MATTER OF CLAN MEMBERSHIP

^^^^^^^^^^

Paula Gunn Allen

Paula Gunn Allen, a Laguna Pueblo/Sioux woman born in 1939 near Cubero, New Mexico, is one of the foremost Native American literary critics. The author of numerous volumes of poetry, a novel, and scholarly works, in her 1986 collection of essays, The Sacred Hoop: Recovering the Feminine in American Indian Traditions, *she defines "family" in the Native American context, a wholly different construct from non-Indian families.*

"Family" did not mean what is usually meant by that term in the modern western world. One's family might have been defined in biological terms as those to whom one was blood kin. More often it was defined by other considerations; spiritual kinship was at least as important a factor as "blood."

Membership in a certain clan related one to many people in very close ways, though the biological connection might be so distant as to be practically nonexistent. This facet of familial ordering has been much obscured by the presence of white Christian influence and its New Testament insistence that the term "family" refer to mother, father, and children, and those others who are directly related to mother and father. In this construct, all persons who can point to common direct-line ancestors are in some sense related, though the individual's distance from that ancestor will determine the "degree" of relationship to other descendants of that ancestor.

Among many American Indians, family is a matter of clan membership. If clan membership is determined by your mother, and if your father has a number of wives, you are not related to the children of his other wives unless they themselves happen to be related to your mother. So half siblings in the white way might be unrelated in an Indian way. Or in some tribes, the children of your mother's sister might be considered siblings, while those of your father's brother would be the equivalent of cousins. These distinctions should demonstrate that the concept of family can mean something very different to an Indian than it does to a non-Indian.

In gynecentric systems, a unified household is one in which the relation-

A family reunion at the Catholic church hall on the Prairie Band Potawatomi Reservation in Kansas. Photograph by M. K. De Montaño.

ships among women and their descendants and sisters are ordered; a split household is one in which this is not the case. A community, then, is an ordering of sister relationships that determine who can depend on whom for what. Male relationships are ordered in accordance with the maternal principle; a male's spiritual and economic placement and the attendant responsibilities are determined by his membership in the community of sisterhood. A new acquaintance in town might be asked, "Who is your mother?" The answer identifies the person and determines the ensuing relationship between the questioner and the newcomer.

From: Gunn Allen, Paula. *The Sacred Hoop: Recovering the Feminine in American Indian Traditions.* Boston: Beacon Press, 1986.

I WAS TAUGHT BY MY MOTHER

^^^^^^^

Sarah Tutube

Sarah Tutube, a Tuquot woman from Port Albion, British Columbia, Canada, was born in 1910. Around 1988, in a conversation with David Neel, a Kwagiutl professional photographer, she emphasized the critical role of extended family in raising children.

I was taught by my mother, grandmother, and grandaunts. They'd come and teach me how to raise up my children. I'm forever thankful for that—the two of them never got tired of telling me over and over again. There was one old guy, this great-grandfather, who used to come in with a cane in his hand, walking in, very old, and he taught me how to raise up my children—what to do and what not to do with them to raise them up to be good men and hard-working, not lazy. So I'm grateful for that old man and another old lady—grandaunt. She used to tell me about my relations. We used to have to know our relationship [genealogy]. We had to respect our relationship up to our fourth cousin. It was a no-no for the first cousin, a no-no for the second, a no-no for the third, and the fourth was just excusable when you couldn't pull them apart any more: "Well, it's alright." They're not teaching them any more like I was taught by my mother, that's the problem. I used to teach mine. The old people used to tell me to pass things on to the next generation when I grew up. My mother used to say, "When they're just big enough to sit up and watch you, don't you ever do something that's wrong because your child will do the same as you're doing." That's the way she taught me.

From: Neel, David. *Our Chiefs and Elders: Words and Photographs of Native Leaders*. Vancouver: UBC [University of British Columbia] Press, 1992.

THERE IS STRENGTH
IN THE FAMILY

Ed Edmo

Ed Edmo, a Shoshone-Bannock poet born in 1946, travels extensively telling native traditional stories to children of all ages as well as teaching about Native American values. In a piece published in the Lakota Times *on December 26, 1989, he explains how some Indian families, split apart by mobility and alcoholism, have found strength in both the old and new ways.*

What parents should help their children understand about being an Indian in a modern world is difficult to say. On one hand, the family will try to hold onto cultural values that have been handed down. On the other hand some of those values have changed.

It used to be that when a family saw visitors approaching, the family would automatically get up and begin cooking a full meal for the visitors. The visitors were then expected to sit and eat; if the family did not cook a meal then the visitor would be offended. Also, if the visitors refused to eat, the family who cooked the meal would be offended.

Nowadays, a family will just ask the visitors, "Have you eaten yet?" If the visitors have eaten, the family would not cook. If the visitors hadn't eaten, the family would cook. Some traditions have changed to suit modern times.

Some families live in a modern, electric house, yet have their children go into the mountains to learn to hunt and gather berries or attend ceremonies at the reservation if they live in an urban setting. Children will watch television and play Pac-Man, but they will also dance at powwows. The child is living in two worlds. Some Indians say that we can take the best of both worlds for ourselves. Maybe the child will be taught how to Indian dance at home and do school work to the best of their ability. Many of the leaders stress to the children the importance of getting an education (meaning a formal education) because the old people know that education offers a person more choices for employment. . . .

There is strength in the family. The Indian family will remain true to itself. Even if there is severe alcoholism, the family will band together to try and help the alcoholic. There is a strong family allegiance among Indian people.

With the modern society, Indians have become mobile and have moved away from the reservations, families, and ceremonial grounds and the extended family are left behind. Many young people do not know where to turn for help in the cities. They were taught who their relatives are on the reservation, but when they move to the city they have no relatives.

Usually those Indians will turn to other Indians for help or to the social programs set up for the whites. Many Indians ask what tribe you are when they meet you, then ask your name to try and find out if you are one of those long-lost relatives.

There is some sense of trying to find our roots in the concrete of a city. In some Indian families, a member will move to the city, find a job, then write home. The economics on the reservation are sometimes so poor that the whole family will find a way to get to the city where a relative is working and will move in on them. I have seen nine people sleeping in a one-bedroom apartment because their relative was lucky enough to have found a job.

On many reservations there is a lack of meaningful recreation for the young people. There is not enough money to fund centers for the youth. Many youths find the reservation boring and will try to escape the reservation through using alcohol or drugs, or sniffing paint, gas, or glue. All this leads to feeling bad about yourself, and when you feel bad, you want to escape. Many Indians try to get rid of their feelings of inadequacy by drinking a lot. What drinking does is split up the family. Many Indian women will not put up with the alcoholism of their husbands or mates. The women will kick out their men. A woman will be left raising children by herself.

When I was young I was told that I should stay with my family. This is a new social problem among Indians. Traditionally, a couple would stay together for life . . . like eagles. But with the introduction of alcohol and mobility of the society, many families do not stay together.

For many reasons Indians have lost their traditional methods for dealing with the world. Many Indians are now looking for their "Indian tradition." They are finding strength in the old ways and beginning to pass those ways on to their children. Today positive parenting is based on both old and new ways. We need to find the best of both worlds.

From: Edmo, Ed. "Finding the Best of Two Worlds; Teaching Children about Prejudice." *Lakota Times*, December 26, 1989.

WE WENT TO LIVE
WITH GRANDMA

∿∿∿∿∿∿∿∿

Ardith Morrow

Ardith Morrow, a member of the Minnesota Chippewa Tribe, published this story, "My Grandmother," in the September 1990 issue of Speaking of Ourselves: Ni-Mah-Mi-Kwa-Zoo-Min, *a publication of the Minnesota Chippewa Tribe. Her work involves interviewing and writing about elders in the Cass Lake, Minnesota, area. Ardith Morrow describes an experience repeated countless times in Indian families across the United States.*

When I was a little girl, my sisters and brothers and I all went to live with my mother's mother in Boy River, Minnesota. Out of respect for my mother and father, I won't go into any detail about why we went to live with grandma, but we were delivered into her care by a couple of uncles. . . . But without any questions, she took us in and did her best to feed and clothe all seven of us.

. . . I don't think she had much money at this time, but she provided us with a roof over our heads and fed us fry bread, wild rice, rabbits, tea and bullheads [catfish], bullheads, and more bullheads. I don't ever recall where she got the darn bullheads from, but we sure had plenty of them to eat!

. . . As her favorite granddaughter, I always slept with grandma and my other two sisters shared a bed together and my brothers shared a bed with my uncles. We didn't have much room, but that was our way of doing things and we were happy.

Grandma couldn't speak much English—she talked to us in a mixture of our Indian language and English. It didn't take us long to pick up her way of talking and pretty soon we were all talking a mixture of Ojibwe and English. She was always busy doing something—cooking, making birchbark baskets, cleaning house, skinning rabbits, tanning hides, and making braided rugs from old rags. She would talk to us the whole time she was doing something.

Oh, those were happy days there in Boy River with grandma. We had fun living and playing and just being children. However, all good things must come to an end and one day the Welfare Department came and removed all of us children from grandma's care. They said she was old and poor and couldn't really properly care for seven grandchildren. So we were all taken and put into foster homes. How we cried when they took us away from grandma. Didn't they realize how happy we were that we were all together? Didn't they realize how much we loved grandma and how much she loved us? Didn't they realize how important our family was to us? Didn't they realize how much we were learning about our culture and our heritage and our language?

Our family was never the same after that. Thanks to Social Services we were split up and two of my brothers were adopted to strangers and we didn't see them for years. We lost our Indian language and to this day none of us speak it as well as we did when we were living with Grandma.

From: Morrow, Ardith. "My Grandmother." In *Speaking of Ourselves* (Minnesota Chippewa Tribe newspaper) 16, no. 6 (September 1990): 6.

LAND AND ITS
RESOURCES

Mitten Buttes in Monument Valley Navajo Tribal Park, located north of Kayenta, Arizona, near the Arizona/Utah border. Photograph by Guy Weber.

*N*ative peoples are related not only to family, but to homelands. The nature of this relationship spells the difference between Indian and non-Indian. Non-Indians buy and sell land and treat it as a quantifiable and measurable entity or as something to be exploited. To Indian people, land is sacred. Traditional accounts relate why certain sites are particularly sacred: a location may be the place where the creation of a specific tribe took place, or the place where an important revelation occurred, or a place through which one enters the next life. Sacred land contains plants, herbs, and waters possessing healing powers, and at certain sites people communicate with the spirit world through prayers and offerings. Native peoples live on and use sacred land, but they are obligated to perform ceremonial or ritual duties in order to honor the land and all it provides.

American Indian people recognize a social contract between themselves and other animals and fish, birds, and plants. When the need is great, Indians will take the life of a tree, animal, or fish, but they use every last shred or eat every edible part of the living creature they kill, and may honor them with rituals after killing them for food. All of these reasons explain why Indians hold steadfastly to their homelands and do battle with Euro-Americans, the federal government, ranchers, miners, the park systems, and others over land ownership.

In this section, Arapooish (Crow) describes why Crow country was exactly the right place to live, and Buck Austin (Navajo) explains how life of all kinds was created. Charles A. Eastman (Dakota) takes us maple sugaring in Minnesota, while Helen Sekaquaptewa (Hopi) tells how her people grew corn. Victor Sarracino (Laguna Pueblo) describes the importance of deer, and Helen Slwooko Carius (Eskimo) discusses the whale. Gregory A. Cajete (Tewa) sees native people's relationship to land as a profound identification with place.

A number of these pieces deal with the ways native people protect their resources. Lucy Thompson (Klamath/Yurok) explains how laws governing fish dams on the Klamath River guaranteed salmon for Indians up and down the river. Dave Elliott (Saanich) and Moses Cruikshank (Athabascan) relate how their peoples were taught not to waste any part of a kill. And Ruby Dunstan (Lytton band of Nlaka'pamux) focuses on the relationship between spirituality and protecting the environment. Selections by Don C. Talayesva (Hopi), Reuben Snake, Jr. (Winnebago), and Louie H. Dick, Jr. (Umatilla) address the need to take care of water, the giver of life.

THERE IS NO PLACE LIKE CROW COUNTRY

_{∧∧∧∧∧∧∧∧∧∧∧∧}

Arapooish

In the late summer of 1833, Arapooish, a Crow chief born about 1790, described to Robert Campbell of the Rocky Mountain Fur Company why his beloved homeland stretching from the Black Hills to the Rocky Mountains was the ideal place to live.

The Crow country is a good country. The Great Spirit put it exactly in the right place; while you are in it you fare well; whenever you are out of it, whichever way you travel, you fare worse. If you go to the south, there you have to wander over great barren plains; the water is warm and bad, and you meet the fever and ague. To the north it is cold; the winters are long and bitter, and no grass; you cannot keep horses there, but must travel with dogs. What is a country without horses? On the Columbia they are poor and dirty, paddle about in canoes, and eat fish. Their teeth are worn out; they are always taking fishbones out of their mouths. Fish is poor food. To the east, they dwell in villages; they live well; but they drink the muddy water of the Missouri—that is bad. About the forks of the Missouri is a fine country; good water; good grass; plenty of buffalo. In summer, it is almost as good as the Crow country: but in winter it is cold; the grass is gone; and there is no salt weed for the horses. The Crow country is exactly in the right place. It has snowy mountains and sunny plains, all kinds of climate and good things for every season. When the summer heats scorch the prairies, you can draw up under the mountains, where the air is sweet and cool, the grasses fresh, and the bright streams come tumbling out of the snowbanks. There you can hunt the elk, the deer, and the antelope, when their skins are fit for dressing; there you will find plenty of white bear and mountain sheep.

In the autumn, when your horses are fat and strong from the mountain pastures, you can go into the plains and hunt the buffalo, or trap beaver on the streams. And when winter comes on, you can take shelter in the woody bottoms along the rivers; there you will find buffalo meat for yourselves, and cottonwood bark for your horses; or you may winter in Wind River Valley, where there is salt weed in abundance.

The Crow country is exactly in the right place. Everything good is to be found there. There is no place like Crow country.

From: Irving, Washington. *Adventures of Bonneville*. New York: G. P. Putnam, 1849.

MAPLE SUGARING

Charles A. Eastman

Charles A. Eastman—or Hakadah, "Pitiful Last,"as his Santee Dakota relatives first called him—was born in 1858, the youngest of five children. Soon after his birth his mother died. He grew to become one of the best-known Indians of his time, receiving a bachelor of science degree from Dartmouth in 1887 and a medical degree from Boston University in 1890. The author of eleven books and numerous articles, in his first book, Indian Boyhood, *published in 1902, he reminisces about maple sugaring in Minnesota.*

With the first March thaw the thoughts of the Indian women of my childhood turned promptly to the annual sugar-making. This industry was chiefly followed by old men and women and children. The rest of the tribe went out upon the spring fur-hunt at this season, leaving us home to make the sugar.

The first and most important of the necessary utensils were the huge iron and brass kettles for boiling. Everything else could be made, but these must be bought, begged, or borrowed. A maple tree was felled and a log canoe hollowed out, into which the sap was to be gathered. Little troughs of basswood and birchen basins were also made to receive the sweet drops as they trickled from the tree.

As soon as these labors were accomplished, we all proceeded to the bark sugar house, which stood in the midst of a fine grove of maples on the bank of the Minnesota river. We found this hut partially filled with snows of winter and the withered leaves of the preceding autumn, and it must be cleared for our use. In the meantime a tent was pitched outside for a few days' occupancy. The snow was still deep in the woods, with a solid crust upon which we could easily walk; for we usually moved to the sugar house before the sap had actually started, the better to complete our preparations.

My grandmother worked like a beaver (or rather like a muskrat, as the Indians say; for this industrious little animal sometimes collects as many as six or eight bushels of edible roots for the winter, only to be robbed of his store by some of our people). If there was prospect of a good sugaring season, she now made a second and even a third canoe to contain the sap. These canoes were afterward utilized by the hunters for their proper purpose.

During our last sugar-making in Minnesota . . . my grandmother was at work upon a canoe with her axe, while a young aunt of mine stood by. We boys were congregated within the large, oval sugar house, busily engaged in making arrows for the destruction of the rabbits and chipmunks which we knew would come in numbers to drink the sap . . . I was then too young to do much except look on; but I fully entered into the spirit of the occasion, and rejoiced to see the bigger boys industriously sharpen their arrows, resting them against the ends of the long sticks which were burning in the fire, and occasionally cutting a chip from the stick. In their eagerness they paid little attention to this circumstance, although they well knew that it was strictly forbidden to touch a knife to a burning ember.

Suddenly loud screams were heard from without and we all rushed out to see what was the matter. It was a serious affair. My grandmother's axe had slipped, and by an upward stroke nearly severed three fingers of my aunt, who stood looking on, with her hands folded upon her waist. As we ran out to the old lady, who had already noticed and reproved our carelessness in regard to the burning embers, pursued us with loud reproaches and threats of whipping. This will seem mysterious to readers, but is easily explained by the Indian superstition, which holds that such an offense as we had committed is invariably punished by the accidental cutting of some one of the family.

My grandmother did not confine herself to canoe-making. She also collected a good supply of fuel for the fires, for she would not have much time to gather wood when the sap began to flow. Presently the weather moderated and the snow began to melt. The month of April brought showers which carried most of it off into the Minnesota river.

Now the women began to test the trees—moving leisurely among them, axe in hand; and striking a single quick blow, to see if the sap would appear. The trees, like people, have their individual characters; some were ready to yield up their life-blood, while others were more reluctant. Now one of the birchen basins was set under each tree, and a hardwood chip driven deep into the cut which the axe had made. From the corners of this chip—at first drop by drop, then more freely—the sap trickled into the little dishes.

It is usual to make sugar from maples, but several other trees were also tapped by the Indians. From the birch and ash was made a dark-colored sugar, with a somewhat bitter taste, which was used for medicinal purposes. The box-elder yielded a beautiful white sugar, whose only fault was that there was never enough of it.

A long fire was now made in the sugar house, and a row of brass kettles suspended over the blaze. The sap was collected by the women in tin or birchen buckets and poured into the canoes, from which the kettles were

Indian Sugar Camp by artist Seth Eastman (1809–1875). Courtesy of the New York Historical Society, New York City.

kept filled. The hearts of the boys beat high with pleasant anticipations when they heard the welcome hissing sound of the boiling sap! Each boy claimed one kettle for his especial charge. It was his duty to see that the fire was kept up under it, to watch lest it boil over, and finally, when the sap became sirup, to test it upon the snow, dipping it out with a wooden paddle. So frequent were these tests that for the first day or two we consumed nearly all that could be made; and it was not until the sweetness began to pall that my grandmother set herself in earnest to store up sugar for future use. She made it into cakes of various forms, in birchen molds, and sometimes in hollow canes or reeds, and the bills of ducks and geese. Some of it was pulverized and packed in rawhide cases. Being a prudent woman, she did not give it to us after the first month or so, except upon special occasions, and it was thus made to last almost the year around. The smaller candies were reserved as an occasional treat for the little fellows, and the sugar was eaten at feasts with wild rice or parched corn, and also with pounded dried meat.

From: Eastman, Charles A. *Indian Boyhood*. Boston: Little, Brown and Co., 1902.

LAWS OF THE FISH DAM

^^^^^^^^^^^^^^^^

Lucy Thompson

Lucy Thompson, or Che-na-wah Weitch-ah-wah, was a Klamath/Yurok woman born at Pecwan village in what is now the state of California. Of "highest birth," she was trained by her father from an early age in all the "mysteries and laws of [her] people." In her book about her people, published in 1916, she argues that she is in a "better position than any other person to tell the true facts of the religion." This she does in describing the strict sacred laws governing the ceremony of putting in fish dams before the ritual White Deerskin Dance, part of the annual World Renewal cycle of ceremonies during which people prayed that earth's resources continue. The strict laws, while guaranteeing that Indians from up and down the river could harvest the salmon, also insured that enough fish were left for spawning the following year.

When the fish dam is put in, they have very strict laws governing it. There are nine traps which can be used, one belongs to Lock [name for the one that handles the putting in of the fish dam] and his relatives, one to Lock-nee [one of Lock's male ritual helpers] and his relatives, one to Nor-mer [maiden of high birth involved in the rituals of putting in the fish dam] and her relatives, and so on down the line. These families come in the morning and each one takes from the trap that which belongs to them, as many salmon as they need, by dipping them out with a net that is made and used for this purpose, and they must not let a single one go to waste, but must care for all they take, or suffer the penalty of the law, which was strictly enforced. After all these get their salmon, then comes the poor class, which take what they can use, some of which they use fresh and the rest they cut up, smoke them lightly, then they are dried. When they are dried up they are taken down and packed in large baskets with pepperwood leaves between each layer, so as to keep the moths out of them, and then they are put away for the winter. The Indians from up the river as far as they are able to come can get salmon, and down the river the same. In these traps there get to be a mass of salmon, so full that they make the whole structure of the fish dam quiver and tremble with their weight, by holding the water from passing through the lattice work freely.

After all have taken what they want of the salmon, which must be done in the early part of the day, Lock or Lock-nee opens the upper gates of the traps and lets the salmon pass on up the river, and at the same time great numbers are passing through the open gap left on the south side of the river. This is done so that the Hoopas on up the Trinity River have a chance at the salmon catching. But they keep a close watch to see that there are enough left to effect the spawning, by which the supply is kept up for the following year.

Katamin Rapids, Siskiyou County, Oregon, 1898. Smithsonian Institution, National Anthropological Archives.

From: Thompson, Lucy. *To the American Indian.* Eureka, California: self-published, 1916.

WATER IS AS PRECIOUS AS FOOD

Don C. Talayesva

Don C. Talayesva (or Sun Chief), a Hopi born in 1890, retained a traditional outlook despite years of Euro-American education. In his autobiography, written by Talayesva himself in English (published in 1942), he provides descriptions of Hopi daily life and rituals as well as the premium Hopi people place on life-sustaining water, a scarce resource in his homeland of northern Arizona.

I also learned that water is as precious as food. Everybody appeared happy after a rain. We small boys rolled about naked in the mud puddles, doused each other with water, and built little gardens. In this way we used too much of the water from the little pond on the west side of the village where the women went to wash their clothes and the men to water their stock. Our parents scolded us for wasting water and once my mother spanked me on account of my dirty shirt.

During droughts we had strict rules for the use of water. Even small children were taught to be careful, and I saw mothers bathe their babies by spitting a little water upon them. By watching the old people I learned to wash my face with a mouthful of water—it is the safest way to wash without waste.

Sometimes water gave out. Then the old men went with their burros to distant springs while the women stayed up all night taking turns to catch a little trickle that came from the Oraibi spring. My grandfather told me about the cistern that he had chiseled out of the solid rock to catch the rain that fell on the mesa shelf. He said that he had done this hard work when he married my grandmother in order that his children and grandchildren might not suffer from thirst. My mother went daily to this well to fetch water. In winter she cut out chunks of ice from the rock ledges and brought them in on her back.

Whenever it rained, we were told to take our little pots and go out on the ledges, scoop up puddles, and fill the cisterns. There were about one hundred of these hewn out of the solid rock by our ancestors. The people pointed out that water is essential to life and taught us what to do in the desert whenever we became so dry and thirsty that we could neither spit nor swallow. Then one should cut twigs off a cottonwood tree and chew them, eat the inner bark of the cedar, or hold dried peaches in his mouth.

The importance of water was impressed upon us by the way the old men prayed for rain and planted pahos [prayer sticks] in the springs to please the water serpents and to persuade them to send larger streams to quench our thirst. We were reminded that all the dances and ceremonies were for rain, not for pleasure. They were held in order to persuade the Six-Point-Cloud-People to send moisture for our crops. Whenever we had a good rain, we were told to show our happy faces and consider ourselves in favor with the gods. We made it a point never to praise the weather on fair, dry days. Whenever it rained during or just after a dance, the people praised highly those who had taken part in the performance. If a strong wind followed the dance, it was a sign that the people who had invited the Katchinas* to come and dance had a bad heart or had done some evil.

We were told that there is health-giving power in water, and that it is a good practice to bathe in cold water, to wash our hands and faces in snow, and to rub it upon our bodies to make them tough. The old people said that warm water made wrinkles and shortened life. I saw them setting bowls of water outside to become ice-cold before using it for a bath. Some old men would go out naked and rub snow all over their bodies. My grandfathers, my aunts' husbands, often took me outside and rolled me in the snow on winter mornings. Talasemptewa did it many times. At first I thought he disliked me, but my mother explained that it showed he loved me and wanted me to grow up strong, healthy, and brave. I could see there was healing power in water, too, for my grandfather often had people drink warm water in order to vomit and clear their systems. Sometimes he prescribed a person's own fresh urine for stomach trouble. Water, then, like food, meant life and health and was a special gift from the gods to use in the desert. The gods could withhold rain when they were displeased, or they could pour it on us when they wanted to.

From: Simmons, Leo W. *Sun Chief: Autobiography of a Hopi Indian.* New Haven: Yale University Press, 1942.

---

*Katchina is a Hopi term (but now a general term by which the outside world calls all spirits of this kind among Pueblo peoples) referring to powerful spirits of the dead that possess power which human beings do not to bring rain and affect fertility, curing, and growth. Although they are not worshiped, they require veneration and respect from human beings or they will not respond. Ritual dancing, ceremonial behavior, and a "good" heart compel Katchinas to reciprocate with the desired benefits.

SHEEP ARE THE HIGHLIGHTS
OF CREATION

~~~~~~~~~~

Buck Austin

Buck Austin, a traditional Navajo medicine man born in 1909 who "grew up in the midst of sheep herds," retold how things were created in his homeland, especially sheep, horses, and cattle. This story was published in 1954 after the federal government, reacting to drought, erosion, and overgrazing on the Navajo reservation in the 1940s, forced a livestock reduction program on the Navajos. To people like Buck Austin, for whom raising stock was the only way of life he knew and sheep, goats, and horses his bank account, livestock reduction spelled tragedy, and Austin and others wept and mourned their loss.

Since time immemorial our grandfathers and our grandmothers have lived from their herds—from their herds of sheep, horses, and cattle, for those things originated with the world itself. With the world the blue sky was created, and between the world and the sky the male and female mountains were placed, with the male and the female water. It is thus that things were created, each with its mate. Placed together were the many kinds of water and the child of the water. Then it was discussed how life might be put into these things. At the time people came into being, there did not exist that upon which we live.

But in the east, Sierra Blanca peak was set, adorned with goods, and Mount Taylor was placed in its position, adorned with jewels. Our mountains were established. San Francisco Peak was set up, adorned with abalone shell; it was a goods-mountain. And La Plata Mountain was established; it was a jet-mountain. Huerfano was another of those adorned with goods, and it too was established as our mountain. Gobernador Knob was set up, adorned with jewels. In this way were the sacred mountains set as a foundation. The question was then, how could holy songs be made that would impart life? What kind of holy prayers would there be? When these questions were asked it was then that the holy songs wherein one says, "With it I live," came to be. And afterward came the prayers. It was then that things took on life.

After these things came about, then were the plants brought into being, male and female. The male plants were created with their mates, and the dark clouds likewise. The male rain was created with its mate; the dark mist was created with its mist. And the prayers followed in the wake of these creations. A rainbow arched over to where Blanca Peak had been placed. It extended to Mount Taylor, to San Francisco Peak, and to La Plata Mountain. It stretched to all of the sacred mountains, and by means of crystal the sacred mountains communicated with one another. It was then that the darkness of dawn was created . . . Changing Woman was created as the mate of the sun and with these things creation was completed.

After these things were done, that which is called "sheep" was discussed and created. These are the highlights of creation, these things which I have described. It was then that life was given to that called "sheep." In the east, chamise was placed for the sheep, and they were freed to go to it. Mormon tea was placed for them in the south, and they were freed to go to it. And in the north, black mountain mahogany was placed and they were freed to go

Navajo woman tending her flock of sheep on New Mexico's Ramah (Navajo) Reservation. Photograph by Paul Conklin.

to it. Thus it was that the sheep were set free to go in four directions. They ate and then they shook themselves, whereupon black clouds came together in a mass overhead, and on the same day hail fell. And on the same day the plants that had been placed with their mates on the world began to multiply and grow. With our sheep we were created, and that is why we weep and mourn. After the plants began to grow, the other kinds of livestock were created. Different kinds of horses, different kinds of sheep, mules and burros all came into being. And creation was finished. We were told that, in the time to come, we would live on these things. And in truth, we live that way today, although alas, we have suffered damage.

I grew up in the midst of sheep herds. The first things of which I became aware were my mother's and my father's flocks and herds. . . . I was reared in the midst of a livestock economy based on sheep, horses, cattle, burros and mules, and to this life I was trained. I was equally well trained to the care of all these forms of livestock. . . . But all these things that we once raised have been taken from us.

From: Austin, Buck. "We Have Lived on Livestock a Long Time." In *Navajo Historical Selections*. Edited by Robert W. Young and William Morgan. Washington, D.C.: Bureau of Indian Affairs, 1954.

CORN: THE STAFF OF LIFE

~~~~~~~~~~~~~~~~

Helen Sekaquaptewa

Helen Sekaquaptewa, a Hopi woman, was born in 1898 in Old Oraibi, northern Arizona. Seventy years later, after her friend Louise Udall suggested she write her life story, Helen started talking and Louise wrote it down. In her book, Me and Mine: The Life Story of Helen Sekaquaptewa, *published in 1969, Sekaquaptewa describes how the land, with coaching from Hopi people, grows corn in sandy, arid soil.*

Corn was literally the "staff of life" in olden days. The Hopis knew how to make their corn grow in sandy, arid soil. Farmers unfamiliar with the situation, who had to depend on the corn they could raise, would surely starve. We had our own native varieties—sweet corn, field corn, blue corn, and yellow corn, red, white, and mixed corn. One aimed to have on hand a supply of corn, enough to last two years, so that if there was a dry year, one's family wouldn't starve. A desperate fear that it might not rain and mature the corn was ever with us. No edible thing was ever wasted. When I was a little girl there were times when we went for weeks without having enough to eat. Then, when the early corn was ripe, the whole family would move out and camp at the cornfield and eat corn on the cob three times a day and be glad to have it.

. . . When warm spring days started to melt the snow back in the mountains, the floodwaters could be seen approaching for miles. A watcher would give the word, and the town crier would give the order from his housetop: "Everybody report for work down in the valley." Men and women, boys and girls, even little children (I remember working there when I was no more than six years old) were required to respond to the call. Very old women and mothers of very young children remained in the village to care for the little ones and to prepare the food for the workers. The few men who were herding the sheep were also exempted. Everyone, taking whatever implements and baskets he had, ran to reach the wash ahead of the floodwaters. The Chief and the head men were there, each to direct the workers where to put dirt and brush in order to spread the water onto his land. First, the land of the Chief was well soaked. Then the water was turned onto the cornland of the next in rank, and then the next. This watering would assure the sprouting of the corn and make it "come up." Every man planted a small tract for early corn, but later was the time for the big planting, and again the whole village was ordered out to plant for the Chief and head men.

Again, when summer brought the hoped-and-prayed-for rains, the community responded to irrigate for their leaders. This time careful tending was necessary to guide the water to each hill of now growing corn. Hoeing and cultivating on these fields was also done by all the people. When the landlord decided the corn was ready, a day was set and the workers gathered the long ears of ripened corn and piled them at the edge of the field nearest the village. The corn was then transported to the door of the owner on the mesa by a line of workers passing baskets and containers from hand to hand. There might be six or eight feet between the workers, but the line stretched from the field to the village. As a container was emptied it was passed back along the line. Now the Chief's corn was ready to dry and store.

There was time for the common man to care for his own cornland. This would be little areas anywhere that floodwaters would flow—sometimes on a hillside, sometimes in the bottom of a little wash. Clans had designated areas for their members. A man farmed a certain farm all his life, and his sons could enjoy the use of it, but it belonged to the clan and could not be disposed of. There was cooperative effort in planting and harvesting within the clan.

Fear of hunger was continuously in the minds of men, and there were no lazy ones. All worked hard and prayed as well for a good harvest. the father led his family to the fields daily to make sure that no weed was allowed to rob the soil of any drop of moisture. Children hoed and threw rocks at rabbits, birds, and rodents. Scarecrows flapped their arms in the breeze, when there was a breeze. Shiny pieces of broken glass and tin were scattered about; the reflection of the sun on these bits had a discouraging effect on some of the pests. . . .

When the corn was harvested and stored, it was a time of joyous thanksgiving. Years of bountiful harvest were happy years.

From: Sekaquaptewa, Helen. *Me and Mine: The Life Story of Helen Sekaquaptewa*. Tucson: University of Arizona Press, 1969.

THE PUEBLOS RELY ON DEER

Victor Sarracino

Victor Sarracino, a 44-year-old member of the Laguna Pueblo Tribe, was the recipient of a Ford Foundation fellowship for leadership training, the first tribal judge of the Pueblo, and a member of his tribal council for 18 years. In 1972 he attended a conference, sponsored by the New York–based Myrin Institute for Adult Education, about the traditional upbringing of American Indian children. In his piece for that conference, Sarracino discusses the importance of deer in Pueblo society.

In the area in which I live, people have great respect for all living creatures on this earth. While many of our neighboring tribes rely on the buffalo for food and clothing, the Pueblos rely on the deer for the food that it brings and the clothing it provides. There are many religious ceremonies performed not only for luck in the hunt, but in tribute to the deer on whom we depend for the necessities of life. One week before a big hunt, there are various groups that have their own dances and ceremonies in which all those who are going on the hunt participate, because dancing is one of the ways of expressing good wishes. At these dances, special songs are sung from early in the evening until midnight. Our people use corn meal, corn pollen and charm stones to bless these preparations, and it is the women who make sure that enough fresh corn pollen and meal are available. They do the grinding and they also cut the charm stones, such as turquoise, into small pieces. Everything has to be freshly made, freshly done; it can't have been sitting around for a year or two. During the purification period prior to the hunt, all the men fill their hearts with respect for the community and their leaders, and for the women folk. Before setting out, they are supposed to have only one thought in mind, and this is the good things out in the mountain; with this good thought they are led out into the mountain.

Upon reaching the hunting ground, each man cleans the area where he will sleep, as well as the fireplace and the place where he will hang his luck. Each one offers prayers, and again corn pollen is used. Then the men get together and sing a song, after which each of them goes off in one of four directions and tries to find the highest hill or peak in the area toward which he is headed. Upon reaching that peak, each man finds an evergreen tree and cleans underneath it and takes this fluffy little eagle feather that he carries with him. He places it right at the top of the evergreen tree, as it was done when he was a young boy. The fluffy feather serves as a messenger to the Almighty Supreme God, who is the provider of all things, and conveys the fact that the hunter is there for one purpose—to receive blessing in getting food plus all the things that go along with it. After he has addressed the Almighty, he goes off to hunt, and in many instances it doesn't take long to make a kill.

If an individual kills a deer, he gives a howl so that everybody in the area will hear it. After the kill, he lays the deer in an easterly direction, or, as we always say, in the direction of the rising sun. All those people in the distance who hear this yell go to where he is and offer prayers and praise the man who made the kill. Of course, everyone is happy, and whoever gets near the deer gives it a blessing.

The person who is to skin the deer makes an imaginary mark indicating where he is going to cut, starting with the four hoofs, then the back, then the neck. Then the skinning begins. When he starts cutting into the animal, everyone asks the Creator for forgiveness for cutting into this carcass—for cutting into the meat of the deer and the skin as well. And when he cuts into the heart, they ask the Creator for an abundance of deer in the future. . . .

As soon as the deer has been cleaned, a small bed is made on the east side of an evergreen tree or a cedar, or whatever nearby is green, and everything from the deer's insides is placed on this soft bed. Prayers are offered once again and charm stones are laid. And any animal that may be served as a result of the luck is invited to enjoy this dinner. Everyone then lends a hand in taking the deer back to camp. Once they reach camp, not a single piece of meat is touched; the men wait to arrive home. . . .

As the hunters approach, they start to build big fires so that the people in the village will know they are on their way. And when those back home see the fires—well, everybody especially the kids, runs out to the hills to greet them, while the old folks offer prayers and sing and prepare for their arrival. They sweep the area where they will lay the deer and spread out a blanket and the things that are of value to them, like silver belts and moccasins.

Upon arrival, the hunters bring in the deer and lay it in a northerly direction. All the valuables are placed on it and the singing begins, and all the neighbors come and join in. If the hunters have been away for quite a long time and have therefore had a chance to cut a deer up and start drying its meat out in the open, they bring this meat along with them and lay it out. They cut a piece of it and give it to the people who are coming to join them—everybody who comes to this gathering gets a piece of meat.

Within four days, or later in the year when it's convenient, we have what we call a deer supper, and everybody in the village is invited. All during the month of November, for example, you can go from one deer dinner to another—everybody's invited. There is a great deal of preparation that goes into these dinners, and it gives you a wonderful feeling that there is this togetherness at home. As we go from dinner to dinner to eat, the old folks have a chance to give us advice; it gives them a chance to talk to us about life's ways. These are quite some occasions, therefore. And, of course, every bit of deer meat is used, from the hoof on up to the tip of the horn. The one who made the kill has godparents and these parents are the ones who are the honored guests. They get the best part of the meat, which is usually from the head area.

When the meal is over, you don't just throw out the bones. All these bones are gathered and put in a basket along with other things that go with them. They are then taken to the nearest river or creek . . . and are dumped in, where they will eventually return to Mother Earth, and become the source of more life and sustenance.

From: Morey, Sylvester M. and Olivia L. Gilliam, editors. *Respect for Life: The Traditional Upbringing of American Indian Children.* New York: Myrin Institute/Waldorf Press, 1974.

WHALE HUNTING SEASON

Helen Slwooko Carius

Helen Slwooko Carius, a Sevukakmet Eskimo born in 1945 at her parents' camp on Boxer Bay, St. Lawrence Island, wrote a book about her life and tribe in 1978. In it, she describes the importance of whales to the Eskimo people in the village of Seevookak, now known as Gambel, Alaska.

Whale hunting season is very special to Seevookak Eskimo because it's a very hard animal to catch. They say only a brave man can kill it. When the skin boat is hunting for whale, other skin boats stay short distance away so they won't scare the big whale. When a man kills the big whale, his crew raise a flag so that the other boats can know the big whale is dead. All those other skin boats now rush to the skin boat which has the whale. The men tie a skin rope to each skin boat like in line. The skin boat that caught the whale is first in line. Some air-filled sealskin pokes are tied to the line between the whale and the last boat. The seal pokes are tied close to the whale so they will keep the dead whale up if the skin rope should break. That way they won't lose the whale. They pull the big whale home that way. When they reach the ice beach, they pull the big whale up on the ice. Then they start cutting it and dividing it up for everyone in the village. Afterward they have a ceremonial dance. The wife of the man who killed the big whale will lead in dance.

A couple of days later, the men go out again to hunt for whale or walrus. When they see a whale, they'll go after it because they would rather catch a whale than a walrus. So they always take a chance on catching a whale. If they lose the whale, they turn to the herds of walrus.

From: Carius, Helen Slwooko. *Sevukakmet: Ways of Life on St. Lawrence Island.* Anchorage: Alaska Pacific University Press, 1979.

The village of Atka, Alaska, on the Aleutian chain of islands. Courtesy of the U.S. Bureau of Indian Affairs.

FIRE AND WATER

Reuben Snake, Jr.

Reuben Snake, Jr., a Winnebago man born in 1937, a much-respected roadman (peyote leader) for the Native American Church, was until his death in 1993 one of the foremost American Indian spiritual leaders. Speaking as vice chairman of the Winnebago tribe in Nebraska, Mr. Snake made the following remarks about fire and water at a landmark symposium on Indian water policy held in Oakland, California, in November 1981.

The way my relatives and I back home try to do things is that we try to think about the traditional things. We Indian people, we have a way of life, we have a culture, and we have values that are taught to us. One of my grandfathers was talking to me about this creation, and what he was telling me is that there are two things that the Indian people really respect in relation to this creation. They know that these things are very sacred. He said they came from the same place, these two gifts that we have. He said one of them is fire and the other is water. On this creation that we walk, my grandfather was saying we cannot live without these two things.

He told me that from time to time you should take a little time out, stop in your everyday life, and think about these things here and try to say something to the Great Spirit in thanksgiving for these gifts that keep us going. Without the fire from the sun, we wouldn't last too long here. Without this water every day, we wouldn't last very long either.

When you come in here and sit down, don't pick up that water glass and drink it right now. Get up some morning before sunrise and say something about this creation. Then try to go from sunrise to sunset without taking a drink of water. Then you might gain a little respect for this creation. These are the kinds of things Indian people think about.

From: Snake, Reuben, Jr. "Luncheon Address." In American Indian Lawyer Training Program, *Indian Water Policy in a Changing Environment*, 1982.

MY PEOPLE NEVER KILLED
A TREE UNNECESSARILY

Dave Elliott

Dave Elliott, a Saanich man born in 1910 at Wjotep ("Place of the Maples"), Tsartlip, British Columbia, Canada, was a commercial fisherman for most of his life. In a 1983 narrative he wrote that when "the need was so great," his people had to take the life of a tree or kill an animal or fish for food, but they used every single shred.

Living the way we did, close to nature, we belonged to the land and the land belonged to us. Land wasn't something to be exploited, bought and sold for profit or gain. Everybody had a right to it whether it was a man or a woman, a bird, an Indian or a white man. The land was here first and it wasn't just for the powerful, corrupt, greedy, dishonest people. . . .

My people never killed a tree unnecessarily. Once in a while the need was so great they would cut a tree. When this had to happen they would speak to the tree. It had a sacred name. Every living thing had a sacred name—streams, lakes, trees, flowers, birds, everything. When your need was great you had no choice. You would stand before the tree and talk to it and tell the tree how sorry you were to take its life. When we took the life of a tree, we used every scrap, every shred right down to the last bit. We used it all. It was wrong to waste something that had been provided for us by this intelligence we didn't quite understand. This is why our people didn't just kill. Sure, they killed ducks, they killed deer, they killed fish and other animals, for eating, for food and other necessities. When they ate the fish they ate the whole thing—the head, tail, skin, many parts of the innards—liver, milt, roe. When we killed a deer, we ate every bit of it that was edible. When there was nothing left but the bare head, we would burn it so it would not be carried around by dogs or lie there in disrespect.

From: Haegert, Dorothy. *Children of the First People*. Vancouver, British Columbia: Tillacum/Arsenal Pulp Press Book, 1983.

THEY'RE TAUGHT NOT TO
WASTE ANYTHING

Moses Cruikshank

Moses Cruikshank, an Athabascan man born about 1906 at Fishhook Town (now called Chalkyitsik), a native village on the Black River northeast of Fort Yukon, Alaska, grew up learning traditional Athabascan customs. Interviewed in the early 1980s by William Schneider, Curator of Oral History, Alaska and Polar Regions, at the University of Alaska at Fairbanks, he told how the traditional people "in the early days" taught that nothing be wasted from animals killed for food.

Those days, you know, it's either feast or famine and those people, in the early days I'm talking about, these people depended upon the country to eat. So while there's a chance to harvest quite a few ducks, why they will. Not one goes to waste. They clean the duck and then dry it. They dry it and save that for times when there is nothing else to eat. The same way with meat, any kind of meat they get, they don't waste it. It don't spoil. Before it spoil they dry it, yes. Then their meat won't spoil; it will keep then.

They're taught not to waste anything, especially animals that we use, animals that we have to kill to eat, small animals like ground squirrels, tree squirrels. On all the other animals, there isn't a thing on that animal that goes to waste. Everything is used, same way right on up the line with bear and moose.

When you kill a moose now, there isn't nothing that you're supposed to waste on that, including the hoofs. If the family happened to have lots to eat, lot of game around to eat and they kill the moose, and they're drying meat, they get the hoofs, they get the sinew on there and cut out this bone and just the feet are left. They tie these sinews together, those four hoofs. They climb a tree and they put it up there, out there in clear view where people can see it from long ways. Now this is what the natives used to do. And that will sound foolish now, to the modern-day society called "sportsman," but that's the way our people used to do. They put them up in the hills. Some starving people see that up there and they can go up there and get the hoofs and they can boil it. They boil it soft and that probably would save their lives, yeah. So like that, they put them up there and the hoofs stay up there three or four years. It don't spoil, it just get harder. But you boil it enough and it'll get soft, yeah. Stuff like that, they stress the importance of saving everything. Not a bit of that moose is wasted. Not only moose, same is true for caribou, bear, sheep, all the animals that they need to eat. They don't believe in killing more than you can use. It will be there when you want it.

From: Cruikshank, Moses. *The Life I've Been Leading.* Oral Biography Series no. 1. Fairbanks: University of Alaska Press, 1986.

SPIRITUALITY AND THE ENVIRONMENT

^^^^^^^^^^^

Ruby Dunstan

*Ruby Dunstan, a woman from the Lytton band of the Nlaka'pamux peo-
ple of British Columbia, Canada, was born in 1941. In 1983, she was
elected chief councillor, the first woman chief in her band's history.
Around 1989, in a conversation with David Neel, a Kwagiutl professional photographer, she shared her opinion that talking about spirituality means talking about the environment—and that both need preserving
and protecting.*

I think the most important thing is the preservation of our spirituality—what's left of it. Without spirituality there really isn't anything else. To
me, spirituality means believing in who you are, what you are, and practising
everything that you've been taught by your elders—how to fish, how to
hunt, how to preserve those fish, how to pick the berries, use the berries and
traditional foods. That's all part of spirituality, because if you don't have spirituality then you don't have those things. When you talk about spirituality,
that also includes the environment. In our language there is no word for the
environment because we have always been taught that it is part of our everyday living. Our everyday teachings from our parents, grandparents, and
great-grandparents show us how to look after the foods that we depend on,
and that's part of the environment, and that's also part of spirituality.
Without spirituality what do you have? You are an empty shell. You're alive,
but you're—almost like a vegetable. You're moving, your heart is ticking,
but you're not really doing anything that is part of you. But if you have that
spirituality, then you understand why you do the things you do every day. I
knew that back in the 1970s people were interested in going into the Stein
Valley and logging. At that point the province had a ten-year moratorium on
it, which was up in 1984–85. They again started talking about going in to log.
By this time the elders were calling me and saying, "You can't let them go
in there and log, because that's our fridge, that's our pantry. If you let them
go in there our people are going to die, they're not going to be able to
survive—not only because of the food, but because of the spiritual things
that are in the valley." That's when we made our position public, saying we

51

wanted no logging in the valley. The province said it was theirs and I said, "No, it's ours." Many times the province has said that they're going to start building roads and have gone so far as putting out construction bids for tender. We've convinced them to at least stop and think about it and take a look at it again. So the province put together this ten-member Wilderness Advisory Committee. . . . They came to Lytton, and we convinced them that because of spiritual concerns that we have in the Stein Valley they shouldn't do anything in there. So their recommendation to the province was that there be no road building in the Stein until there was a formal agreement with the Lytton Band. We met with the Minister of Forests Dave Parker in 1988. It was just a big fight—it was a waste of time because he really didn't care. They said, "If that's how you feel, show us there is an alternative." So we got together as a tribe and got a consulting firm to put a study together for us on some of the uses that we could have without logging, without building roads or anything as destructive as logging. We ended up with a seven-volume report. . . . In our fight for the Stein, Dave Parker and other people in the provincial government have always called us environmentalists—as a derogatory term. I went to an environmental conference recently, and the provincial and federal governments were calling themselves environmentalists—in such a different way. The thing we have tried to do with this Stein issue is show that we do not want confrontation, we do not want roadblocks—only as a last resort. I said I would try to do everything that I could to receive recognition for something we believe is ours.

From: Neel, David. *Our Chiefs and Elders: Words and Photographs of Native Leaders*. Vancouver, UBC [University of British Columbia] Press, 1992.

WATER IS THE GIVER OF LIFE

Louie H. Dick, Jr.

Louie H. Dick, Jr., formerly a firefighter with the United States Forest Service, and in 1990 vice-chairman of the board of trustees of the Confederated Tribes of the Umatilla Indian Reservation in Oregon, offers his views about water, published in Oregon Humanities *in the winter of 1990.*

Well, in 1985, the Gramm-Rudman Bill caused budget cuts. I was "eligible" to retire from fire fighting because I had twenty years in and was fifty years old. I said I didn't want to retire, but they retired anyone who was "eligible" anyway. I knew I would not have the opportunity to express the Indian values again, so I decided to leave a memo.

My wife Iwatsimai and my niece, Sandy Craig—both artists—drew a map of our land on a hide. When I retired I gave it to the Forest Service and I said, "This is an Indian memo saying that water is a priority. Water is the giver of life. The map that you see shows you something basically the same as the veins in my body which give every portion of my body life. Water enters and is the only thing that can touch the heart. The river runs through the land to give it life." The hide is still on the wall, so I am fortunate that my memo is seen every day. . . .

The Indian believes that seven generations in the past we had good water. Seven generations in the future we should give back that same water that was given to us. So we think about fourteen generations of clean water. We should be able to go anywhere and get a cup of water. Ninety-eight percent of the water should be clean. Creator's standard is much higher than the EPA's.

We need to plant native plants along the streams. They are already designed to live in harmony here. The Indian thinks in terms of the circle. If we take care of the water and the land, it will take care of us. We can look at the Umatilla River today. . . . My example is the sucker fish. It is tremendously abundant. The sucker is telling us that the water is a good place for suckers to live; the water is warm. The trout and steelhead cannot live in the warm water. Too many trees have been cut. For example, at Meacham Creek in the Blue Mountains, the water has been pushed out of its bed to the west so that the Union Pacific Railroad could come through. So now it warms up two degrees. The water can only give life on one side of the

53

canyon; the rest is all destroyed. We are trying to reestablish vegetation there now so the water can be shaded. . . .

Indian beliefs are the same and different. For us the sacred food is salmon; for the Plains Indians it was buffalo; in the Southwest it was corn. Other Indians call us "fisheaters" and we smile. We all see food as part of our religion, but different foods give us our strengths. Each tribe has its own way, but if we move around from place to place, we become separate from our sacred foods; we become weak. . . .

Water and food are energies you use in following the path to the other world. In the sweat house first you sit on the earth. Then the water enters every part of your being. Third, you have an elder talking to you to fix your mind. You are in total darkness, committed to listening to whoever is doing the talking.

The women sweat together; the men sweat together. The women learn about their duties, about cleaning their bodies. The men learn not to go hunting when they are angry. Only the ones who are happy and free should hunt. If a man is angry when he hunts, he will put anger in the food. If a man is sad when he hunts, he will put sorrow in the food. . . . In the sweat house, the water touches every part of the body and the anger and the sorrow are taken away. An Indian should go to the sweat house every day, and the sweat house should be open to everyone, just as the water should be free to everyone. No one should tell you, "You can't drink this water."

We have to learn to share more than we have shared before. If we don't take care of the water, we have no fish. We, as a tribe and as a people, need to tell the fish that we are still here. The water touches the land and it touches certain things in that land which mark it. When it gets down to the Columbia, the salmon recognizes that marking in the water and follows it. Now we owe water to the mouth of the river, water that will identify Umatilla country. If we use all the water before it gets to the mouth, the salmon looks at the opening and says, "My water is not here." We owe the salmon a signal; we can't just abandon him and use all the water for cows.

When we pray before fishing, we are really saying, "The salmon returned just like he promised." He says back to us, "When I return to you, you will honor me." Water goes into food to make it easier for us to eat. It carries food into us. The elders told us, "If you change the food, it will make you sick and hurt you. If you change the water, it will make you sick and hurt you."

From: Dick, Louie H., Jr. "Water is a Medicine, It Can Touch Your Heart." *Oregon Humanities: A Journal of Ideas and Information* (Winter 1990): 8–10.

ENSOULMENT OF NATURE

Gregory A. Cajete

Gregory A. Cajete, a Tewa man from Santa Clara Pueblo in New Mexico, has been an educator for many years and also operates his own business, Tewa Educational Consulting. He is the author of Look to the Mountain: An Ecology of Indigenous Education, *published in 1994, in which he writes about the Native American identification with the natural world, a relationship he calls ensoulment, a kind of spiritual or sacred ecology. This excerpt is from Dr. Cajete's two-part series on this subject, published in the Winter 1994 journal of the American Indian Science and Engineering Society.*

The Native American identification with Place presents some of the most viable alternative paradigms for practicing the art of relationship to the natural world. American Indians have consistently attempted to maintain a harmonious relationship with their lands in the face of tremendous pressures to assimilate. Traditionally, Indian people have expressed in multiple ways that their land and the maintenance of its ecological integrity is key to their physical and cultural survival. The importance American Indians traditionally put on *connecting* with their Place is not a romantic notion which is out of step with the times. It is rather the quintessential ecological mandate of our times.

Indian people expressed a relationship to the natural world that can only be called *ensoulment*. The ensoulment of nature is the most ancient foundation of human psychology. This projection of the human sense of soul and its various archetypes has been called "participation mystique."*

Participation mystique for Indian people represented the deepest level of psychological involvement with their land and in a sense also reflected a kind of map of their soul. The psychology and spiritual quality of Indian behavior, with its reflections in symbolism, were thoroughly "informed" by the depth and power of their participation mystique and their perception of the Earth as a living soul.

It was from this orientation that Indian people believed that they had responsibilities to the land and to all living things, similar to those which

---

*Abt, Theodor. *Progress Without Loss of Soul*. Wilmette, Ill: Chiron Publisher, 1989.

they had to each other. In the Indian mind, spirit and matter are not separate; they are one and the same.

Indian people projected the archetypes which they perceived in themselves onto the entities, phenomena and places that were a part of the natural environment which they encountered. Indian people traditionally understood the human psyche and the roots of human meaning as grounded in the same order which they perceived in nature. They experienced nature as a part of themselves and themselves as a part of nature. They understood themselves as literally born of the earth of their Place. That children are bestowed to a mother and her community through direct participation of "earth spirits," and that children come from springs, lakes, mountains, or caves embedded in the earth where they existed as spirits before birth, was a widespread Indian perception. This is the ultimate identification of being indigenous to a place and forms the basis for a fully internalized bonding with Place. It is also a perception that is found in one variation or another among the traditions of indigenous people throughout the world, even in the archaic folk traditions of Europe. The very word *indigenous* is derived from the Latin roots *indu* or *endo* which are related to the Greek word *endina*, which means entrails. "Indigenous" means being so completely identified with a place that you reflect its very entrails, its insides, its soul. . . .

People make a place as much as a place makes them. Indian people did indeed interact with the places in which they lived for such a long time that their landscape became a reflection of their very soul. So phrases such as "Land of the Hopi" or "Land of the Sioux" or "Land of the Iroquois" have a literal dimension of meaning, because there was a cocreative relationship between Indian people and their lands. We know that all Indian groups literally managed their territories in what today can only be termed ecologically elegant ways. Through long-term experience with the ecology of their lands, and the practical knowledge that such experience brings, they interceded in the creation of habitat and the perpetuation of plant and animal life toward optimum levels of biodiversity and biological vitality. . . .

Ultimately, there is no separation between humans and the environment. Humans affect the environment, and the environment affects humans. Indigenous practices were founded on this undeniable reality and sought to perpetuate a sustainable and mutually reciprocal relationship.

Indian people practiced a highly sophisticated, very competent land stewardship that was universal and indigenous to this hemisphere. The precontact landscapes of America were as much an expression of Indian cultures as their arts and ceremonies. Today, the artifacts of Indian cultures are legally protected. Yet the wellsprings from which such cultural expressions come—the land, the plants, the animals and the waters—are generally viewed by mainstream society as being outside the realm of cultural preservation.

The historic relationship between Indians and their environment was so deep that separation from their home territory by forced relocation of many tribes in the last century constituted literally a kind of soul loss for that whole generation. Indian people were joined with their land with such intensity that many of those who were forced to live on reservations suffered a form of soul death. The major consequence was the loss of a sense of home and the expression of profound homesickness with all its accompanying psychological and physical maladies. As one elder put it, "They withered like mountain flowers pulled from their mother soil." When Indians talk about restoring or preserving their cultures, they talk about restoring their lands in the same breath. . . .

Traditionally, the connection of Indian people to their land was a symbol of their connection to the spirit of life itself. The loss of such a foundational symbol for Indian tribes led to a tremendous loss of Indian meaning and identity which only with the most recent generations has begun to be revitalized. Indian loss of their homelands took such a toll, because inner kinship with the world is an ancient and natural extension of the human psyche. The disconnection of that kinship can lead to a deep split in the inner and outer consciousness of the individual and the group. It also brings with it a whole set of social and psychological problems which can ultimately only be healed through reestablishing the meaningful ties to the land that have been lost. Reconnecting with nature and its inherent meaning is an essential healing and transformational process for Indian people.

From: Cajete, Gregory A. "Land and Education." *Winds of Change* (American Indian Science and Engineering Society journal) 9, no. 1 (Winter 1994): 42–47.

LANGUAGE

The Cherokee syllabary created by Sequoyah, a Cherokee, in the early 1820s. U. S. Bureau of American Ethnology, Nineteenth Annual Report, Plate 5.

*N*ative Americans do not speak "Indian." Estimates vary as to the total number of American Indian languages in North America north of Mexico at the time of first contact with Europeans, but it is generally held that there were between 500 and 600 mutually unintelligible languages belonging to more than ten language families. Some of the languages, which still exist today, are related. For example, Navajos and Apaches in Arizona, who both speak an Athabascan language, can understand one another. But more often, native languages are worlds apart: dialects spoken for thousands of years by native peoples diverged and evolved into many different languages. Tlingits in Alaska who speak an Athabascan language do not understand Navajo speakers. And the Hopis of Arizona cannot understand the Siouan language any more than the Spanish can understand the Tibetan language.

Traditionally, native languages were passed orally from generation to generation. Spoken for thousands of years, these languages have complex and precise systems of grammar and vocabularies with thousands of words. Some of these grammars and vocabularies have been written down: missionaries, among others, captured on paper the words they heard native people speak. Preserving native languages was not U.S. government policy, however. Many Indian languages were lost in the 1800s and early 1900s, when the federal government forced Indian children to go to boarding schools. From 1886, when federal policy first forbade the use of any Indian language, through the 1950s, the U.S. government prohibited or discouraged Indian languages in schools and public settings. The ban on Indian languages caused the loss of more than 150 languages.

Despite destructive policies, ancient native languages continue to be spoken in many Indian, Inuit, and Aleut communities. On some reservations, quiet revivals of languages once forbidden in schools reflect the resurgence of interest in preserving and protecting native languages in native communities throughout the country. Many of the excerpts following also reflect the energies being put into regaining and relearning traditional languages.

Speaking one's tribal language rates high on the agenda with many tribes, because it is one of the most important ways native peoples express their identity and ensure the life of their unique cultures. Information about the past and about the spiritual, ceremonial, and natural worlds is passed through language. For some tribes, religion cannot be practiced without tribal spoken languages. Ties to the land weaken. Without language, native cultures can be irreparably damaged.

For all Native Americans, the spoken word or oral tradition has been a way of life inseparable from culture. In this section, Don Wanatee and Mrs. Brown (Mesquakies) attest to this in their testimony before a Senate subcommittee, while Acoma poet Simon Ortiz calls his native language life itself. A group of Ögwehö:weh *(people from eight native nations in New York State) describe the importance of language curriculum for their children, and Anna Lee Walters (Pawnee/Otoe) writes eloquently of her reverence for the spoken word.*

Peter Webster (Ahousaht), once "kicked" and "slapped" for speaking his language, now teaches that same language to his own tribe. Lydia Whirlwind Soldier (Lakota), also subjected to punishment and ridicule in boarding school, believes tribal language should be used outside the home. Jill Sherman Fletcher (Hupa/Yurok) describes with enthusiasm a Hupa language immersion camp, while Deborah Decontie (Algonquin), a high school student studying her tribal language, regrets how little school time there is for language instruction.

For hundreds of years, native people have expressed their love for their languages and this section includes some of those observations. Kah-ge-ga-gah-bowh, or George Copway (Chippewa/Ojibway), lauds the Algonquian language, perhaps the most widely spoken of any native language in North America, for its force of expression. James Kaywaykla (Apache) points out that his language contains no profanity. N. Scott Momaday (Kiowa) compares the legal language of diplomacy with the beauty and power of oral tradition, and Percy Bullchild (Blackfeet) describes the origin of sign language.

THE OJIBWAY LANGUAGE

Kah-ge-ga-gah-bowh [George Copway]

Kah-ge-ga-gah-bowh, or George Copway, a Chippewa or Ojibway Indian born about 1818 near the Trent River in Canada, did not have "the happiness of being able to refer to written records in narrating the history of [his] forefathers." He chose, therefore, to "reveal to the world what has long been laid up in memory." In the following excerpt taken from his work Indian Life and Indian History, *published in 1858 (first published in 1850), Copway reveals a great deal about Algonquian, the language of his people.*

The Ojibway language, or the Algonquian stock, is perhaps the most widely spoken of any in North America. The Atlantic tribes partook of this idiom when they were first discovered.

The snows of the north bounded the people who spoke this language on that side, while in the south as far as the Potomac and the mountains of Virginia, down the Ohio, over the plains of Illinois to the east of the upper waters of the Father of Rivers, nations resided three or four hundred years ago who could speak so as to be understood by each other. A person might have travelled nearly one thousand miles from the head of Lake Superior and yet not journey from the sound of this dialect. . . .

Mr. H. R. Schoolcraft, who has studied the language more than any other person, and to some purpose, has often said through the press, as well in private conversation, that there is in it that which few other languages possess; a force of expression, with music in its words and poetry in their meaning. I cannot express fully the beauty of the language, I can only refer to those who have studied it as well as other languages, and quote their own writing in saying "every word has its appropriate meaning, and with additional syllables give additional force to the meaning of most words." After reading the English language, I have found words in the Indian combining more expressiveness. There are many Indian words which when translated into English lose their force, and do not convey so much meaning in one sentence as the original does in one word.

It would require an almost infinitude of English words to describe a thunder storm, and after all you would have but a feeble idea of it. In the Ojibway language, we say *"Be-wah-sam-moog."* In this we convey the idea of a continued glare of lightning, noise, confusion—an awful whirl of clouds, and much more.

. . . It is a natural language. The pronunciation of the names of animals, birds, and trees are the very sounds these produce; for instance, hoot owl, *o-o-me-seh;* owl, *koo-koo-ko-ooh;* river, *see-be;* rapids, *sah se-je-won.* *"See"* is the sound of the waters on the rocks. *"Sah-see"* the commotion of waters, and from its sound occurs its name.

The softness of the language is caused, as I have before said, by the peculiar sounding of all the vowels, though there is but little poetic precision in the formation of verse, owing to the want of a fine discriminating taste by those who speak it.

From: Kah-Ge-Ga-Gah-Bowh, or Copway, George. *Indian Life and Indian History by an Indian Author—Embracing the Traditions of the North American Indians Regarding Themselves Particularly of that Most Important of all the Tribes—The Ojibways.* Boston: Albert Colby and Co., 1858.

IN OUR LANGUAGE THERE
IS NO PROFANITY

James Kaywaykla

James Kaywaykla, a Warm Springs Apache, born in New Mexico about 1873, shared the story of his life in the southwest. During this time, Apache families were driven from their homelands, hunted like animals, and eventually herded aboard a train and shipped to Florida prisons in 1886. In his story, dictated between 1956 and 1963, when he was nearly 90 years old, he describes his pride in the Apache language.

One morning I was awakened by the sound of Grandfather's voice. He sat in the opening of our brush arbor, facing the rising sun, and singing The Morning Song. This is a hymn to Ussen [Creator of Life] thanking Him for one of the greatest of his gifts—the love between a man and woman, which is to Apaches a sacred thing. Never do they make obscene jokes about sex, and the fact that White Eyes consider conception and birth a matter of levity is something they cannot understand. It is, to them, on a level with taking the name of God in vain. I am very proud of the fact that in our language there is no profanity. For the privilege in sharing the creation of new life we give thanks to the Creator of Life.

From: Ball, Eve. *In the Days of Victorio: Recollections of a Warm Springs Apache.* Tucson: University of Arizona Press, 1970.

THE MESQUAKIE LANGUAGE

Don Wanatee and Mrs. Brown

Don Wanatee, a Mesquakie* man from the Mesquakie Tribe in Tama, Iowa, secretary of the tribal council, and Mrs. Brown, a Mesquakie woman, appeared on February 18, 1969, before the legendary hearings held by the Senate's Special Subcommittee on Indian Education during the 91st Congress. Answering Senator Edward Kennedy's questions, they testified about the need for Mesquakies to go to their own schools, not public schools, so their children could speak their own language, participate in their own religion, and be free from subtle discrimination.

Senator Kennedy: As I understand it, the Indian children that go to the first grade can only speak the language of the tribe; is that correct?

Mr. Wanatee: Yes . . .

Senator Kennedy: As I understand further, the children go to these schools but, unlike other children, they haven't the background in language and understanding of English and that in the schools that are provided to the Indian Settlement, they try to teach them the language. Isn't that right; they try to teach them English, as well?

Mr. Wanatee: Yes; they try to teach them English as a secondary language. Of course, we need it.

Senator Kennedy: What are the reservations that you, or members of the tribe, after the first few grades, have on going to the public schools in the area? Why don't the families and the parents of the children want them to go into the public schools?

Mr. Wanatee: Basically, the attitude of the Tama community I might say has not been too receptive to the Indians.

Senator Kennedy: Could you be more specific?

***Mr. Wanatee:** We consider ourselves Mesquakie. Let me try to explain. The Fox was derived from the French word *renard*. When the French first met with a clan of Mesquakies in the early 1600s they saw a sign that these particularly strange-looking people were carrying, which was the sign of a fox. So the French right away recognized the animal and said, "It is a fox." From then hence, we were known as the Fox through the translation of the word *renard* into fox. You see, the other tribes of the United States know us as Algonquins. The French know us as *renard*. The English-speaking people know us as Fox. The Bureau knows us as Sac and Fox.

Mr. Wanatee: May I say that the Indians have a different culture than the white community. In the time that we have spent with the Tama people they have not attempted to understand our viewpoints on education or on the basis of our cultural heritage. . . .

Mrs. Brown: I have a statement here. It is a short one that I want to read first.

The Mesquakie language, our ways, our religion are interwoven into one. All are significant to our religion. With another language we cannot perform our religion. This is taught right from the beginning.

I want the school to keep our language and also at this age and grade level the children need the natural environment to learn a basic fundamental of education, free from subtle discrimination, being made to be aware that he is Indian or different.

When we speak Mesquakie, we think in Mesquakie. When we enter school, it is very difficult to respond in English and during that process in the public schools the Indian child in his hesitation is very noticeable; the student knows the answer but in that hesitation the teacher will disregard him even though he knows the answer. . . . I would like to point out right now before I forget, in the Headstart Program of 1967 I had worked with the preschoolers. These were small children. I had the job of taking these kids to their dental appointments. When I entered that room these kids, as soon as they saw me, talked in Mesquakie. The teacher, with her finger in her mouth, said, "Don't speak Mesquakie; don't speak Mesquakie."

Senator Kennedy: As I understand it, you have to be able to speak Mesquakie to practice your religion; is that right?

Mrs. Brown: This is true.

From: *Indian Education*, part 1. U.S. Congress. Senate Special Subcommittee On Indian Education. *Hearings.* 91st Cong., 1st sess., 1969.

TEACHING HIS LANGUAGE
BACK TO HIS TRIBE

Peter Webster

Peter Webster, an Ahousaht man born in 1908 in Bedwell River, Vancouver Island, Canada, was an independent fisherman, a carpenter, an author, and an actor. The holder of an honorary degree in linguistics from the University of Victoria, he taught his native language in his own school in Ahousaht. In this excerpt from an essay published in 1983, Webster writes about his pride in being a language teacher.

I am fully educated, with my knowledge of the traditions, culture, history and songs that belong to my Indian way and language. But I haven't got much white man's language because I only spent two years in a boarding school. It was Ahousaht School. I didn't even know how to say "yes" and I used to get kicked or slapped or sent to bed without supper if the staff heard me use my own language. So if any of those teachers are alive today, I wish they could take a look at Peter Webster. What is he doing in university? He's a man who didn't know a word of English and he's teaching his language back to his tribe. . . .

I've been a language teacher for the past three years and children today are having a hard time. In the writing of the songs, some kids are really good but some don't know what they write.

I believe we need more teachers to teach them our language back. First teach them what we were taught by our grandparents in the past. This might be the only way to get them to change. If we don't it's going to get worse. So if I live another ten years, I hope I'll see a difference in the future. Again, if any of these young children of school age would get interested in it—teaching the language—if one of them gets the idea, I'll help them. I'm saying this because I want somebody to finish the Indian dictionary.

From: Haegert, Dorothy. *Children of the First People.* Vancouver, British Columbia: Tillacum/Arsenal Pulp Press Book, 1983.

THE ORIGIN OF SIGN LANGUAGE

Percy Bullchild

Percy Bullchild, a 66-year-old Blackfeet man born in Montana, passes on the oral history of his tribe in traditional stories he himself heard from his elders. In one of his stories, published in his 1985 book, The Sun Came Down, *he explains the origin of sign language, an elaborate means of silent communication that circumvented the multiplicity of languages spoken in the Plains region of the United States.*

All of the children of Mudman [son of Creator Sun] and Ribwoman [wife of Mudman] scattered ever so wide. Up to this time there wasn't any contact with those very first groups that left their parents. They had gone too far to be met again any time by their folks.

At the very beginning of the lives of Mudman and Ribwoman, when the few children born to Mudman and Ribwoman began this life we are in on Mother Earth, the words of their spoken language were very few. It was a real simple language. As the children of Mudman and Ribwoman scattered ever so far apart from one another, their languages changed more and more until none of them could understand the other. This happened to almost all of those small groups that had separated from one another. In time, none of those groups could even begin to understand the others.

Communication with one another was impossible. This language barrier existed between those first people until they learned to talk to one another with their hands. The Native sign language began over this language barrier in that beginning. Today, too, there are language barriers between all nations of this world. Translators or interpreters are needed to understand one another. . . .

Mudman and Ribwoman, being told to go spread the good news of more variety of food for all by his father, Creator Sun, left the children they were living with at that particular time. Telling them they were going to seek their brothers and sisters that left a long time ago, to give them the good news about more food for all.

Readying themselves the night before, the two left just before sunrise for their long journey to find all of their children.

For many, many days they traveled, and always on foot, before they came to the very first of their children's group. This group hadn't gone too far away, yet it still knew the spoken language. They told them of the food animals and fowls they were given to eat, and also more of the vegetation. Not abiding too long in one place, they went on to find more of their children.

For many, many more days they went on before coming to more of their children. As the two came within hearing distance of the camp, they heard the children talking. The language these children were using differed somewhat from the language they spoke.

On and on the two went, Mudman and Ribwoman, trying to find all of their children that had left them many, many years ago, to give them news of the new food and what it was. As they went further and further away from their camping area, the two learned of the different languages being spoken by their very own children that had left them long ago. This different language became stranger the further it got away from their home.

It was in this time that the hand language first came into existence, to make their own children understand what they were talking about. With this newer language with the hands, the sign language, the two told their children about the food.

In sign language, the talker spoke out audibly, and at the same time made signs with his hands of what was being said. For example, if the talk was about a bear, he would be talking about the bear and at the same time making like a bear, his finger curled to his palms and hands held even with his chest, and then a sign of the bear's teeth in its mouth. If it was a bird of some sort, big or small, the sign of big or the sign of small would be used. And then the hands and fingers to the shoulders and flapped like wings for the bird sign.

So a new language was made by Mudman and Ribwoman to communicate with their own children in that time. This hand sign language soon was used by all of those that couldn't understand one another, and it still goes on today among many Native Americans.

From: Bullchild, Percy. *The Sun Came Down: The History of the World as My Blackfeet Elders Told It*. New York: Harper and Row, 1985.

LANGUAGE IS LIFE

~~~~~~~~~~~~

Simon Ortiz

Simon Ortiz, born in 1941 at Acoma Pueblo in New Mexico, deserves recognition as one of the United States' foremost contemporary poets. The author of many books of poetry and short fiction—his book of poetry From Sand Creek *(1981) received the Pushcart Prize for Poetry. In a 1985 interview with Laura Coltelli that took place in Mission, South Dakota, in the heart of the Rosebud (Sioux) Indian Reservation, where the poet was teaching creative writing at Sinte Gleska College, Mr. Ortiz explains his love of language.*

Lc: You describe the English language as a very definite one, "useful in defining things," which in other words means also "setting limits." "But language is not definition . . . language is all-expansive." Language, then, "as perception and expression of experience." Does it go back to your people's use of language?

Ortiz: I guess all my perceptions and expressions do go back to what I was born into and what I was developed through, that is, the original experience. That is really what I know. That is, that I was born of the Acoma people, and that my name comes from them. My mother and my father were the most immediate teachers. The elders of my clan were the stuff of life, so to speak, in every way, personal and social. My formation with regards to language was the *dzehni niyah* of the Acoma people: "the way they spoke," the way they thought and felt, the way they perceived. So the writing cannot help but be fundamental. I can only be who I am as an Acoma person. I cannot be anything else. *Tzah dze guwaah ihskah nudahsqkunuuh,* "I cannot be anything else." The language I use is English. Nevertheless, my English language use is grounded on the original and basic knowledge of myself as an Acoma person. I cannot be anything except an Acoma man in nature, philosophy, and outlook and so forth. Although, obviously, in terms of technical linguistics, there are going to be influences and implications from other sources. There may be colorings that are not so easily interchangeable and are not synonymous from one language to another. But my frame of reference, being Acoma originally, determines what and how I write today. Even if I did not write anything Acoma, even if I did not write anything about Native America, I would still have that prior knowledge. Unless I was just totally brainwashed, which is not very far from possibility; I mean, Indian people have changed, but I think consciously and conscientiously they refer to what is fundamental. *Acquumch sthudhah*, "I could not be anything else." As long as I believe that I cannot be anything else, then whatever I say—I may write about MX missiles or about Italy or I may live in Italy—cannot be anything else; I couldn't fail to use language according to my original identity.

LC: In [Kenneth] Rosen's anthology, *The Man to Send Rain Clouds*, you said that language is a way of life, which in my opinion is one of the most beautiful definitions of language.

Ortiz: It's true, and I have sort of refined that in a way, to mean that by language we create knowledge. Our language is the way we create the world. And I don't mean just spoken language or heard language, but language as the oral tradition, in all of its aspects, qualities, and dimensions. Scott Momaday, in his essay "The Man Made of Words," talks about this particular magic process of language. The process being the act of language; man exists because of language, consciousness comes about through language, or the world comes about through language. Life-language. Language is life, then.

From: Coltelli, Laura. *Winged Words: American Indian Writers Speak.* Lincoln: University of Nebraska Press, 1990.

THE POWER AND BEAUTY
OF LANGUAGE

N. Scott Momaday

N. Scott Momaday, a Kiowa writer born in 1934 in Lawton, Oklahoma, is considered one of the greatest writers in North America. Possessing, even as a child, extraordinary gifts of language and poetic insight, he won the Pulitzer Prize for fiction in 1969 with his first book, House Made of Dawn. *Momaday, whose fiction, poetry, essays, and paintings have earned him an international reputation, has also won Italy's highest literary award. A professor at the University of Arizona, Momaday often writes about language and oral tradition.*

The American Indian has a highly developed oral tradition. It is in the nature of oral tradition that it remains relatively constant; languages are slow to change for the reason that they represent a greater investment on the part of society. One who has only an oral tradition thinks of language in this way: my words exist at the level of my voice. If I do not speak with care, my words are wasted. If I do not listen with care, words are lost. If I do not remember carefully, the very purpose of words is frustrated. This respect for words suggests an inherent morality in man's understanding and use of language. Moreover, that moral comprehension is everywhere evident in American Indian speech. On the other hand, the written tradition tends to encourage an indifference to language. That is to say, writing produces a false security where our attitudes toward language are concerned. We take liberties with words; we become blind to their sacred aspect.

By virtue of the authority vested in me by section 465 of the Revised Statutes (25 U.S.C. #[section 9 of this title]) and as President of the United States, the Secretary of Interior is hereby designated and empowered to exercise, without the approval, ratification, or other action of the President or of any other officer of the United States, any and all authority conferred upon the United States by section 403(a) of the Act of April 11, 1968, 82 Stat. 79 (25 U.S.C. #1323(a) [subsec. (a) of this section]): provided, That acceptance of retrocession of all or any measure of civil or criminal jurisdiction, or both, by the Secretary hereunder shall be effected by publication in the *Federal Register* of a notice which shall specify the jurisdiction retroceded and the effective date of the retrocession: Provided further, That acceptance of such retrocession of criminal jurisdiction shall be effected only after consultation by the Secretary with the Attorney General.

Executive Order No. 11435, 1968

I have heard that you intend to settle us on a reservation near the mountains. I don't want to settle. I love to roam over the prairies. There I feel free and happy, but when we settle down we grow pale and die. I have laid aside my lance, bow, and shield, and yet I feel safe in your presence. I have told the truth. I have no little lies hid about me, but I don't know how it is with the commissioners. Are they as clear as I am?

Satanta, Kiowa Chief

The examples above speak for themselves. The one is couched in the legal diction of a special parlance, one that is far removed from our general experience of language. Its meaning is obscure; the words themselves seem to stand in the way of meaning. The other is in the plain style, a style that preserves, in its way, the power and beauty of language. In the historical relationship in question, the language of diplomacy has been determined by the considerations that have evolved into the style of the first of the examples. It is far removed from the American Indian oral tradition, far from the rhythms of oratory and storytelling and song.

The fundamental difference in ways of looking at the world, as those differences are reflected in the language of diplomacy, seem to me to constitute the most important issue in Indian-white relations in the past five hundred years.

From: Momaday, N. Scott. "Personal Reflections." In *The American Indian and the Problem of History*, edited by Calvin Martin, 160–161. New York: Oxford University Press, 1987.

ÖGWEHÖWE:KA:? LANGUAGES

Ögwehö:weh People

In 1989, a group of Ögwehö:weh* people developed a New York State syllabus entitled ÖGWEHÖWE:KA:?: Native Languages for Communication, a framework for the development of local curricula that integrated principles of second language acquisition with New York State program requirements and goals for elementary and secondary education. Under the topics "philosophy" and "historical background" the writers stress the importance of languages to the eight native nations in New York State.

Ögwehöwe:ka:? is our connection to our community and to the world. Through language we identify the world around us, express our concerns and dreams, and share our experiences and ideas.

The ability to communicate in a native language provides a unique opportunity to maintain access to *Ögwehöwe:ka:?*. Language is inseparable from culture and is a living part of one's being. . . .

Ögwehöwe:ka:? has always been an oral tradition. The need to preserve the oral tradition/language of *Ögwehöwe:ka:?* has become imperative because many native children speak only English. There are historical reasons for this, such as the boarding school era when *Ögwehö:weh* were punished for speaking *Ögwehöwe:ka:?* and were, in essence, "immersed" in English.

In many cases, *Ögwehö:weh* experienced a loss of pride because they were taught that their languages and cultures were inferior to the dominant society.

In the past, the educational process, with its emphasis on assimilation and acculturation, had long-term negative effects. The people who experienced this process continued to speak *Ögwehöwe:ka:?* among themselves. However, they did not teach their children and grandchildren in an effort to spare their descendants the ridicule and punishment they experienced.

**Ögwe'ö:weh* means "The Real People/The Original Beings," in Seneca. *Ögwehö:weh* means "The Real People/The Original Beings" in Onondaga, Oneida, Cayuga, and Mohawk. The Tuscarora say *Agwaha:weh* for "The Real People/The Original Beings." There are eight native nations in New York State: Onondaga, Mohawk, Seneca, Oneida, Cayuga, Tuscarora, Shinnecock, and Unkechaug (Poospatuck Reservation). In the syllabus *Ögwehö:weh* refers to all of the eight native nations in New York State. *Ögwehöwe:ka:?* refers specifically to the languages of the eight Native nations.

Today, there is a resurgence among the people to strengthen *Ögwehöwe:ka:ʔ*. Language programs have been developed since the early 1970s among the Mohawk, Seneca, Onondaga, Cayuga, Tuscarora, and Oneida.

In former times, children grew up thinking and speaking *Ögwehöwe:ka:ʔ*. In some communities, the Elders feel the language should not be taught in public schools and regret that this point in history has been reached. The Elders, however, recognize the need to preserve their languages. This necessitates the present method of teaching language in the schools.

From: *Ögwehöwe:ka:ʔ: Native Languages for Communication, New York State Syllabus*. Albany: New York State Education Department, 1989.

THE SPOKEN WORD IS REVERED

Anna Lee Walters

Anna Lee Walters, a Pawnee/Otoe woman born in 1946 in Pawnee, Oklahoma, is a poet, essayist, novelist, and scholar. In her 1992 book, Talking Indian: Reflections on Survival and Writing, *she begins her collection of autobiography, short stories, historical tribal documentation, and archival family photographs with a discussion of oral tradition. Descended from two tribal cultures that have revered the spoken word and existed for millennia without written languages, Walters explains, "It is through the power of speech, and the larger unified voice of oral tradition, that we exist as we do."*

My first memories are not so much of *things* as they are of *words* that gave shape and substance to my being and form to the world around me. Born into two tribal cultures which have existed for millennia without written languages, the spoken word held me in the mystical and intimate way it has touched others who come from similar societies whose literature is oral.

In such cultures, the spoken word is revered, and to it are attributed certain qualities. One quality is akin to magic or enchantment because the mystery of language and speech, and the processes of their development, as well as their origin, can never be fully explained. For the same reason, the spoken word is believed to be power which can create or destroy.

Members of nonliterate societies spend their lifetimes reaffirming that the spoken word lives of its own indescribable power and energy, floating apart and separate from individual human voices who utter it. Yet, paradoxically, we are also shown that it is through the power of speech, and the larger unified voice of oral tradition, that we exist as we do.

Listening is the first sense to develop in the womb. It is not surprising, then, that I was conscious of sounds earlier than anything else as an infant. Mainly, these were the sounds of the universe, the outdoors. They included whishing bird wings rising up into the sky, rustling trees, the cry of the mourning dove, and the rippling wind. They were the first nonhuman sounds I heard because my family spent most of the time outdoors. This awareness was followed by other sounds of life embracing me with deep sighs and measured breaths. Those human sounds then became syllables, or vocables, and voice patterns with intonations and inflections. Eventually and inexplicably they turned into words such as Waconda, meaning Creator, or the Great Mystery of Life, and *waduge*, meaning to eat, and *Mayah*, the Earth. Single words became explosions of sounds and images, and these traveled outward in strings of sentences or melodies and songs.

There were many individual voices, male and female, old and young, scattered about me, and these voices expressed themselves in two languages, Otoe and English. Some of the people were literate in English. Otoe was unwritten for the most part. But more often than not, as if by some magnetic pull of oral tradition, the individual tribal voices unconsciously blended together, like braided strands of thread, into *one* voice, story, song, or prayer. That thread stretched, unbroken, to a pretime and origin that still lived in the mystery and power of the Otoe language, their *spoken* word, even translated into English as it had been for well over a century before I was born. The echo of that tribal voice, in Otoe or English, never disappears or fades from my ear, not even in the longest silences of the people, or in my absences from them.

In the Pawnee culture, the experience with that language and their spoken word, and their numerous voices flowing into one, was identical to the Otoe experience, though Pawnee culture and language are distinctly different because the two tribes are unrelated. The Pawnees had also adopted English to a certain extent by the time I was born. But before that, daring Frenchmen and Spaniards had mingled among them and intermarried with them, thereby introducing those languages. French and Spanish intermarriage had also occurred among the Otoe, but even with these influences, as well as those of other tribal cultures through adoption and intermarriage, the Pawnees and the Otoes retained their own unique voices, their own memories, consciousness, and spirits. In their approaches to the world, reality, and existence, and through the spoken word, they were alike. They both had extended a pattern of life over countless generations, through the centuries, and credited their survival and continuity to the power of their oral traditions. These are haunting and powerful voices that still recall prehistoric tribal visions and experiences that are the core of their identities today.

The Otoe voice seemed to originate and drift from the north, much further away from Oklahoma where the Otoes then resided. Nevertheless, I was able to hear it when I was alone in the cotton fields north of my grandparents' house. It whispered of a time before Indian territory, before the Oklahoma hills where I was born, and I'm certain, too, that this was the same voice of a relative who retold old stories with a new twist. He often sat at our table speaking to us in whispers, and occasionally in shouts from across the fields, of the life, history, and fate that we all shared as one tribal people.

Most of the time, the Otoe voice was as fluid as the water from which we were told that we came. In water we were conceived, and we made our first appearance on its shorelines in clans of totem beings who have since not ceased to be. The clans of Bear, Elk, Buffalo, and others traveled in circles for a while, leaving their imprints deeply impressed in mud. Their totem voices swirled visibly overhead in the immenseness of the universe, and this is how the clans knew they lived. Silence and speech at the water's edge alternated here. Remember that we need both, we are told. The totem voices took turns speaking—the Bears roared, the Eagles screeched, the Pigeons cooed—until all the clans had spoken. Silence followed. *Silence.* Then all the totem beings spoke at once. Yes, through their speeches and voices, and through the ensuing silence, the people, the clans, knew they lived. This is the power of language, but often it is not realized until silence prevails. Silence. *Remember both, we are told.*

It is understandable that the Otoe voice did pause from time to time. In its place silence reigned, and in these periods, other affirmations about the universe and life were absorbed through the other senses. These affirmations always seemed to correspond to oral tradition. Then the Otoe tribal voice began again, sometimes at the periphery of my world, and other times it seemed to come from deep inside *me.* Later when I began to write, it is what I drew upon.

From: Walters, Anna Lee. *Talking Indian: Reflections on Survival and Writing.* Ithaca, New York: Firebrand Books, 1992.

MY ALGONQUIN VOCABULARY

Deborah Decontie

The following essay was written by 14-year-old Deborah Decontie, an Algonquin, in an English class at the Kitigan Zibi School in Maniwaki, Quebec, Canada. It was first published in Turtle Quarterly *magazine, in Spring/Summer 1993.*

*K*itigewinini obimiwidon toshanabo-atagan was the first sentence I learned to speak in Algonquin, my Native language. I remember learning it in Grade one and being very happy about my little accomplishment. I was taught Algonquin since I was in Nursery. I was just learning the basics such as my numbers and colors and then words I could use everyday, like "please" and "thank you." Progressively, I began to learn more.

In spite of my Algonquin lessons, my vocabulary is very limited. Allow me to explain "limited." "Limited" in the sense that if someone would come up to me and start talking to me in Algonquin I would not understand a word he or she said. "Limited" in the sense that I had to ask someone how to spell the sentence mentioned at the onset. "Limited" in the sense that I cannot tell someone something in Algonquin that he or she would understand or that would be understood clearly. So, my Algonquin vocabulary is very "limited" and perhaps it's my fault or perhaps it's not. The purpose of this essay is not to point the finger at anyone. However, I do realize that I do not know my language and I can honestly say that I regret not having put more of an effort to learn it. So I'm writing this essay from my viewpoint, my perspective, as a fourteen-year-old Algonquin girl who lives on an Algonquin reserve, and goes to an Algonquin school, and does not know her language.

I still have memories about my Algonquin classes and teachers and the things they used to teach us. I had much fun in nursery. In the afternoons we would go downstairs and we'd sing songs and learn legends and play "pretend." My language didn't mean much to me, at that time it just meant having fun. I didn't realize how important it is to learn your language or the impact language has on your culture. It is through language that legends are passed on. It is through language that we learn about traditions. And, it is through language that we pass on to the next generation, our children and grandchildren, our culture.

Now, more than ever, the people in my area are becoming concerned with preserving the language that makes our culture unique and in effect, makes every individual who knows the language unique. I believe that I would like to learn my language but I don't think I'm motivated enough to actually do something about it, and that bugs me. It bugs me because it leads me to ask questions that I don't know the answers to and can do nothing about. Why, for example, in elementary, were we taught Algonquin for half an hour every day whereas we would be taught English, Language Arts and how to write for longer periods of time? When I entered High School, why was English taught for an hour every day while Algonquin was taught for an hour every two days? And in Grade nine why was Algonquin replaced with Native Studies where we'd learn about other cultures such as the Beothuks?

Isn't it ironic that we're learning about how the Beothuks lost their entire nation when the same is happening to us? The slow erosion of our culture and language is a psychological genocide. The fuuny thing about it is very few people realize that this is happening to us on our reserve because it is happening at a slow rate. However, the people that do realize this are doing something about it and it gives a hope that there is still time for me to learn the language I was originally supposed to learn. Maybe someday I can rewrite this essay in my Native language.

From: Decontie, Deborah. "My Viewpoint on Native Languages." *Turtle Quarterly* 5, no. 2 (Spring–Summer 1993): 37.

WE MUST ENCOURAGE THE
USE OF OUR LANGUAGE

Lydia Whirlwind Soldier

Lydia Whirlwind Soldier, a Lakota woman who is Indian Studies Curriculum Coordinator for the Todd County School District in South Dakota, also sits on the Board of Regents of Sinte Gleska University (one of the 31 Indian-controlled colleges in the United States and Canada), located in Rosebud, South Dakota. In her 1993 piece "Lakota Language Survival and Restoration—Lessons from the Boarding School" in which she campaigns for the preservation of the Lakota language, she decries the "reprehensible practices" of Euro-American boarding schools and religious institutions that tried to eliminate native languages and install English in their place.

I will never forget the Catholic nun dressed in black garb, her face tightly wrapped in white material that seemed to cut into her face. Taken from my family and locked in the St. Francis boarding school, I remember standing under this person, her mouth moving, enunciating words directly at me that I did not understand. But I felt her words, harsh, cold, and bludgeoning. After that first year at St. Francis, I never felt quite the same about myself, my language and my culture.

We still feel the ripples from the reprehensible practices of the educational and religious institutions. The generational damage cloaked by good intentions still haunts us.

In those days we didn't see the school as instruments of forced assimilation. Our families believed they had come to help us. Yet those apostles attempted to "wipe clean our heathen minds." Their efforts permeated every aspect of our lives, language, homes, families, education and religion.

Their approach for teaching English was the sink-or-swim method, today called submersion. The philosophy was based on the belief that the more complete our exposure to English, the better and faster we would learn the language. Instead, it led to more punishment and ridicule.

We were expected to learn the English content of educational materials, and be as competent as those who already spoke the language. The distinct message was that English verified our abilities, competence and intelligence. I struggled, not really becoming a strong swimmer but managing not to sink.

The divide-and-conquer tactic was used repeatedly. English speakers were treated more favorably and were often more successful in receiving approval. This eroded the tribal bond within the group and encouraged students to think negatively about their own language. The Lakota language became an obstacle for access to social, educational, and economic opportunity. I still carry the scars of having my loyalty and spiritual attachment to my language ripped from me.

I often recall my Grandfather Whirlwind Soldier's words, "Remember who you are. Remember you are a Lakota." However, as a young mother I overlooked the importance of preserving our Lakota language. When my children were young we moved back to the reservation so they could be raised with their relatives. I thought there was plenty of time for them to learn Lakota, but time quickly passed. Today, although they are familiar

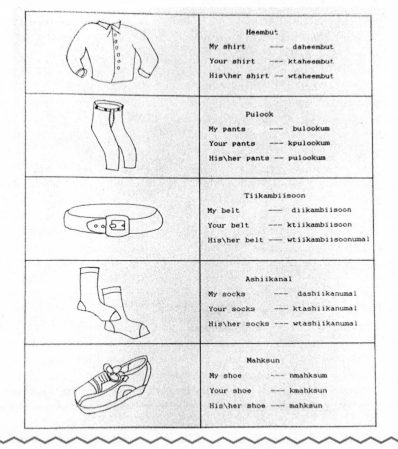

Heembut	
My shirt	--- daheembut
Your shirt	--- ktaheembut
His\her shirt	-- wtaheembut

Pulook	
My pants	--- bulookum
Your pants	--- kpulookum
His\her pants	-- pulookum

Tiikambiisoon	
My belt	--- diikambiisoon
Your belt	--- ktiikambiisoon
His\her belt	--- wtiikambiisoonumal

Ashiikanal	
My socks	--- dashiikanumal
Your socks	--- ktashiikanumal
His\her socks	--- wtashiikanumal

Mahksun	
My shoe	--- nmahksum
Your shoe	--- kmahksun
His\her shoe	--- mahksun

Page from a Delaware-English dictionary used in Delaware language classes by the Moravian of the Thames Indian Band of Ontario, Canada. Photograph by Georgetta Stonefish Ryan.

with the ceremonies, they cannot join in conversations with their grandparents. Now my *takoja* [grandchildren] know even less than their parents.

As parents and grandparents, we survived the onslaught against our culture and language. But our children experience the consequences of our attempts to protect them from undergoing the malevolent policies of forced assimilation. We found we cannot be Native American in name only. Our language is an integral part of our identity. . . .

In 1984, Sinte Gleska University conducted a literacy and demographic survey. We found 30 percent of the homes on the Rosebud reservation listed Lakota as the language spoken in the home. These families actively retained our language and culture. The churches and government boarding schools had not been able to crush the spirit and pride of these families. They sustained our language despite all outside pressures to assimilate and even ridicule within.

I have long wondered just what it would be like to have control over our own education. The tribal colleges now have that opportunity to stop the course of our assimilation.

Integration of language and culture concepts can be mandated into all college courses. Teacher preparation programs can be developed to work within the cultural framework of our languages and culture. These courses will instruct prospective teachers to explore methods of restoring and sustaining our language. Language teaching methods and development can be researched. Our opportunities are limitless.

Sinte Gleska University is already training Lakota linguists and Lakota language teachers for grades K–12. The university's Lakota Studies Department, and Albert White Hat in particular, developed an exemplary orthography, the first by a Lakota-speaking tribal member. All the other orthographies were developed by non-Indians, the Catholic and Episcopal churches, and the University of Colorado. These orthographies lack an insight into our Lakota values and sacred language. Sinte Gleska is recording oral tradition for future generations and working with local schools, providing resource people to teach all areas of cultural education. These are only a few of the university's accomplishments. . . .

In order to help our children value and preserve our tribal languages, we must share with them what our people experienced because of the assimilationist ideology. Our children must realize the sadness and despair of losing what we had, so they may respond actively, saving what we have left. They then will come to understand and articulate the philosophical aspects and spiritual attachments we feel toward our language, the heart and mind of our culture.

If we are to teach our language in public schools we must consider the differences between the basic everyday language and sacred language used in ceremonies. Public schools can teach basic everyday language, but our sacred language should be taught by a qualified instructor who understands Lakota thought and philosophy.

We must be careful the public schools do not use our language to teach concepts that contradict our Lakota values. For example, the traditional concepts of cooperation over competition, generosity and compassion over materialism must be maintained. The desires of the individual ego over the welfare of the tribe is against our philosophy.

We must encourage the use of our language beyond home, intimate family settings and ceremonies. We must continue to encourage the use of our language in public gatherings and conversations. Our people need positive role models speaking our languages in public places. These are only a few of the considerations. We will learn from risk taking and experiences.

In the next decade we will lose many of the elders who have preserved our language and culture. I commend and thank those families for their vision and determination to preserve our language, for their pride and strong convictions. *He lila wopi-la tanka heca.* (This is something for which to be thankful).

From: Whirlwind Soldier, Lydia. "Survival and Restoration: Lessons from the Boarding School." *Tribal College* 4, no. 4 (Spring 1993): 24–25.

HUPA LANGUAGE
IMMERSION CAMP

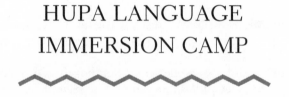

Jill Sherman Fletcher

Jill Sherman Fletcher, a Hoopa tribal member, is Hupa and Yurok. She directs the Hoopa Tribe's teaching program for all pre–high school students. One of about 50 native Californian languages spoken in the state today, Hupa is believed to have only between 12 and 25 fluent speakers. In a 1994 article published in a newsletter of The Advocates for Indigenous California Language Survival, Fletcher describes language immersion camps conducted by the Hoopa Tribe during the summer of 1993. These camps and other community-based native language programs are sure signs of native Californians battling to keep their languages alive.

The camp was held on the village of *Me'dil-din*, meaning "place of the boats." At one time it was the largest populated Hupa village. Today its residents consist of squirrels, lizards and an occasional snake. On that day not so long ago those squirrels, *mikye'ne:s*, watched as we diligently worked around the village. It was unusual for them to see people here unless there was a "Brush Dance" taking place. I am sure they wondered about us as we posted signs, moved garbage cans, set up tables and chairs, hauled water and moved tents. . . .

In the excitement of the camp, many of the elders arrived by five instead of six. They came with new ideas and small suggestions for the camp. They talked to one another about the "old days." They thought about families that came from the village. They thought about their own relatives. They cautiously made their way around the whole village looking at the signs we had carefully made. One sign posted in front of a tree read KIN. Another sign posted near a rock read TSE'. There was even a sign placed in the river which read HAN. They wondered and laughed at the cleverness of how each sign was posted. They also quietly shared hopes that this "language thing" would work so the people could again speak their language—after all, theirs had not always been a written language. . . .

A slight wind blew as the families arrived in the warmth of summer in the early evening. They were greeted in Hupa, *"hey-yung, tse' diyay-niwh-tsa:n,"* which means "Hello, I am glad to see you." I greeted them initially but then the participants went to sit with the elders, who had been patiently awaiting their arrival for over an hour. Everyone smiled, laughed, and listened to stories of yesterday. While laughter was in their eyes, pangs of hunger lurked in their stomachs. . . .

Dinner was finally ready. Elders were strategically placed, one to each table. Each table was served with the evening's meal: salmon, bread, salad, corn, coffee, juice, milk, water, salt, pepper, and butter. The elders understood what needed to be done. Not only the ingestion of food would take place but of language too.

"*Xwi=ching'ya:ng-xa:wh*," meaning "pass the . . ." in Hupa. Hupa language was being poured out along with the coffee and milk. Children boldly repeated words while the parents tentatively followed behind. Elders smiled and gently corrected mispronounced words. . . .

The campfire was started to announce the arrival of story time. Ray Baldy prayed a blessing for the camp while families nestled in each others' arms listening to words their hearts understood although their ears did not. . . . Jimmy Jackson and Herman [Sherman Sr.] shared a story about ol' coyote, then teased each other in Hupa and English about being a coyote. Jimmy spoke up and told the families about the importance of learning the language and using the language as a family. Jimmy said, "Sitting around the table, being told what to do, that's how I learned." He said it would take more than this camp. He was right: for people to learn the language it would take time and commitment, but it could be done. The families were encouraged by his genuine desire to see them learn. Somehow the stars seemed brighter in the night-darkened sky as the fire's flames danced warmly around, sowing the seeds of hopes for the future. . . .

Please know that not only did this camp introduce and familiarize the families with a language that was once theirs, but it also established the belief that the language can and will be learned.

From: Fletcher, Jill Sherman. "Na:tinixwe:Xonta—Hupa Home." In *News From Native California* 7, no. 4 (Fall/Winter 1993/94): 49–51.

NATIVE EDUCATION

Grey Squirrel, Navajo medicine man, making a sandpainting under the watchful eyes of a young boy. Photograph by George Hight. National Museum of the American Indian Smithsonian Institution.

Traditionally, Native American children were educated by their families, and espe-cially by grandparents, tribal elders, and religious and social groups, whose job it was to pass on to youngsters the world view, values, attitudes, beliefs, rules, roles, and skills that each group prized. Family and community exposed children to kinship roles, life-cycle rituals, religious ceremonial events, storytelling, and hands-on instruc-tion. Tribal educators taught tribal history, what would now be called earth or phys-ical sciences, physical education, codes of social behavior, religious training, health care, and many other subjects. And when relatives were not exposing them to these things, children played "tipi," "potlatch," and "family," trying on grown-up roles and preparing themselves for the time they would become adults with work responsi-bilities. Girls helped their mothers and grandmothers; boys assisted fathers and grandfathers. While they helped, they observed and listened to the words adults spoke.

Relatives practiced in the art of noninterference often stood back and allowed chil-dren to explore and experience things on their own. They permitted children to make their own decisions. When a child showed an aptitude for skills that the parents did not possess, they might arrange for that child to spend time with an expert. Native education practices ensured that another generation of Indians would inherit the knowledge and beliefs that were the basis of native identity and tribal survival.

This section begins with one of the first Indians schooled by missionaries, Hendrick Aupaumut (Mahican), describing how Indian children were traditionally taught by their parents. Ernest Benedict (Mohawk) also describes how oral traditions instruct children.

An anonymous Fox woman remembers helping her mother do spring planting, Pretty Shield (Crow) recalls playing with tiny tipis that mirrored real-life Crow villages, and Anna Price (Apache) describes imitating adults and playing wickiup. Charles James Nowell (Kwakiutl) describes playing potlatch. Anna Moore Shaw (Pima) describes how Pima girls learn the art of making baskets from the elderly women of the tribe. Mary Annette Clause (Tuscarora) tells of teaching her daughter to bead, while Jennie Weyaus (Chippewa) and Trudie Lamb-Richmond (Schaghticoke) describe how grandmothers pass down tribal ways. Alexander Saluskin (Yakima) tells how his uncle tutored him; John Thomas (Nitinaht) praises women as "the first teachers in our lives."

Several excerpts contrast native and non-native education. Wilfred Pelletier (Odawa) describes learning through experience, and Terry Tafoya (Taos/Warm Springs/Skokomish) advises Native educators to rely on the traditional Native way of learning; Leona Okakok (Inupiaq) contrasts "education" and "schooling." Cornel Pewewardy (Comanche-Kiowa) explains how Native American values per-meate the curriculum in a public magnet school in St. Paul, Minnesota. Finally, Ann Renker (Makah) warns readers that in Makah country traditional knowledge is not available to everyone.

TEACHING THE CHILDREN

Hendrick Aupaumut

Hendrick Aupaumut, a Mahican man born around 1757 in Stockbridge, Massachusetts, was an influential chief, translator, missionary, Indian agent, and diplomat. He received a mission school education at Stockbridge, serving as an assistant and translator under Congregational missionary John Sergeant. In the following historical sketch of the Mohegans, written around 1790 and published in 1854 as part of Electa Jones's Stockbridge Past and Present, *Aupaumut describes the traditional teachings parents handed down from generation to generation— teachings believed to be communicated to them from the Supreme Being.*

In order to please the Great, Good Spirit which they acknowledged to be their dependence, and on the other hand to withstand the evil one—therefore, the following custom was observed, which was handed down to them by their forefathers, and considered as communicated to them by Good Spirit.

The Head of each family—man or woman—would begin with all tenderness, as soon as daylight, to waken up their children and teach them, as follows:—

"My Children—you must remember that it is by the goodness of the Great, Good Spirit we are preserved through the night. My children you must listen to my words. If you wish to see many good days and evenings you must love to all men, and be kind to all people.

"If you see any that are in distress, you must try to help them. Remember that you will also be in distress some time or other. If you see one hungry you must give him something to eat: though you should have but little cake, give him half of it, for you also liable to hunger. If you see one naked, you must cover him with your own raiment. For you must consider that some future time you will also stand in need of such help; but if you will not assist, or have compassion for the poor, you will displease the Good Spirit; you will be called *Uh-wu-theet*, or hard-hearted, and nobody will pity on you the time of your distress, but will mock at you.

"My little Children, if you see aged man or woman on your way doing something, you must pity them, and help them instantly. In so doing, you will make their hearts glad, and they will speak well of you. And further, if you see your neighbors quarreling, you must try to make them to be good friends again. And you must always listen to the instruction of old folks: thereby you will be wise. And you must not be hasty to speak, when you hear people talking, nor allow yourself too much laughing. And if you find any that will speak evil against you, you must not speak evil words back, but shut your ears and mouth as though you hear nothing, and shun such people. And you must never quarrel to any person for quarreling belongs to evil spirit, and beast. But live in peace with all people: thereby you will please the Great, Good Spirit, and you will be happy.

"My little Children—you must be very kind to strangers. If you see stranger or strangers come by the side of your fireplace, you must salute them, and take them by the hand, and be friendly to them; because you will be a stranger some time or other. You must never speak any harsh words to strangers, but use them well as you can; thereby they will love you and will speak well of you wherever they be; and if you ever come into a strange country you will meet with such kindness. But if you will not be friendly to such, you will be in danger wherever you go.

"My Children—again listen. You must be honest in all your ways. You must always speak nothing but the truth wherever you are. But if you should love to tell lie, everybody will take notice of it; thereby you will bring a bad name to yourself. For instance—whenever people shall see you walking, they will say one to another with scorn, and point at you 'Look at that liar!' and even when you should bring tidings of importance with the truth, they shall not regard what you say.

"My Children—you must never steal anything from your fellow men, for remember this—you will not be pleased if some of your neighbors should take away your things by way of stealing; and you must also remember that the Great, Good Spirit see you. But if you will allow yourself to steal, you will hurt your name, and disgrace your parents and all relations; and you will be despised by all good people.

"My Children—you must always avoid bad company. And above all, you must never commit murder, because you wish to see long life. But if you commit murder, the Great, Good Spirit will be angry with you, and your life will be in great danger; also the life of your dear relations.

"My Children—you must be very industrious. You must always get up early morning to put on your clothes, *muk-sens*, and tie your belt about you, that you may be ready to do something; by so doing you will always have something to eat and to put on. But if you will be lazy, you will be always poor. Your eyes shall be on those who are industrious, and perhaps you will be shamefully beg or steal; and none will give you anything to eat without grudging.

"And further, my Children—when you grown up, you must not take wife or husband without the consent of your parents and all relations. But if you will do contrary to this, perhaps you will be joined to one who will bring great darkness to you, and thereby you will be very unhappy. . . ."

Thus they inculcate instruction to their children day after day until they are grown up; and after they are grown, yet they would teach them occasionally. And when young people have children they also teach theirs in like manner.—This custom is handed down from generation to another; at the same time it may be observed that there were some that did not take no pains to instruct their children, but would set bad examples before them, as well as there are such among civilized nations. But such men were roving about, and could not be contented to stay at one place.

From: Aupaumut, Hendrick. *History of the Muh-He-Con-nuk Indians.* In *Stockbridge Past and Present,* edited by Electa Jones. Springfield, Mass.: S. Bowles & Co., 1854.

YOU WILL MAKE YOUR OWN POSSESSIONS

~~~~~~~~~~~~~~

Anonymous

A Fox woman born about 1875, who preferred to remain anonymous, was interviewed through an interpreter in 1918. In a narrative looking back at her life, presented in Fox and English texts, the woman provides information about the way she was educated.

Well, when I was nine years old I was able to help my mother. It was in spring when planting was begun that I was told, "Plant something to be your own." Sure enough, I did some planting. When they began to hoe weeds where it was planted, I was told, "Say! You weed in your field." My hoe was a little hoe. And soon the hoeing would cease. I was glad.

When (we) ceased bothering where it was planted, I was unwilling to do anything. But when I would be told, "When you finish this, then you may go and play with the little girls," I was willing. I then surely played violently with the children. We played tag as we enjoyed it.

And at the time when what we planted was mature, I was told, "Say! You must try to cook what you have raised." Surely then I tried to cook. After I cooked it, my parents tasted it. "What she has raised tastes very well," they said to me. "And she has cooked it very carefully," I would be told. I was proud when they said that to me. As a matter of fact I was just told so that I might be encouraged to cook. And I thought, "It's probably true."

And when I was ten years old I ceased caring for dolls. But I still liked to swim. But when I said to my mother, "May I go swimming?" she said to me, "Yes. You may wash your grandmother's waist for her, and you may wash mine also," I was told. I was made to wash (anything) little. Surely I would not feel like asking, "May I go swimming," as I was afraid of the washing. Now as a matter of fact the reason why I was treated so was to encourage me to learn how to wash.

"That is why I treat you like that, so that you will learn how to wash," my mother told me. "No one continues to be taken care of forever. The time soon comes when we lose sight of the one who takes care of us. I never got to know how my mother looked. My father's sister brought me up. To-day I treat you just as she treated me. She did not permit me to be just fooling

95

around. Why, even when I was eight years old I knew how to cook very well. When my father's sister was busy with something, I did the cooking," she said to me. I did not believe her when she said that, for I was then ten years old and was just beginning to cook well, and I knew how to sew but I was poor at it. At that time when my mother woke up, she said to me, "Wake up, you may fetch some water. And go get some little dry sticks so we may start the fire," she said to me. When I was unwilling I was nevertheless compelled. That is the way I was always treated. . . .

And when I was eleven years old I likewise continually watched her as she would make bags. "Well, you try to make one," she said to me. She braided up one little bag for me. She instructed me how to make it. Sure enough, I nearly learned how to make it, but I made it very badly. I was again told, "You make another." It was somewhat larger. And soon I knew how to make it very well. . . .

She would be very proud after I had learned to make anything. "There, you will make things for yourself after you take care of yourself. That is why I constrain you to make anything, not to treat you meanly. I let you do things so that you may make something. If you happen to know how to make everything when you no longer see me, you will not have a hard time in any way. You will make your own possessions. My father's sister, the one who took care of me, treated me so. That is why I know how to make any little thing. . . . And that is why I treat you so to-day. . . . It is because I am fond of you and wish you to know how to make things. If I were not fond of you, I would not order you around (to do things) . . . I desire that you take care of yourself quietly," my mother told me.

And again, when I was twelve years old, I was told, "Come, try to make these." (They were) my own moccasins. "You may start to make them for yourself after you know how to make them. For you already know how to make them for your dolls. That is the way you are to make them," I was told. She only cut them out for me. "This is the way you are to make it," I was told. Finally I really knew how to make them. . . .

Soon I was told, "Well, begin to try to weave; you may wish to make these mats." Then I began to try to weave. Later I knew how to weave very well. Then I began to help my mother all the time. She was proud when I continued to learn how to make anything.

From: Michelson, Truman, *The Autobiography of a Fox Woman*. U.S. Bureau of American Ethnology, 40th Annual Report. Washington, D.C.: Government Printing Office, 1925.

I TRIED TO BE LIKE MY MOTHER

~~~~~~~~~

Pretty Shield

Pretty Shield, a Crow medicine woman, was born "across the Big [Missouri] River from the mouth of Plum Creek in the moon when the ice goes out of rivers [March]," around the year 1857. In 1932, when agency rolls showed her age as 74, using sign language she told her story to Frank B. Linderman through an interpreter. In her account of her people's cultural life before Euro-Americans disrupted it, she tells how childhood play prepared—and educated—Crow children for adulthood.

I tried to be like my mother, and like another woman, besides . . . I carried my doll on my back just as mothers carry their babies; and besides this I had a little teepee [lodge] that I pitched whenever my aunt pitched hers. It was made exactly like my aunt's, had the same number of poles, only of course my teepee was very small. My horse dragged the poles and packed the lodge-skin, so that I often beat my aunt in setting up my lodge, which she pretended made her jealous. And how I used to hurry in setting up my lodge, so that I might have a fire going inside it before my aunt could kindle one in hers! I did not know it then, but now I feel sure that she often let me beat her just to encourage me. Each year, as was our custom, I made myself a new lodge and set it up, as the grownups did, when we went into our winter camps. Each time I made a new one I cut my lodge-skin larger than the old one, took more and more pains to have it pretty. I played with these little lodges, often lived in them, until I was a married woman, and even after. I have never lost my love for play.

Once several of us girls made ourselves a play village with our tiny teepees. Of course our children were dolls, and our horses dogs, and yet we managed to make our village look very real, so real that we thought we ought to have some meat to cook. We decided to kill it ourselves. A girl named Beaver-that-passes borrowed her father's lance that was very sharp, and longer than both our bodies put together. We caught and saddled two gentle packhorses; and both the old fools went crazy before we managed to kill a calf. I helped all I could, but it was Beaver-that-passes who wounded a big calf that gave us both a lot of trouble before we finally got it down, and dead. I hurt my leg, and Beaver-that-passes cut her hand with the lance. The calf itself looked pretty bad by the time we got it to our play-village. But we had a big feast, and forgot our hurts. . . .

Cheyenne girls playing with their toy tipi and dolls around 1900. Smithsonian Institution, National Anthropological Archives.

And sometimes . . . we made ourselves into mud-clowns and entertained the village, riding double on old horses that we made to look as funny as ourselves. There was one old man who would always drum for us, because drumming is not for women; and we would sing and dance through the village, stopping to show off before the lodges of our particular friends. Often women would come out and as though to pay us for our performances, give us meat and berries to eat. [The Crows are fond of clowning. With mud alone they are able to transform themselves, and even their horses, into grotesque figures] . . . one day several girls and a boy were going to have a play sun-dance. . . . Our lodges were pitched on Spotted-fish creek [Judith country], a nice place for us children to play. The day was warm. Flowers were everywhere, and birds were singing in the bushes and trees. There is a cliff not far from where the Crow lodges were pitched that day, and we children pitched our brush-lodge for our play sun-dance at the foot of this cliff. We believed that our dance was real. We felt very serious. I said that there was but one boy with us. There were two, one to beat the drum, and one who danced. The dancer wore only his moccasins and breech-clout, as men do, and of course, he was painted. We girls wore our usual clothes, as dancing women do, painting our faces to please ourselves.

The dance made us forget everything else . . . The beating drum, our whistles, made from the big bone of an eagle's wing, our dancing, made us grownups whose hearts were in the sun-dance. . . .

From: Linderman, Frank B. *Pretty Shield: Medicine Woman of the Crows.* Lincoln: University of Nebraska Press, 1974.

PLAYING WICKIUP

Anna Price

Anna Price, or Her Grey Eyes, an Eastern White Mountain Apache woman born around 1837 in Arizona, was a trusted informant of anthropologist Grenville Goodwin. In his interview with her in 1937 when she was about one hundred years old, Price gives an account of her childhood, which included playing wickiup *[the Apache word for dwelling]. She points out how closely children imitated such Apache cultural realities as marriage negotiations, quarreling with spouses, and butchering cows.*

We children used to play wickiups. Some of them were as high as one arm span. We built little fires inside them, just like a real wickiup. We played at getting married and having families. Girls and boys played together at this. When we played at marriage, we were always careful not to marry some child who was of our own clan, just as big people were. We played at marriage negotiations, the girl's family and boy's family exchanging gifts of food. The food was made of mud and water. When it came time for the presentation of these gifts, the members of the family receiving them would all line up on one side to get their share. Sometimes we would make a gift of horses to the other family. The horses were boys. After the marriage, the husband would call his wife's mother and father *ca da ni* [proper affinal term]. If a boy passed his mother-in-law, both he and she would hide their faces in their hands, so they would not look upon each other. We used to use the polite form of the third person in talking between son-in-law and parent-in-law, just like grown people. In the same way we joked a woman or man whom we called . . . [terms for woman married to relative and man married to relative], and they us, because they were married to someone we pretended was a relative. We also pretended we had cross-cousins with whom we joked.

After a boy got married, he would pretend to go hunting with other men [boys]. They used other boys as their horses. They would make bundles of soft *k'ai* bark [a willow], large ones, and pack them on their horses. This was the meat. When he arrived home, the husband would have his wife take the meat as a gift to his relatives-in-law. The relatives-in-law divided the meat among themselves. They would pretend to be waiting for a few days, and then the man's wife would go among her relatives who had been given the meat and tell them to go hunting for her husband's family. The men started off. When they returned with their meat, it was brought over to the husband's mother and presented to her. That was how they got even again. Sometimes a boy went out hunting in an irrigated field and killed a gopher. He would send it over by his wife to his mother-in-law. His mother-in-law would skin and butcher it. Then she would start to tan the hide, scraping it and all. It was easy to tan these gopher hides, and the mother-in-law sometimes would remark sarcastically, "This hide must be rotten. It tans too easily."

You know how some men quarrel continually with their wives? Well, we used to play that this happened. A boy would fight his wife until her father would take her away from him. Boys took their daughters back just like grownups. A boy would speak angrily to his son-in-law, "I have never received anything from you, so I am going to take my daughter back." In the evening the husband would go to his wife's parents' home where his wife had been taken. He would want his wife back and say . . . ["look, come here"], just like a real man does. But the girl's mother would say, "No, I won't let her go with you any more."

When we played family with a boy for a husband, we used to have children. We had dolls as well. Each family had its own wickiup. We pretended there were many camps together and lots of people about. There were even old men and old women among us. We used to play that our husbands went out hunting. They would kill a lot of young bats, if they could find them, or small birds or gophers. They brought them home. The wives played at making buckskin of the gophers' hides. When a husband came home with meat, he or his wife might tell another boy living close by, "Don't leave your camp. I want you to stay there, for I am going to give you a lot of fine meat in a little while."

Generally, boys pretended to be horses, but sometimes girls played at being mares, while the boys were stallions and geldings. They would run about holding two sticks in their hands for the front legs. In the morning the man owning the horses went out after them. When he drove them to camp, we would try to catch them. Some were wild and ran about. We couldn't catch these. Whenever we moved camp, we tried to pack our belongings on our horses. Some of the wild horses would run away with the packs. Boys pretended that they were cattle sometimes. When we wanted one to eat, we would catch him, tie his legs together, and throw him. Then we would start to cut his throat, as you do in butchering a cow. The boys would begin to bellow just as a cow does. We pretended to skin one side of the carcass, and then, before rolling it over to skin the other side, we pretended to lay brush down beneath it so the meat would not be soiled. As we butchered, we called out the name of each part we took out, even each internal organ.

Among other things, we pretended we had farms and that we raised large crops. We would gather little bunches of green weeds and stick them up in the ground. We put wild gourds at the ends of these to make them look as if they grew there. These we called squash. We broke off black walnut branches with green nuts on them and stuck them in the ground for corn. We played at hiring girls and boys to work in our fields for us and to build little fences about them, just like grownups do. We women [girls] would pretend to fight among ourselves about the division of the irrigating water and our turns at using it. When harvest time came, we gathered all our crops out of the fields. We bundled the walnuts together and hung them up to dry, just as is done with corn.

When we found stones with hollow places in them, we pretended that they were pots. We made little pots and baskets of mud also, and we used to make play coil baskets and water bottles out of needles of the yellow pine, of yucca leaves, or leaves of the narrow-leafed yucca, even sometimes the cottonwood. Boys made knives of the sharp-edged leaves of bear grass. The children had play skirts and women's poncho capes of the inner bark of *k'ai* and wore them in our play. We made braided headbands from the same material, and sometimes we shredded it out and wore it on our heads, pretending it was long hair. . . .

At times we were gone all day. When we got home, some children would say to their parents, "We've been having a good time all day . . ." The parents might get mad and scold them, but it wasn't for playing. . . . That was all right. It was because the children had been gone all day without anything to eat.

From: Goodwin, Grenville. *Social Organization of the Western Apache.* Chicago: University of Chicago Press, 1942.

PLAY POTLATCHES

Charles James Nowell

Charles James Nowell, a Kwakiutl man born in 1870 at Fort Rupert, in what is now British Columbia, Canada, was interviewed in English in 1940. His narrative, published in book form, tells about Kwakiutl beliefs and values, especially the legendary potlatch, a ceremonial event combining feasting and the formal distribution of gifts according to a person's rank. Gifts are presented before an audience serving as witnesses. In his description of playing potlatch, Nowell shows just how closely young boys imitated the behavior of older men in potlatches, owing to the instruction of fathers and older brothers.

When I was a boy we used to give potlatches of small canoes to imitate the potlatches of older people. I had small canoes made for me just the shape of the big ones. My second brother made some of them, and I paid other older people tobacco and things to make some others for me. When I have enough to give my potlatch, I go around to all the boys of the other tribes at Fort Rupert. I call my own tribe boys to come in front of my house and to count these small canoes and put them in rows according to the rank of the fathers of the boys. This imitates the real potlatch of canoes that the older men have. Then some of the older boys of my own tribe make speeches like those of the men as they speak in their potlatches. In the potlatch I gave, they made speeches telling them I am giving away these little canoes, and that my name will be "Devil-fish" from now on.

Now when we have these boys' potlatches, we all get names of different kind of fishes or things like that. These are our names amongst the boys when we give these potlatches. This kind of potlatch is a play potlatch, and after the older boy that is taking the part of the chief speaks, then they begin to sing my song for this potlatch. The older boys give this kind of play potlatch with boxes and shirts and other things, so that they have these different kinds of names. These are not real potlatches. I gave mine before I came to Alert Bay to school. The older women have the same kind of potlatch even when they are married. They used to give away dishes, spoons, boxes, and those things that belong to them, and they called it by the same name.

Our fathers and older brothers teach us to give these potlatches, and help us do it, telling us all about what we should do to do it right. That is just like teaching us what we should do when we get grown up and give real potlatches. My older brothers were the ones who taught me, but they didn't come and watch us while we gave them. They only heard about it and how we did afterwards. When I come home, they tell me that is fine. They are the ones that started it—I wouldn't have done it if they hadn't started it—and they helped me all the time with my play potlatches.

If any of us has a quarrel between us, regarding our potlatch, then the other one that I have quarreled with would give his potlatch and try to make it bigger than mine. That is, he wants to get ahead of me. He wants to get in a higher place than me, even though we didn't have any real places in our clan yet. If he gives a bigger potlatch than me, I go to my father's brother to help me give another potlatch that is bigger than his. For this we use little canoes and other things, until one of us has to quit. The other fellow's parents help him and so on back and forth till one couldn't do any more. The one that gives the most is supposed to be higher than the other. The other goes lower down. Every time we pretend to quarrel, or really do quarrel, if I give more than he does, I keep telling him he is lower than me.

From: Ford, Clellan S. *Smoke from Their Fires: The Life of a Kwakiutl Chief.* Hamden, Connecticut: Archon Books, 1941.

LEARNING THROUGH LISTENING

Wilfred Pelletier

Wilfred Pelletier, an Odawa Indian born in the village of Wikwemikong on Ontario's Manitoulin Island, Canada, wrote "Childhood in an Indian Village" for a Toronto magazine about 1966, while on the staff of the Institute for Indian Studies at Rochdale College in Toronto.

I have been to numerous communities across Canada and I still do not find where Indians teach. All young children were allowed to grow, to develop, to learn. They didn't teach you that this was mommy, daddy, desk, ash tray, house, etc. We learned about these things by listening to the words adults spoke, what they said when they were talking, and built our own kind of relationship with the article. If you observe your children now you will see a child turn a chair over, cover it with a blanket and use it for a house. He can relate many ways to a chair. As we get older we have only one relationship and that is to stick our rear ends on that chair. It's for no other purpose, and, in fact, we tell our kids that that is what it is, and it belongs in a corner and don't move it out of there.

These things I remember very well. We were brought up to have a different relationship to a house and to all the things that surrounded us. That is, the values that adults placed on things in the community did not necessarily carry over into their child and lead him to place the same values on them. Children discovered the values of these things on their own, and developed their own particular relationships to them.

This is very closely related to the religion of the community, which centered entirely on man. One of the practiced ethics of the community was non-interference. No one interfered with us, and this way of living still exists today. If you go to an Indian home the kids don't come up and bug you while you are talking to someone else. They might come and stand by you quietly, just as an adult might. If you observe Indians someplace, they will stand quietly, and only when they are acknowledged will they speak. If they get into a group session, they will act the same way. They will sit and listen to people talk, and when they get the opportunity they will speak, but they won't cut you off or interfere. There are some who do this now, but not very many. Most of them will just wait.

And part of the reason our parents say so little is that that's their way. They don't teach like white people. They let their children make their own decisions. The closest they ever got to formal teaching was to tell stories. Let me give you an example. We had been out picking blueberries one time, and while sitting around this guy told us this story. The idea was that he wanted to get us to wash up—to wash our feet because we had been trampling through this brush all day long. He talked about a warrior who really had a beautiful body. He was very well built, and he used to grease himself and take care of his body. One day this warrior was out, and he ran into a group of other people whom he had never seen before. They started to chase him. He had no problem because he was in such good shape. He was fooling around and playing with them because he was such a good runner. He ran over hills and over rocks, teasing them. Then he ran into another group. The first group gave up the chase. But now he had to run away from this other group, and he was fooling around doing the same thing with them. All of a sudden he ran into a third group. He ran real hard and all of a sudden he fell. He tried to get up and he couldn't. He spoke to his feet and said, "What's wrong with you? I'm going to get killed if you don't get up and get going." They said, "That's alright. You can comb your hair and grease your body and look after your legs and arms but you never did anything for us. You never washed us or cleaned us or greased us or nothing." He promised to take better care of the feet if they would get up and run, and so they did.

This is one of the stories we were told, and we went up and washed our feet right away and then went to bed. Maybe this happens among other ethnic groups, I don't know, but this is the kind of learning we had. I will never forget the kinds of things we learned, because to me it all belongs to me. It isn't something that someone says is so; it's mine. I'd wanted to go hunting, and the guys would know I couldn't get across the stream because it was flooded, but they wouldn't say anything. They'd let me go, and they'd say O.K. knowing all the time I couldn't get through. But they wouldn't tell me that. They'd let me experience it. And I'm grateful to these people for allowing me to have this kind of exploration/learning situation. Secondly, of course, that fact is that maybe I could have gotten across where they couldn't, discovered something different, a method that was new. I think this kind of learning situation is one of the really important things that Indians have today and which could contribute to the society we have today. That is, a learning situation *For people*, instead of teaching or information giving.

From: Pelletier, Wilfred. "Childhood in an Indian Village." In *This Book Is about Schools*, edited by Satu Repo. New York: Pantheon Books, 1970.

TRAINED BY AN EXPERT

Alexander Saluskin

Alexander Saluskin, a Yakima man in his seventies from Toppenish, Washington, participated in a 1968 conference sponsored by the New York–based Myrin Institute for Adult Education. During the week-long meetings, a group of Indian leaders discussed problems of education and tradition. Mr. Saluskin, who planned to attend the University of New Mexico to obtain his BA in language, shared the traditional way he was educated by a tutor, his uncle, an expert in Yakima ways.

In our tribal custom, which was handed down to my grandfather, Chief Saluskin Wee-al-wick, each of his children were assigned to a tutor, like he had been by his grandparents, so that each child, each of his descendants, should be trained by an expert. These experts were proficient in hunting and everything for survival, as well as teaching the blessing of the Great Creator. I was assigned to my uncle and his name was Twi-nant in Indian name, in English they call him Billy Saluskin. So he and his wife had undertaken to bring me under their wing for a season. This was after I had one year of schooling.

My grandfather came and asked my father if I would make a trip with them to the mountains where they hunt for deer, as well as mountain sheep, and gather huckleberries. They caught salmon from the spawning beds there and dried them for their provisions while they were staying in the mountains. Naturally, they depended for their livelihood on what they could catch and kill, as well as catch small fish from the streams.

When we began, first I was to learn how to control my horse, which was given to me with a complete outfit, as well as a gun. Then we came to the first camp. Early in the morning my uncle started to assume his responsibilities, got me out of bed, and he says, "Nephew, let's hurry down to the creek. It's my duty now to train you, to equip you with the wisdom and knowledge that I had acquired. First of all, we're going to go down to this swift stream and we're going to plunge in that stream and we will disturb the old lady." (We referred to the stream as an old lady). "We'll disturb her and the old lady will rub you down and soothe up your sore muscles and give you an endurance for the rest of the day." I knew I had to do the things that I was told. We went down and we stripped off and jumped into this swift water, very cold. We stayed in the water until my body was numb. We came up and pranced around, jumped up and down to get our circulation going. We put on our clothes and by the time we got back to camp, the breakfast was ready.

Again we were taught how to care for the horses and how to handle them. As we traveled, the same processes were conducted until we reached our destination.

As soon as we reached our destination, I was told that the sweat house and the hot rocks which were prepared for the sweat house were blessings taught and handed down from the Great Spirit. This hot water caused by cold water on the hot rocks would cleanse you and purify your scent, so the wild animals wouldn't detect you. You would have the scent the same as the fir bough and reeds that grow in the mountains. So naturally I had to believe that this was the case. I followed through this system and we had to do this every morning about three o'clock while we were in the mountains.

At the end of our trip, I was wiry; I could walk probably for days and weeks if I had to. I had gone through my course of training for survival. I learned every herb, root, berries, and how to take care of them. This kind uncle of mine and his wife took time to explain these things step by step. They didn't leave one thing untold and it was shown physically to me, then asked me if I could do it.

From: Morey, Sylvester M. *Can the Red Man Help the White Man?: A Denver Conference with the Indian Elders*. New York: Myrin Institute, 1970.

MAKING PIMA BASKETS

Anna Moore Shaw

Anna Moore Shaw, a Pima woman, was born about 1898 in a tradi-
tional brush dwelling on the Gila River Reservation in Arizona. At the
age of seventy, she wrote an autobiography in which she describes the tra-
ditional education of Dawn, a fictionalized but typical Pima girl, who
learns the art of making baskets from the elderly women of the tribe.

. . . Dawn's life did not become complete until the day dear Grandmother
Red Flowers decided that her young fingers had reached the stage where
they could learn to weave the magnificent Pima baskets.

Dawn helped gather river willow twigs and cattail reeds with eager glee.
She gladly picked the black devil's claws at the edges of the irrigated fields,
for these weeds would form the striking black designs on her beautiful baskets. Red Flowers showed her granddaughter how to place the devil's claws
in water for a week, to soften the tough thorns. After the two had stripped
the sides of each claw with sharp awls, they threw the rest of the plant away.

Next came preparation of the cattails. Red Flowers demonstrated the trick
of splitting the weeds with the teeth, then spreading them in the sun to dry.
The young willow twigs were stripped free of leaves, then split in half with
the teeth. These were rolled up while damp and flexible, then tied with
string or strips of willow bark and hung on the rafters of the *olas kih* [brush
roundhouse] to dry until they were needed.

At first it was hard for Dawn's untrained fingers to learn the complex art.
"Have patience, my dear," grandmother would say. "Basket-weaving is to
teach you patience, my granddaughter."

But it took such infinite patience! To weave intently, then unravel when
it was not perfect, was the hardest thing for Dawn. But in time her fingers
grew supple and skillful. When Grandmother Red Flowers finally nodded
with prideful approval upon seeing a finished basket, Dawn knew she was
ready to go to *Nahsa*, the famous weaver, who lived in Slippery Rock Village.

"Please, grandmother," Dawn said humbly. "I would like to learn the art
from the great Nahsa."

"You are ready, my child," replied grandmother with love, "but you know
you must stay with her for one whole moon in order to learn properly. Are
you ready to leave us for such a time?"

Dawn looked up at her grandmother respectfully. "I wish to learn to weave, grandmother," she said simply. "I wish to become expert like the great Nahsa."

So it was that Red Flowers took Dawn to Nahsa. The old lady lived in an *olas kih* of her son's household and spent all her days weaving the most beautiful of baskets. She was an exacting but patient teacher. How many times she said softly, "No Dawn, the devil's claw goes this way in this design—in a circle, not an oval. This is the ancient maze pattern of Pima legend. You must make it right, Dawn, exactly right."

After one month of weaving, Dawn's basket was perfect. The traditional Pima patterns of long ago marched along the sides of it in beautiful symmetry. When Red Flowers came to get her granddaughter she marveled at the work. She said nothing, but in truth she could not tell this basket from one of Nahsa's.

Dawn wanted to keep her masterpiece, but for years she had been told that she must give her first great finished basket to her teacher for good luck. In this way, Nahsa's talent would rub off on her, and in her time she would gain the skill and renown of an expert.

From: Shaw, Anna Moore. *A Pima Past.* Tucson: University of Arizona Press, 1974.

THROUGH THESE STORIES WE LEARNED MANY THINGS

Ernest Benedict

Ernest Benedict, a 56-year-old Mohawk from the St. Regis Reservation in New York State, taught Introductory Indian Studies at Trent University in Peterboro, Ontario, ran the education department on the Canadian side of the St. Regis Reservation, and around 1972 founded and headed the North American Indian Traveling College, located on Cornwall Island, that takes Iroquois history, language, and culture to Indian communities. As a participant in the 1972 conference on the traditional upbringing of American Indian children sponsored by the New York–based Myrin Institute for Adult Education, he spoke about the role storytelling plays in instructing Mohawk children.

Among my people, not only lullabies but stories play a very important role in instructing children. Fall and winter are storytelling time, the time of legends. During the summer, I guess, children are expected to be much too busy and active for stories, and anyway, by the time it gets dark, it's bedtime.

The real old legends that still survive almost always have a moral. Many of them are about various birds and animals and are meant to teach children about virtues and faults. The story of how the robin got his red breast, for example, really tells you how to take care of birds and animals, and how you should try to treat them almost as people, as guests.

Then there's the story of the rabbit who wanted to show off. He was showing how fast and how long he could run. He ran so long that eventually it began snowing and the snow got packed underneath him and lifted him way up. It snowed and snowed and soon he found himself up in the branches of the trees. So he jumped into a tree and fell asleep. While he was sleeping, the snow melted and there he was still up in that tree. Since he had no claws with which to climb down, he eventually had to jump out of the tree. His tail and ears got caught in a branch so that his ears stretched way out and his tail got permanently stuck up there. Then he fell and hit his nose against a sharp object and split his face. That explains his split nose and his stretched-out ears and why his tail comes out every spring in the pussy willows. And so a lesson is learned about showoffs and smart alecks.

Some of these stories are purely for entertainment. Then, of course, there are the tall stories, some of which have been modernized. For instance, a man was telling about how well he tended his garden. He got a potato out of it that was big enough to fill a wheelbarrow. So another man says, "I got one so big that when I dug it up out of the garden, I hit it with a shovel and it sounded hollow. So I cut a hole and got down inside of it and found another garden in it with a potato field!"

These are some of the stories that are told during the winter. Children are usually encouraged to stay up. The evenings start early and are long, and so the children can stay up and listen to them. Now that I look back on it, the grownups would rather have been doing something else, but they told stories for the benefit and entertainment of the kids, and it was through these stories that we learned many things. Even the tall tales contained a lesson. Youngsters were shown that a lie is so ridiculous that you shouldn't give it any belief at all, that it isn't worthy of serious thought. So we received a kind of moral teaching through our legends and tales.

From: Morey, Sylvester M., and Olivia L. Gilliam, editors. *Respect for Life: The Traditional Upbringing of American Indian Children*. New York: Myrin Institute, 1974.

THE OLD WAYS TEACH US

Terry Tafoya

Terry Tafoya, of Taos, Warm Springs, and Skokomish heritage, has been a freelance consultant on native and bilingual education throughout western Canada and the United States. In his speech at the 12th General Assembly of the Union of British Columbia Indian Chiefs in September 1980, he speaks about being a prophet, with a small "p." In his own words, "prophets with a little p look ahead and warn people of dangers that are coming and say, 'here are some of the ways you might act.'" In his speech, Tafoya warns native educators against relying on non-Indian educational methods that emphasize product. He advises native educators to focus on process, the traditional native way of learning.

Education, as practiced by our ancestors, does not correspond with "education" as non-natives define it . . .

Product and process are two different things. White culture teaches us to evaluate or judge by *Production*. If the number of logs in the timber industry drops, something is wrong. But we cannot judge our children's achievement by the number of baskets they make or the salaries they can earn. Beware that you do not end up only looking at the end of a process. Life itself is the journeying, not the destination. The things that have traditionally been done within the tribes are a training process—the sweat lodge, old-fashioned methods of hunting and fishing, storytelling, Indian dancing—all these teach discipline, teach an attitude towards the Mother Earth, and an understanding of what our place is with all our relations. In short, the old ways teach us our purpose for being. White society has always shied away from understanding the purpose of life in terms of the everyday person. The business of life is life. The traditional native way maintains and renews life. This is the focus of our ceremonies, public renewals not only of our own lives, but the renewal of the Earth Mother's life. White people use terms like "ecosystem" or "biosphere" as a limited way of understanding what we mean when we speak of the Earth. But they only look around them. Thus it is all right to pollute one stream, because the majority of people don't live near there; it is all right to build a nuclear plant in a desert because few people (besides Indians) live there. When you understand that all of our lives are only a small part of a greater life—the Earth herself—your attitude changes.

You take a larger view—see with the eyes of an eagle, like our old people tell us. When you destroy life, it is like throwing a stone into a pond. The ripples cannot be stopped. To pollute or dam a stream destroys a salmon run, and will therefore change the lifestyle of a people where culture, economy, and religion are based on salmon. What we call "witch-fires," the nuclear energy with which the Whites play in the interest of economy, cannot be made safe, but only buried. If we see the Earth as a living body, we can understand that putting poison within any part of that body will eventually infect the whole.

This is the ultimate danger of separating process from product. To only see the end means we are blind to the path that leads to the end we feel we should seek. To be blind to the path means you fail to see other possible avenues and destinations. . . .

All the elements of traditional life contributed in making a complete Indian in the old days. I've heard old people say that discipline begins on the board, meaning that a tiny baby strapped to the cradleboard is already being taught certain things that are valued by his or her tribe. The rituals of fasting, spirit quests, giveaways, and feasts all taught things that cannot simply be summed up and poured into a child's ear the way conventional education pours in arithmetic. They are all processes of learning. The skills learned in beadwork, tanning hides, and traditional fishing all teach patience as well as physical coordination. Beadwork, weaving, and basketmaking all teach a way of seeing the world in a different way, of being able to visualize what does not yet exist, learning to see how patterns can be made or taken away to build something that can be recognized and understood. . . .

If you want to end up with a traditional Indian person you're going to have to provide all those things which form those values, behaviors, and thought patterns that we so loosely call "traditional." Otherwise it's like trying to come up with a chocolate cake and neglecting to add baking powder, eggs, and sugar. You get something, but not what you wanted.

Ask yourself honestly if you really think a child who lacks the discipline that used to begin on the board and which was enhanced by the skills of beadwork, tanning, fishing, and hunting, is going to listen respectfully to an elder who comes into the classroom or sit quietly and watch a videotape of how canoes were made. *I am not saying books, videotapes, or culture programs are not needed.* I am saying we need to look very closely at how we can best use these things within a school and community setting. With the small number of elders we have, and the mortality rate what it is, I think it is vital that we record as much as we can from our old people before they are gone. It is a tragedy that so many tribes have to record artificially what would have been taught and remembered in the old days. But we have to act swiftly. I would prefer to see that what we gather be used more as a resource and reference, where we train teachers, aides, and older students what was recorded there, and then have those people work directly with our young children, so they may experience the exchange of knowledge firsthand. No videotape can possibly replace the presence of an elder. Use elders if they are willing, but a younger person working with the teaching of an elder is going to be more effective in some ways than a videotape of an elder saying the same thing. This goes back to the concept of interactions between people. Those personal interactions have always been important to native people. . . .

From: Tafoya, Terry. "The Directions of Indian and Native Education: Culture, Content, and Container." *Bilingual Resources* 4, nos. 2–3 (1980): 45–47.

TRADITIONAL TRAINING

~~~~~~~~~~~~~~~~~~~~~

John Thomas

John Thomas, a Nitinaht man, was born in 1913 at Clo-oose on Vancouver Island. A fisherman, logger, and a linguistics teacher at the University of Victoria and at Neah Bay in Washington State, he describes in a narrative written in 1983 the role of women, the "first teachers in our lives," and the traditional way Indian children over six years old were often trained by family members other than their mothers and fathers.

As far back as I remember, we were still practising the old way of being with our mothers for the first six years of our life. At that time women had equal standing in the band—very important because they were the first teachers in our lives. In the life of an Indian growing up, she was considered to be the first teacher of mankind. So her position was as important, maybe more so, than the men. She taught us everything that a young child should know, even helped us to start walking and start talking. We learned our language from her. This took about six years of our lives and then we were turned over to our uncles for training. It was never the father who trained you because they're too personal. This was traditional in certain families. I come from a whale hunter's family, so I'll talk about that kind of training. If I was a fisherman's son or a hunter's son, I would have been initiated differently and trained differenly. My uncle trained me in getting along in life so it would be easier to survive. At that time we had no supermarkets or places where you could go to buy meat and things. We had to live off the land. In order to do this, we had to be trained. My uncle and my grandfather taught me the physical and spiritual sides of life. They taught us at equal rates. So we were taught to pray while building up our physical strength.

For about four years I went through the training with my uncle. He was real impersonal. He wouldn't think anything of shoving me into the river. My father would never do that. Many of these things were harsh and hard to take. For instance, I was hit with a switch, a spruce limb, while I was standing there naked. He told me to look across the river and not to holler whatever happens—don't cry out. He gave me a piece of stick to put between my teeth—if it fell out, I failed. You were never to cry out, no matter how much the pain or how uncomfortable you were. There were about eleven kids in our group, and just seven of us got through because the others dropped the sticks out of their mouths and cried out. When he hit me with the switch on my back I jumped, and I'm not ashamed to say that I pretty near swallowed the stick. But I didn't make a noise. Next thing I knew I was being lifted up bodily and thrown into the river. My uncle came in after me to see that I didn't stay under. Then he told me what to say—the first words for when you come out. You have to face the east where the sun comes up, and pray, pray for a successful life and pray that you're not going to fail. These words are secrets within families and among families and nobody else repeats it because that's your own personal kind of prayer. We were taught to pray and to keep ourselves clean—to sort of purify our bodies and minds at the same time, and not to think different thoughts. Certain thoughts in your mind were forbidden. We were separated from our sisters who went to their aunts and their grandmothers where they had their own way of learning how to get along in this world.

I was sent to school when I was ten years old, so I didn't complete the training. I was learning to make tools, hunting implements, bows and arrows, different spears—especially the whale spear which is part of our ancestral heritage. There is a lot to whale hunting. You don't just go out and catch a whale. You had to be physically and spiritually fit. You had to know what you were doing. One mistake could be your last, so you were told over and over again how to perform certain rituals to get the power to go out and hunt the whales. To this end, we were taught how to make the tools, even pieces of rope. We learned what to say to the tree before cutting it down, which way to fall it. You didn't just cut it down. It took four days just to cut down a tree for a whale spear. You had to fall it toward the sun, just when the sun was coming up over the mountain. You treated it like a person coming home. You talked to it and you continued to talk to it even when you were using it to spear a whale. So things like this were part of it all. Every little piece of equipment was spoken to. You were old enough to go hunting when you finished the training. You had to go through a lot of things before you touched the whale gear. You had to wait till you had twenty-odd years of training. If you failed—like some of the kids in our group—then it took longer. It wasn't a disgrace or a shame to fail because of the harsh things you go through, but if you failed two, three times, then you weren't good enough.

From: Haegert, Dorothy. *Children of the First People*. Vancouver, British Columbia: Tillacum/ Arsenal Pulp Press Book, 1983.

INDIAN WAYS

Jennie Weyaus

In 1985, the Minnesota Chippewa Tribe published a history of the Mille Lacs Band of Anishinabe (or Chippewa) who lived along the southwestern shores of Lake Mille Lacs. Included with the history were reminiscenses of Mille Lacs elders who told about the past as they experienced it. In sharing her memories, Jennie Weyaus, who was born and grew up in Mille Lacs, explains how she was educated.

I was raised by my grandmother. That's who instilled the Indian ways in me. My mother died when I was about two years old, I think. My dad went to White Earth [another Chippewa reservation in Minnesota]. My real grandfather died when my mother was just a little girl. I just had a stepgrandfather, but he was a real grandfather to me, though. She (grandmother) talked about her growing up days. How they never had a permanent home. In the winter, they moved around a lot where the game was plentiful. In the fall, they moved here and there to gather wild rice. Same thing in the spring to gather maple sap. They went across the Lake for that. She told me they had to travel by foot, carrying everything on their backs.

She made maple syrup. My uncles and I would help her gather maple sap, bring in wood for her. She made those spigots out of wood and tapped the trees by hand. I think the spigots were made of basswood.

She gathered roots and flowers for her medicine. To this day, I don't know what she gathered. She used skunk oil. It used to taste awful. She'd stick it way down my throat. She gathered bulrushes to make mats. I used to carry the bundles in for her. . . .

They got about two hundred pounds of finished wild rice every year. It was more than enough. She gave some to her parents who were old and couldn't do things for themselves. We had a sixteen-foot canoe for gathering. When you bring it home, you spread it on a tarp to let it dry out. Then you take out the sticks. You parch the rice in a kettle 'til it's nice and brown. Then the old men used to thrash it by foot. They used moccasins made out of old blue jeans, tie those and stomp on the rice 'til it's all cleaned out. Then you winnow all those hulls out. You lift it up so the wind blows all those husks out.

A mother and her two daughters dancing at the Thunderbird Powwow at the McBurney's YMCA in New York City. Photograph by Georgetta Stonefish Ryan.

They used to bring fish in. She (grandmother) would clean the fish and I'd help her. Then hang the fish on racks to smoke. My Uncle Jim used to set nets—in wintertime, too, he'd string a net under the ice. We had rabbits, deer, and ducks, too. He'd trap muskrat and sell the hide. We'd get our staples from that, like flour and lard and tea.

The most important thing we were taught was to respect the elderly. Help them if you can. If you see they're having a hard time. So I tried to teach the same to my kids. I was taught to respect and obey the elderly.

From: Minnesota Chippewa Tribe. *Against the Tide of American History: The Story of the Mille Lacs Anishinabe.* Cass Lake, Minnesota: Minnesota Chippewa Tribe, 1985.

DEAR WUNNEANATSU

Trudie Lamb-Richmond

Trudie Lamb-Richmond, a former tribal chair of the Schaghticoke Tribe of Connecticut, writes in a 1987 letter to her granddaughter, one of the youngest in a long line of Schaghticoke women, how she neglected her obligations to pass down her tribe's rich cultural heritage.

Dear Wunneanatsu,*   April 1987
    I fear that as a grandmother, as an elder, I have been remiss in my duties and responsibilities toward you. In order to ensure the survival of our children and protect their inheritance for generations to come, there are certain instructions and teachings which must always continue to be passed down. There are so many lessons to consider, so many directions to take; . . . In our way of life it is the elders, the grandparents who are seen as the bridge to the past just as the young are the bridge to the future. And both are necessary to complete the circle of life. I have been neglectful because I have not always been that bridge for you. It is my responsibility as a grandmother to show and guide you as you are growing up. My own grandmother did not talk a great deal. We really learned by watching her and following her about. And sometimes the things we saw did not have great meaning until we were grown up ourselves. . . . There is so much you need to know, and so much I need to share; for it is that understanding, that attitude, that consciousness, which is the most valuable of our legacy. . . . Here at Schaghticoke we have the land, but we are lacking in a stronger community. Our people are scattered off in many directions with other greater priorities. And like you, they live off the reservation. We need to continue to build and strengthen our Indian community. But that will remain an impossible task as long as our younger generations remain ignorant of their history and culture. And even more important, maintaining and passing down our centuries-old attitudes and world view—a legacy that deserves protecting and inheriting. Your Duda†

From: Lamb-Richmond, Trudie. "An Open Letter to My Granddaughter." In *Rooted Like the Ash Trees: New England Indians and the Land*. Edited by Richard G. Carlson. Naugatuck, Connecticut: Eagle Wing Press, 1987.

*Wunneanatsu—means one who is beautiful or good inside
†Duda—means grandmother or elder.

EDUCATION: A LIFELONG PROCESS

Leona Okakok

Leona Okakok, an Inupiaq* woman who was deputy director of the North Slope Borough School District in Alaska, wrote an article about Inupiat educational philosophy for the Harvard Educational Review *November 1989 issue. Her 19-page article includes a discussion contrasting Inupiat and Euro-American definitions of education.*

To me, educating a child means equipping him or her with the capability to succeed in the world he or she will live in. In our Inupiat communities, this means learning not only academics, but also to travel, camp, and harvest wildlife resources in the surrounding land and sea environments. Students must learn about responsibilities to the extended family and elders, as well as about our community and regional governments, institutions, and corporations, and significant issues in the economic and social system.

"Education" and "schooling" have become quite interchangeable in everyday speech. When we talk of a person being educated we usually mean he or she has gone through a series of progressively higher formal systems of learning. Although a person may be an authority on a subject, we don't usually think of him or her as "educated" if he or she is self-taught. Since all of our traditional knowledge and expertise is of this latter type, the concept of "an educated person" has worked against us as people, creating conflicting attitudes, and weakening older and proven instructional methods and objects of knowledge. Therefore, we, the North Slope Borough School District School Board, have defined "education" as a lifelong process, and "schooling" as our specific responsibility. This is expressed in our Educational Philosophy statement:

> Education, a lifelong process, is the sum of learning acquired through interaction with one's environment, family, community members, schools and other institutions and agencies. Within the Home Rule Municipality of the North Slope Borough, "schooling" is the specific, mandated responsibility of the North Slope Borough School District

---

*If one talks about an individual, the term *"Inupiaq"* is used. If one talks about a people, one uses "Inupiat."

Board of Education. . . . (North Slope Borough School District Policy Manual, Adopted 10/13/76, Revised 8/11/87).

We decided that our role is to control the environment of the schooling process: the building, the equipment and materials, the quality of teaching and counseling services—everything about our schools—to ensure that education can take place in the classroom.

Remember that education is also the passing down of a society's values to children. Although I suppose there are people who would disagree, I think teachers pass down values by what they do in certain situations. Showing approval to a child for quickly attempting to answer a question—even wrongly—is valuing a quick answer to questions. At home, this same child may have been taught not to say anything until he or she has observed and observed and *observed*, and feels certain that his or her answer is correct. At home, the parents value accuracy more highly than a quick answer. They know that accuracy may mean the difference between life and death in the Arctic. In grade school, however, many of us learned that the teacher would "reward" us when we spoke up, whether we were right or wrong. Only by hearing our responses could she determine whether or not learning was taking place. If the answer was correct, she would have the opportunity to praise us. If a wrong answer was given, this gave her the opportunity to correct us. . . .

It is interesting that the root of the English word "educate" is very similar to our Inupiat concept of education. According to Webster:

It has often been said that *educate* means "to draw out" a person's talents as opposed to putting in knowledge or instructions. This is an interesting idea, but it is not quite true in terms of the etymology of the word. "Educate" comes from Latin *educare*, "to educate," which is derived from a specialized use of Latin *educere* (from *e-*, "out," and *ducere*, "to lead") meaning "to assist at the birth of a child." (*Webster's II New Riverside University Dictionary* [Boston: Houghton Mifflin, 1984], 418.)

This old meaning of the English word "educate" is similar to our own Inupiat Eskimo word "*iñuguq-*"*—which literally means "to cause to become a person." It refers to someone who attends to the child in the formative years and helps him or her to become a person. In our Inupiat Eskimo society, the first few years of a child's life are a time when they are "becoming a person." Anyone who attends to the child during that time of his or her life is said to cause him or her to become a person, "*iñuguġaa.*"

---

*Inupiaq words followed by a hyphen are stems that need at least an ending to make sense.

We Inupiat believe that a child starts becoming a person at a young age, even while he or she is still a baby. When a baby displays characteristics of individual behavior, such as a calm demeanor or a tendency to temper tantrums, we say "he or she is becoming a person." In our culture, such characteristics are recognized and accommodated from early childhood. As each child shows a proclivity toward a certain activity, it is quickly acknowledged and nurtured. As these children and adults in the community interact, bonds are established that help determine the teacher and the activities which will be made available to that particular child. As education progresses, excellence is pursued naturally.

Parents often stand back and let a child explore and experience things, observing the child's inclinations. If a child shows an aptitude for skills that the parents don't possess, they might arrange for their child to spend time with an expert, or an adult may ask to participate in the education of the child. Thus, many adults in the community have a role in the education of our children.

When you hear the word "educate," you may think more often of the primary Webster definition which is "to provide with training or knowledge, especially via formal education." In the Western tradition, educating children depends heavily on a system of formal schooling with required attendance until a certain age. . . .

Though most of the education in our traditional society was not formal, it was serious business. For us, education meant equipping the child with the wherewithal to survive in our world. Because social interaction is a part of survival in the Arctic, this included education in proper social behavior, as well as equipping the child with the means with which to make a living. In the traditional Inupiat Eskimo culture, education was everybody's business. It was okay to admonish, scold, or otherwise correct the behavior of any child, whether or not one was a relative. The success of the child's education depended in large part on how well his or her parents accepted admonishment of their child by other members of their own community. We as a people valued this acceptance highly because we knew that every member of our village was involved in some way with equipping our child for success.

From: Okakok, Leona. "Serving the Purpose of Education." *Harvard Educational Review* 59, no. 4 (November 1989): 405–422.

KNOWLEDGE IS NOT AVAILABLE
TO JUST ANYONE

Ann Renker

The Makah Nation Tribal Council in Washington State chartered the Makah Cultural and Research Center to oversee and coordinate programs affecting the culture and cultural education of the Makah people. The center records oral histories on audiotapes as part of the creation of a tribal archive. Unlike most non-Indian archives, however, the audiotapes will not be made available to the general public, researchers, or even other tribal members unless permission is expressly given by the contributing elder. This is because within the Makah Nation (and other native nations as well), different kinds of knowledge are the property of particular age, sex, or kin groups. Ann Renker of the Makah Nation explains the policy in the 1990 volume Keepers of the Treasures, *a report about the cultural and historic preservation needs of this nation's native peoples.*

As a cultural institution, we would make a big mistake if we start to institutionalize and make decisions for the families who are the traditional units of government in the Makah community. We make sure, when it comes to this kind of information, that the rights of dissemination and access remain with the families and remain with the elders. Our elders are not afraid of death. What they are afraid of is having their words and their things used wrong later on.

In our case, in Makah country, knowledge was not available to [just] anyone. And it was not available to everyone. And that's the way it has been since the beginning of time. Men were only allowed to know some things. Women were only allowed to know some things. And then even within a family there might be only one person at a time who could have access to information. We feel that it is not our responsibility to change that system. As a cultural facility it is our job to make sure that system stays in place.

Tribes also must make very firm decisions about how they record their oral histories and the access within their own archives. Consequently, in our archives, regardless of what the Society of American Archivists says, regardless of what the American Association of Museums says, we have the responsibility to protect the ancestral information management system and we do that in our facility today. When an elder agrees to do an oral history for us [he or she must specify] if the information is ever to be committed to writing and if this information is ever to be published. And I know it might sound morbid to some people, but we make an arrangement for that elder for a beneficiary in their family, . . . who, when [the elder] passes on, will then have the responsibility to tell us what to do with that information.

I think in the Indo-European community that, as regards to information, things have been switched around some. In the Indo-European community, many people believe that the person that writes the information down owns the information. In our case that is not correct. It's the person who speaks the information that has control over that information.

From: Parker, Patricia L. *Keepers of the Treasures: Protecting Historic Properties and Cultural Traditions on Indian Lands*. Washington, D.C.: National Park Service, Interagency Resources Division, Branch of Preservation Planning, 1990.

BEADWORK: PASSING ON TUSCARORA CULTURE

Mary Annette Clause

Mary Annette Clause, a Tuscarora woman, was born in Niagara Falls, New York, in 1958. In 1992, she wrote about the ways her mother taught her beadwork when she was in grade school and how she in turn taught her six-year-old daughter to string up beads and handle needles and thread. For Clause, teaching her daughter to do beadwork means transmitting Tuscarora culture along to the next generation, continuing a family tradition stretching back to her great-grandmother.

My mother, Marlene Printup, taught me how to do beadwork when I was in grade school. My great-grandmother, Harriet Pembleton, and my grandmother, Doris Hudson, taught my mother how to do beadwork. Doris Hudson was one of the original beadwork teachers to teach the beadwork class at the Tuscarora Indian School. I enrolled myself and attended the beadwork classes. I learned how to do the raised beadwork technique and other complicated styles of beadwork.

The first pieces of beadwork that I was taught to do were daisy chains and rings made out of beading wire. Also, I learned to make jitterbugs as a child. Jitterbugs are little people made out of beads. Beads, big enough for a child to learn how to handle a wire and go through the big holes inside of the beads. The bead wire is sturdy enough to hold and still pliable to bend. We would use large-sized beads and dish-shaped beads to make the hats on these jitterbugs. My mother always had my brothers and I busy doing beadwork at home. Whenever we went to the fairs we sold our goods and had our own spending money.

I'm teaching my six-year-old daughter, Jacqueline, to do beadwork. She's been doing it since she was about three years old. She sat by me and thread up strings of beads to learn how to manipulate a needle and thread. This past summer, I taught her to do beadwork on a loom. I bought her a loom kit which included a loom, thread and beads. She learned the loom work and quickly became bored with it. I showed her how to do a daisy chain stitch, just to see if she could do it. Surprisingly, she did it. Now, she knows how to make a daisy chain bracelet about three inches long. When she finishes a bracelet, she puts it on her wrist and off she goes.

I know there's a lot of people out here that are not interested in doing the beadwork art. It requires a lot of time and patience. There's only a few people on the reservation still doing the beadwork. Some parents who do know how to make beadwork are not teaching their children the art. The Tuscarora Indian School still offers beadwork classes to adults. Only a few children attend. . . .

I have patterns from my grandmother that I use for some of my beadwork designs. She always said she never had a pattern. She would draw a circle first and then by tracing her little finger or her pointer finger, go around the outside of the circle. That's how she would make her flower pattern. She said, "Nothing is perfect. We're not perfect. And don't try to be perfect, either. There's always a mistake in everything we do!" If I make a mistake, I just leave it because she said that's the way life is. People make mistakes. You just keep going with what you're doing. She said, "If you make a flower and don't like it, don't take it apart. Just leave it because everybody has a different taste. You might not like it but somebody might come along and think it's just gorgeous."

The colors of the beads that I prefer to use are the earth tones or colors similar to nature. Leaves are green and the flowers are done in pastel colors. Today, there's many different colors of beads. Looking at old beadwork, you'll see just the white chalk beads and the clear glass beads. They were the only kind of beads around. . . .

I have some pink glass beads that can't be purchased or are hard to find in a bead shop. They were my grandmother's beads that she had before she passed away. She left the beads to her children and they divided the beads amongst themselves. My father received these beads from her. This is what I'm using to make Jacqueline's dress. I also have some iridescent beads that my grandmother gave to me. I have some patterns that have been passed along from generation to generation. I don't even know who designed some of these patterns. I feel that it is very important to pass our culture along to our children. That's why I'm teaching my daughter, Jacqueline, to do beadwork, like my mother taught me.

From: "Circle of Unity: Portraits and Voices of Seven Native American Women—Mary Annette Clause, Tuscarora Beadworker." *Turtle Quarterly* 4, no. 3 (Spring–Summer 1992): 22–23.

AN AMERICAN INDIAN
MAGNET SCHOOL

Cornel Pewewardy

Cornel Pewewardy, a Comanche-Kiowa man born in 1952 in Lawton, Oklahoma, was principal of the American Indian Magnet School in the St. Paul, Minnesota school district. His life-long work in Indian education earned him the 1991 National Indian Education Association "Educator of the Year" Award. In this 1992 article written with Mary Bushey, Pewewardy describes the Native American program at the school.

St. Paul's American Indian Magnet School is the first magnet school of its kind in Minnesota and the second in the entire nation—initiating "placing education into culture" rather than continuing the practice of placing culture into education. Students from kindergarten to eighth grade study the rich history, culture and heritage, and contributions of the Native American with emphasis on the Ojibwe, Dakota and Lakota, and Winnebago tribes.

The magnet school concept is not new. Magnet schools are designed to meet particular needs and interests of students and parents, working like magnets to attract voluntary student enrollment. At ours, it is the school's philosophy—the Native American world view—which makes the American Indian Magnet School a sought-after learning environment for all those who attend, Native and non-Native. This world view stresses respect for elders, the importance of family, the values of giving and sharing, and living in balance and harmony with oneself, animals, and all nature.

In Native American philosophy and thought, "medicine" is a vital energy source that we draw upon and use for direction and for wholeness. Holistic education equates to responsibility for the whole universe. We are all related—*Mitakuye oyasin*. This Lakota saying speaks of our interdependence upon one another and is whispered in supplication or prayer: "Understand me and help me, all my relatives."

The circle is a sacred symbol of life and its interdependence. Sections within a medicine wheel circle are all connected to each other, and what happens to one section affects the others. The circle is a key symbol in Native American spirituality, family structure, gatherings of people, meetings, songs, and dances. Native American symbolism is used in the architectutral design of our school, which incorporates a new 16,000-square-foot addition to a 1924 school building that had been vacant for nearly a decade. Origin myths

A small boy learning about singing and drumming from a member of an Iroquois dance group. Photograph by Georgetta Stonefish Ryan.

helped to teach the architects and builders many methods in collecting building materials, good construction techniques, and blessing the finished building. Sometimes a myth was recited before construction began.

The significance of the circle dictated the design of our large, circular All-Nations Room as it was constructed and painted. It also regulated each phase of construction, described the prayers that were uttered, and dictated how the room (its doors, four brick pillars, multicolored tiles, and four-pointed wooden cross in the ceiling) were to be aligned with the four cardinal directions. The All-Nations Room is a special place where we connect persons to each other and to technology in a culturally responsible way.

From: Pewewardy, Cornel, with Mary Bushey. "A Family of Learners and Storytellers: The American Indian Magnet School." *Native Peoples: The Arts and Lifeways* 5, no. 4 (Summer 1992): 56–60.

TRADITIONAL
STORYTELLING

Martha Kreipe de Montaño at weekend storytelling program, Museum of the American Indian, New York City. Photograph by Julia V. Smith. National Museum of the American Indian, Smithsonian Institution.

Native Americans pass on their histories, cultural traditions, and laws by telling stories. Stories explain how the world was created, how the first people of the tribes originated, and how the sun, moon, stars, rainbows, sunsets, sky, thunder, lakes, mountains, and other natural occurrences came to be. Tribal stories explain the origin of every landmark, every plant, and every animal. Some stories tell about greed, selfishness, or boastfulness and show the correct way for people to treat one another and other beings in the world. Stories may also contain practical advice, such as how to hunt or fish. Some include "recipes" for ways to heal—how to find the proper roots and medicinal herbs. Some teach tribal laws and the consequences for violating them. Some stories are so sacred and powerful that they are treated with special respect: creation stories are often recited in a ritual way and told in a serious manner. There are also stories about dying and how to prepare for death.

Stories are told during designated periods, usually winter, when snakes and stinging insects are asleep. Ancient traditions forbid summer storytelling. "All the world stops work when a good story is told and afterwards forgets its wonted duty in marveling," noted Seneca scholar Arthur Caswell Parker. Listening to good stories would make animals forget their place in nature and wander dazed through the forests. Likewise, plants would forget to grow, birds would forget to fly south when winter came, and people would become lazy. During the cold winter months, people believed there was more time to relax and receive the teachings in stories. The restriction on storytelling is still honored by many Native American people to this day.

The stories from more than 400 oral traditions of North America have been recited from memory again and again and passed from generation to generation over hundreds of years to the present day. All the information native peoples knew and needed was held in the collective memories of the individual communities, where it was always available through storytelling.

Here, George Copway (Chippewa) writes about stories that both instructed and amused, Chief Elias Johnson (Tuscarora) and Arthur Caswell Parker (Seneca) describe Iroquois storytelling customs, and Anna Price (Apache) speaks of storytelling rituals. Janet Campbell Hale (Coeur d'Alene) writes that her father and uncle, knowing the power of Coyote stories to worsen weather, told them only when the temperature had already hit 40 below.

Maria Chona (Papago) recalls her father's stories, "Chris" (Apache) remembers his favorite Apache storytellers, and Helen Swan Ward (Makah) reminisces about the stories of her grandfather and step-grandmother. Sadie Brower Neakok's (Iñupiaq) favorite storytellers were an old man of the tribe and her father; Wilma Mankiller (Cherokee) especially liked her Aunt Maggie's stories; Asa Daklugie (Apache) memorized stories he heard repeatedly from narrators who never deviated by even one word. John Stands in Timber (Cheyenne) also memorized his people's stories, while Luci Tapahonso (Navajo) explains that ancient Navajo stories retold today are essentially the same as they were hundreds of years ago. Leslie Marmon Silko (Laguna Pueblo) stresses, however, that each telling of a story is a new experience.

OJIBWAY LEGENDS

Kah-ge-ga-gah-bowh [George Copway]

*Kah-ge-ga-gah-bowh, or George Copway, a Chippewa (or Objibway)
Indian born about 1818, published* Indian Life and Indian History *in
1858, in which he describes different aspects of his tribal culture. Here, he
writes of their "legendary" stories.*

The Ojibways have a great number of legends, stories, and historical tales,
the relating and hearing of which form a vast fund of winter evening instruction and amusement.

There is not a lake or mountain that has not connected with it some story
of delight and wonder, and nearly every beast and bird is the subject of some
story-teller, being said to have transformed itself at some prior time into
some mysterious formation—of men going to live in the stars, and of imaginary beings in the air, whose rushing passage roars in the distant whirlwinds.

I have known some Indians who would commence to narrate legends and
stories in the month of October and not end until quite late in the spring,
sometimes not till quite late in the month of May, and on every evening of
this long term tell a new story.

Some of these stories are most exciting, and so intensely interesting, that
I have seen children during their relation, whose tears would flow quite plen-
tifully, and their breasts heave with thoughts too big for utterance.

Night after night for weeks have I sat and eagerly listened to these stories.
The days following, the characters would haunt me at every step, and every
moving leaf would seem to be a voice of a spirit. To those days I look back
with pleasurable emotions. . . .

These legends have an important bearing on the character of the children
of our Nation. The fire-blaze is endeared to them in after years by a thousand happy recollections. By mingling thus, social habits are formed and
strengthened. When the hour for this recreation arrives, they lay down the
bow and the arrow and joyously repair to the wigwam of the aged men of the
village, who is always ready to accommodate the young.

From: Kah-Ge-Ga-Gah-Bowh, or George Copway. *Indian Life and Indian History by an Indian
Author—Embracing the Traditions of the North American Indians Regarding Themselves Particularly of
that Most Important of All the Tribes—The Ojibways*. Boston: Albert Colby and Co., 1858.

TELLING STORIES

Chief Elias Johnson

Chief Elias Johnson, a Tuscarora man, published in 1881 an account of the legends, traditions, and laws of the Iroquois, or Six Nations, of New York State. In it he explains the tradition of storytelling, especially noting restrictions that govern the time of year when stories may be told.

On long winter evenings the Indian hunters gathered around their fireside, to listen to the historical traditions, legends of war and hunting, and fairy tales which had been handed down through their fathers and fathers' fathers, with scarcely any variation for centuries, kindling the enthusiasm of the warrior and inspiring the little child some day to realize similar dreams, and hand his name down to posterity as the author of similar exploits.

They have superstitious fears of relating fables in summer; not until after snow comes will they relate of snakes, lest they should creep into their beds, or of evil genii, lest they in some way be revenged.

It is very difficult for a stranger to rightly understand the morals of their stories, though it is said by those who know them best, that to them the story was always an illustration of some moral or principle.

To strangers they offer all the rites of hospitality, but do not open their hearts. If you ask them they will tell you a story, but it will not be such a story as they tell when alone. They will fear your ridicule and suppress their humor and pathos; so thoroughly have they learned to distrust pale faces, that when they know that he who is present is a friend, they will still shrink from admitting him within the secret portals of their heart.

From: Johnson, Chief Elias. *Legends, Traditions, and Laws of the Iroquois, or Six Nations, and History of the Tuscarora Indians.* Lockport, New York: Union Publishing Co., 1881.

SENECA STORYTELLING
TRADITIONS

Arthur Caswell Parker

Arthur Caswell Parker, Gawaso Wanneh, a Seneca man born in 1881 on the Cattaraugus Seneca Reservation in New York, worked for years as an archaeologist at the New York State Museum in Albany. A renowned scholar of his people, in his 1923 work, Seneca Myths and Folk Tales, *Parker describes storytelling customs of the Seneca people, traditions still observed today.*

Among the Seneca, in common with other Iroquois tribes, each settlement had its official story tellers whose predecessors had carefully taught them the legends and traditions of the mysterious past.

According to ancient traditions, no fable, myth-tale, or story of ancient adventure might be told during the months of summer. Such practice was forbidden by "the little people," the wood fairies. Should their law be violated some [little people] flying about in the form of a beetle or bird might discover the offender and report him to their chief. Upon this an omen would warn the forgetful Indian. Failing to observe the sign some evil would befall the culprit. Bees might sting his lips or his tongue would swell and fill his mouth, snakes might crawl in his bed and choke him while he slept, and so on, until he was punished and forced to desist from forbidden talk.

Certain spirits were reputed to enforce this law for two purposes; first, that no animal should become offended by man's boasting of his triumph over beasts, or at the same time learn too much of human cunning, and fly forever the haunts of mankind; and second, that no animal, who listening to tales of wonder, adventure or humor, should become so interested as to forget its place in nature, and pondering over the mysteries of man's words, wander dazed and aimless through the forest. To listen to stories in the summer time made trees and plants as well as animals and men lazy, and therefore scanty crops, lean game and shiftless people resulted. To listen to stories made the birds forget to fly to the south when winter came, it made the animals neglect to store up winter coats of fur. All the world stops work

when a good story is told and afterwards forgets its wonted duty in marveling. Thus the modern Iroquois, following the old time custom, reserves
his tales of adventures, myth and fable for winter when the year's work is
over and all nature slumbers.

The story teller (*Hageotă'*) when he finds an audience about him or wish-
es to call one, announces his intention to recite a folk tale by exclaiming,
"*I'' newa' eñgegě' odě, Hau'' nio'' djado*ⁿ *"diiⁿus!"* The auditors eagerly reply
"*Hěⁿ'*" which is the assenting to the proposed relation of the folk tale.

At intervals during the relation of a story the auditors must exclaim
"*hěⁿ'*." This is the sign that they were listening. If there was no frequent
response of "he," the story teller would stop and inquire what fault was
found with him or his story.

It was not only considered a breach of courtesy for a listener to fall asleep,
but also a positive omen of evil to the guilty party. If anyone for any reason
wishes to sleep or to leave the room, he must request the narrator to "tie the
story . . ." Failing to say this and afterwards desiring to hear the remainder of
the tale, the narrator would refuse, for if he related it at all it must be from
the beginning through, unless "tied . . ."

A story teller was known as *Hagé otá* and his stock of tales called *ganon-
das' hago*. Each listener gave the story teller a small gift, as a bead, small
round brooch, beads, tobacco, or other trinket. . . .

From: Parker, Arthur Caswell. *Seneca Myths and Folk Tales*. Buffalo Historical Society
Publications 27. Buffalo: Buffalo Historical Society, 1923.

TELLING THE STORY
STRAIGHT THROUGH

Anna Price

Anna Price, or Her Grey Eyes, an Eastern White Mountain Apache woman born around 1837 in Arizona, was interviewed by anthropologist Grenville Goodwin when she was nearing the hundred-year mark. Here Anna Price briefly speaks about the rituals of storytelling among her people.

In the old days when a person got ready to be told a story, from the time the storyteller started no one there ever stopped to eat or sleep. They kept telling the story straight through till it was finished. Then when the story was through, the medicine man would tell all about the different medicines. There would be a basket of corn seeds there, and for each line that was spoken, that person who was listening would count out one corn seed. This way there would be sometimes two hundred corn seeds. Then that person would have to eat them all. If he could eat them, then he would remember all the words he had been told. If you fell asleep during this time, then the story was broken and was no good. That's the way we used to do.

From: Goodwin, Grenville. *Apache Raiding and Warfare.* Edited by Keith Basso. Tucson: University of Arizona, 1971.

MY FATHER TOLD US
THE STORIES

Maria Chona

Maria Chona, a Papago woman born about 1846, was interviewed from 1931 to 1935. With the help of an interpreter, she told of her life and her people, who now call themselves Tohono O'odham.

I knew all about Coyote and the things he can do, because my father told us the stories about how the world began and how Coyote helped our Creator, Elder Brother, to set things in order. Only some men know these stories, but my father was one of them. On winter nights, when we had finished our gruel or rabbit stew and lay back on our mats, my brothers would say to him: "My father, tell us something."

My father would lie quietly upon his mat with my mother beside him and the baby between them. At last he would start slowly to tell us about how the world began. This is a story that can be told only in winter when there are no snakes about, for if the snakes heard they would crawl in and bite you. But in winter when snakes are asleep, we tell these things. Our story about the world is full of songs, and when the neighbors heard my father singing they would open our door and step in over the high threshold. Family by family they came, and we made a big fire and kept the door shut against the cold night. When my father finished a sentence we would all say the last word after him. If anyone went to sleep he would stop. He would not speak any more. But we did not go to sleep.

My father's story told us all about why we hold our big feasts, because Elder Brother showed us how in the beginning of the world. My father went to those feasts and he took us, too, because my father was a song maker and he had visions even if he was not a medicine man. He always made a song for the big harvest festival, the one that keeps the world going right and that only comes every four years.

From: Chona, Maria. *Autobiography of a Papago Woman.* Edited by Ruth Underhill. Menasha, Wisconsin: American Anthropological Association Memoirs, vol. 46, 1936.

UNCLE AND AUNT, TELL
US STORIES

"Chris"

"Chris" (a pseudonym), a Chiricahua Apache born about 1880, was interviewed during the mid-1930s by anthropologist Morris Edward Opler. In his autobiographical account, largely spoken in English, Chris talks about some of the Apache storytellers he heard.

Natsili was really a good leader in all things. He showed us how to hunt, to ride horses, to make saddles, bows and arrows, ropes, quirts, head bonnets, shields, and many other things; and in the making of these things he showed us what to use, the stoutest buckskin and sinew that would last a long time. He also told stories, such as the Coyote stories, the moccasin game stories, the tales of the killing of the monsters, the rearing of Water's Child, and of the Foolish People, and also some stories about one of the Chiricahua Apache bands. And we sat there day and night listening. Sometimes we'd get sleepy. A head would begin to go forward; a boy would be asleep. Rap! he'd get it on the head, and that head would come up again. He tapped me on the head many times. I stayed longer than any of them. All the other youngsters would go, but I would stay. My father, Swinging-Lance, and others also used to tell us boys stories. . . .

I didn't care so much for the war stories, but I just couldn't listen enough to the animal stories. I often stayed up all night to hear them. Some of the stories used to scare us. When they told a story about Owl and Coyote, Owl's part would be spoken in a loud voice, and we would be quiet. When we'd hear an owl out in the woods after that, we'd sure scatter and go for camp. . . .

They always made some boy who wasn't paying attention chase after something they called "that which one smokes with." They had me chasing it once. Natsili told me, "You go and get it." I kept asking for it at one camp after another. They kept me going! At every place they told me that they had just given it to someone else. It was what you call a wild goose chase. I was pretty well tired out. Finally I came to my own camp, and I asked for it, and the whole family laughed and said old Natsili had it. . . .

Old Man Luntso and his wife, who knew power from Goose, were good storytellers too. They said that Goose was the best of all powers and led the others. We used to get these old people to tell us about Goose. I'd go to their camp and say, "Uncle and Aunt, tell us stories." They were no relatives to me, but I'd call them this just so they wouldn't refuse. . . .

If they were willing, a whole bunch of us would come to their camp. Then they'd begin the story and take turns telling it. They would often stop right in the middle of a story to explain the meaning and give a lesson. In the story of Goose, where the smallest goose does not obey, they would say, "Don't laugh at us. We have lived long. We know what happens to young people who don't say good words. Look what happened to this little goose! Never say that you going to do a thing at a certain time in the future or that a thing will surely happen at a certain time. Say 'bye-and-bye.' . . ."

They would tell stories till dawn. During the night when anyone got sleepy or wanted to go, they'd say, "We've got some yucca fruit we'll give you pretty soon." They promised us chokecherries, dried fruit, and everything else that children like. But it never came. At dawn they'd say, "That's all. Now you can go. We're not going to feed you. All you do is sleep." Some would hang around, but I was always the first one to go. When I got home, my folks would ask me where I had been, and I'd say, "Over to see Old Man Luntso." Then we'd go to bed and sleep all day.

From: Opler, Morris Edward. *Apache Odyssey: A Journey Between Two Worlds*. New York: Holt, Rinehart and Winston, 1969.

EACH STORY WAS A SACRED THING

Asa Daklugie

Asa (Ace) Daklugie, a Nednhi Apache born about 1870, who was "the dominant patriarch" of the Mescalero Apache Reservation in New Mexico, pretended for four years that he couldn't speak English, trying to avoid Eve Ball, who had made it her life's work to interview dozens of Apaches whom she persuaded to talk with her. Having served as interpreter for Stephen M. Barrett, to whom Geronimo, his uncle, dictated his life's story, Daklugie actually spoke English quite well and finally broke down and agreed, in 1954 and 1955, just before he died, to dictate information about his personal experiences and the Apache side of conflicts with the "White Eyes." Here he speaks about storytelling.

Next to our religion, I learned of my people and their brave men and deeds. As we ate our evening meal around the fire, an older man recited the stories of our people. Sometimes my father recited these stories, or sometimes one of his warriors did; sometimes a visitor was given the honor. We heard these stories until we memorized them. The narrator never deviated by one word. He, too, had memorized the account; each account was a sacred thing that must be handed down word for word as it happened. Occasionally some child went to sleep during the recital, but I did not. My mother had impressed upon me that the son of a chief must stay awake and learn. But I think I stayed awake largely because I loved hearing of the brave deeds of our brave people.

We had no written language and were forced to remember what we heard or were told. Our lives depended on accurate recall of such information, and particularly upon the reliability of messages sent by a chief to his people by runners. They had to accurately record his orders in their heads.

When I was very young I could not distinguish between fictional stories told for entertainment and true stories told to teach.

From: Ball, Eve. *Indeh: An Apache Odyssey*. Provo, Utah: Brigham Young University Press, 1980.

Apache men listening to a storyteller (second from right). Library of Congress.

CHEYENNE STORIES

~~~~~~~~~~~~~~~~~~

John Stands in Timber

*John Stands in Timber, a Northern Cheyenne man born in Montana around 1884, whose grandfather was killed in the Custer battle, appointed himself tribal historian in 1905. He spent a lifetime listening to tribal stories with the intention that they be published. In 1956 and 1957, he realized his dream when he teamed up with anthropologist Margot Liberty and for the next decade tape-recorded in English Cheyenne traditions and history as Cheyennes recalled them. Mr. Stands in Timber died in 1967 as the book he cherished—*Cheyenne Memories—*was in press.*

When I was just a little boy, I began to listen to old men and women of the Cheyenne tribe telling stories that had been handed down from earlier generations. Many of them used to visit my grandparents who raised me— my parents died before I was ten years old. And I could listen and listen; if they talked all day I would be there the whole time.

I memorized some of the stories that way. And when I came back from school in 1905, I thought I could write some of them down, so I went back to these old people to get the details straight. I have been doing it ever since. That is why the Cheyennes call me their historian, both the Southerners in Oklahoma and the Northerners in Montana. There is still much to learn. I talk to old-timers and their sons and daughters whenever I can, getting it straight about this or that battle and other things that happened long ago. I have helped many others to collect our history. Now I am glad to finish a book of my own, with all the Indian stories in one place.

An old storyteller would smooth the ground in front of him with his hand and make two marks in it with his right thumb, two with his left, and a double mark with both thumbs together. Then he would rub his hands, and pass his right hand up his right leg to his waist, and touch his left hand and pass it on up his right arm to his breast. He did the same thing with his left and right hands going up the other side. Then he touched the marks on the ground with both hands and rubbed them together and passed them over his head and all over his body.

That meant the Creator had made human beings' bodies and their limbs as he had made the earth, and that the Creator was witness to what was to be told. They did not tell any of the old or holy stories without that. And it was a good thing. I always trusted them, and I believe they told the truth.

Now I am one of the last people who knows some of these things. I am telling them as they were told to me during more than eighty years among the Cheyenne people. I can tell only what I know; but I have not added anything or left anything out.

The old Cheyennes could not write anything down. They had to keep everything in their heads and tell it to their children so the history of the tribe would not be forgotten. There were tales of the Creation, and the early days before the Cheyennes lived in the Plains country. Many of these have been forgotten, but some have lasted to this day. And there were tales of the hero Sweet Medicine, the savior of the Cheyenne tribe, who gave us our laws and way of living. And there were history stories, of travels and fights, and stories of a funny person, *Wihio*, told for the children. . . .

When I talked to the old people about stories like the Creation, or the Seven Stars or Sweet Medicine, I always tried to ask them, "Can you estimate how many years ago that happened? Or can you just guess?" And they would say, "No, all we can say is that from many generations before our grandfather's time this story has been handed down." Even the famous storytellers like Stands All Night—they mentioned his name often—lived far back. They did not know when, though they often said after they told a story, "That was told by Stands All Night." He lived before their grandfather's time. That was all they knew. And his stories were even older. . . .

There was one more kind of story told just for fun, and to teach the children about a funny person—a trickster—who lived among the people. In a way he was an animal, but in another way he was a Cheyenne. He was very clever, but he was always getting into trouble because he thought he was so smart. His name was *Wihio* or *Veho*, the same word the Cheyennes use for White Man.

From: Stands in Timber, John. *Cheyenne Memories, A Folk History*. With Margot Liberty and Robert M. Utley. New Haven: Yale University Press, 1967.

STORIES HAVE A LIFE
OF THEIR OWN

Leslie Marmon Silko

Leslie Marmon Silko, a woman from Laguna Pueblo, was born in 1948 in Albuquerque, New Mexico. Growing up in the pueblo, she once wrote "This place I am from is everything I am as a writer and human being." The recipient of a MacArthur Foundation fellowship in 1981, she left teaching at the University of Arizona to pursue writing. Author of the celebrated novel, Ceremony *(1977), Silko also has written short stories and* Storyteller, *her retellings of the stories she heard as a child. In the following excerpt from a 1986 interview, in her answer to a question put to her about* Storyteller, *she discusses the reasons stories stay alive in a community.*

Every time a story is told, and this is one of the beauties of the oral tradition, each telling is a new and unique story, even if it's repeated word for word by the same teller sitting in the same chair. I work to try to help the reader have the sense of how it would sound if the reader could be hearing it. That's original. And no matter how carefully I remember, memory gets all mixed together with imagination. It does for everybody. But I don't change the spirit or the mood or the tone of the story. For some stories, I could just hear Aunt Susie's voice reverberating. The challenge was to get it down so you could have a sense of my Aunt Susie's sound and what it was like. Earlier you [referring to interviewer, Kim Barnes] said something about writing the stories down in some way that they would be saved. Nobody saves stories. Writing down a story, even tape-recording stories, doesn't save them in the sense of saving their life within a community. Stories stay alive within the community like the Laguna Pueblo community because the stories have a life of their own. The life of a story is not something that any individual person can save and certainly not someone writing it down or recording it on tape or video. That's a nice little idea, and in some places where they've had these kind of archival materials, younger people can go and see or listen to certain stories. But if for whatever reasons the community no longer has a place for a story or a story no longer has a life within that particular period, that doesn't mean that the story no longer has life; that's something that no single person can decide. The old folks at Laguna would say, "If it's important, you'll remember it." If it's really important, if it really has a kind of substance that reaches to the heart of the community life and what's gone before and what's gone later, it will be remembered. And if it's not remembered, the people no longer wanted it, or it no longer had its place in the community.

People outside the community are often horrified to hear some old-timer say, "No, I won't tell my stories to the tape recorder. No, I won't put them on videotape. If these younger folks don't listen and remember from me, then maybe these stories are meant to end with me." It's very tough-minded. It flies in the face of all the anthropologists and people who get moist-eyed over what a good turn they're doing for the Native American communities by getting down these stories. I tend to align myself with the tougher-minded people. The folks at home will say, "If it's important, if it has relevance, it will stay regardless of whether it's on videotape, taped, or written down." It's only the Western Europeans who have this inflated pompous notion that every word, everything that's said or done is real important, and it's got to live on and on forever. And only Americans that America, which has barely been around two hundred years, which is a joke, what a short period of time, only Americans think that we'll just continue on. It takes a tremendous amount of blind self-love to think that your civilization or your culture will continue on, when all you have to do is look at history and see that civilizations and people a lot better than people building the MX [missile system] have disappeared. The people at home who say the story will either live or die are just being honest and truthful. But it's a pretty tough statement the Western European notion that something just has to live on and on and on. People at home say some things have their time and then things pass. It's like Momaday when he writes about the Kiowa, how the horse came and they became masters of the Plains. He says their great heyday lasted one or two hundred years. It passes and it's gone, you know? You could feel sad about it, but that's the way it is.

From: Barnes, Kim, "A Leslie Marmon Silko Interview." *Journal of Ethnic Studies* 13 (Winter 1986): 83–105.

STORIES WERE TOLD IN THE WINTERTIME

~~~~~~~~~~~~~~~~

Sadie Brower Neakok

Sadie Brower Neakok, an Iñupiaq woman born in Barrow, Alaska in 1916, was over a 40-year period as a schoolteacher in Barrow, a nurse, social worker, coroner, and a justice of the peace, as well as Barrow's magistrate, for 20 years. The wife of a respected whaling captain, the mother of 13 children and numerous foster children, she was voted Alaska's Mother of the Year in 1968 and twice chosen Alaska Native Woman of the Year. In her life story, shared with anthropologist Margaret B. Blackman, Sadie speaks about storytelling time in Barrow before the era of movies.

Stories were told in the wintertime—only in the wintertime, never in the summertime. Storytelling was done on long nights when we couldn't go out and enjoy ourselves in the dark, and it was mainly old people that had hand-me-down stories, legends, or where they came from and how they got there. Stories were told during hunting season; if you were a successful hunter or had a good hunting trip, you were entitled to invite some storyteller to your house. And it was an honor, like giving out candy to a bunch of kids if you were successful. Whoever was successful would pick out his favorite story-teller and say so-and-so is going to tell a story at so-and-so's house. It didn't matter where. The houses were small, but those of us that could get in, we could sit there and listen until it was time to go home.

Mom used to invite this one old man, Suakpak. That was because my brothers used to go out trapping and hunting. And if they were successful, they would bring in that old man to our house and we'd sit all evening, listening to his yarns and stories and hand-me-downs and all types of stories about animals and about boogie-men; the boogie-men stories would scare us half the time. I remember him so well—and we'd sit there along with some of our next-door neighbors' kids and listen to this man tell his stories. We were given dried fruit—raisins and dried prunes—saying this was the part of the catch that was to be given to him. We enjoyed it. Pass the evening

listening to that old man. And we were supposed to learn those stories. I
don't think I even remember one whole one.

Dad used to tell stories to us kids, too. I used to just sit there by the hour
and pump Dad about his life, and it was so interesting. The others weren't
as interested as I was. I was more attentive and curious. And then my mom
would be sitting there, be playing solitaire, and let him tell his stories in the
evening when he came home from the store and have his midnight snack,
whatever he wanted. He'd just talk away [in English], and when he would
say names, Mom would want to know what he was talking about. She would
ask questions in her native tongue, and Dad would answer back, verify in
Eskimo, and then she'd frown: "It wasn't quite like that; it was this way."
"Aha, aha, aha," and they would agree it was like that. Oh, it was interesting!

From: Blackman, Margaret B. *Sadie Brower Neakok: An Iñupiaq Woman*. Seattle: University of
Washington Press, 1989.

NOW, YOU TELL A STORY!

Helen Swan Ward

*Helen Swan Ward, a Makah Indian born in the village of Neah Bay,
Washington in 1918, grew up listening to Makah stories told in the
Makah language. In a narrative published in the catalog of the 1989
Washington State Centennial exhibit, she reminisces about her stepgrand-
mother and grandfather and how they signaled neighbors and relatives to
come for storytelling time.*

Her name was Katie, Katie Anderson, and she was my step-
grandmother. She was our storyteller. She was a beautiful storyteller! We
used to love to listen to her when we were kids, because she could really put
expression into her stories. You could sit and listen to her anytime. But she
wouldn't tell stories just anytime. She used to say, "I can't tell stories unless
it's dark!" We had to wait till after dark to listen to her. There were times
also when there were a dozen or more couples (neighbors and relatives) and
they would all come over and they'd start telling stories.

Sometimes when my grandfather, Charlie Anderson, got through doing
his chores, like fixing his garden, or tilling, or after haying season, when the
hay was all in the barn, he often felt like he wanted to tell stories, so then he
and his wife would get ready. My step-grandmother would fix some food
. . . she always made two or three great big buckskin breads, just big and
round, like that. She'd know just about how many were coming and she'd be
ready for them.

Those relatives and neighbors were scattered all around out there . . . so
my grandfather had to let them know he wanted them to come over for
storytelling. Well, in order to signal the people, if it was dark, he'd use a light
. . . because they could see his house up on top of the hill there. He'd invite
them by so many flashes—he'd cover the window, you know. My grandfather also had a big triangle-shaped iron out there which he would sound. It
would all depend on which way the wind was blowing—he'd always watch.
That triangle iron rang so loud they could hear it clear up the river. He'd
have to use it maybe two or three times, waiting for the wind to carry.
That was the way he'd carry these invitations to them and then they'd come
up about an hour later.

When they arrived, my grandfather would feed them first, give them a good feed, you know, then he'd roll out a mat. They used mats made out of cattail. Some of them were four foot wide, some they made about a foot and a half wide. Every person had one of these mats. They'd take off their shoes at the door and leave them there. Then they'd roll the mats out and everybody would sit down on a mat. The short mats they'd leave rolled up for pillows. Then they'd all lay down and then they'd say, "Now, you tell a story!" And they'd take their turns going clear around the room counterclockwise—each one of them telling the same story, but yet it came out a little different.

My friend, Ramona, and I used to fight to be next to my grandfather. So he'd say, "Well, you get on one side and she'll get on the other side." Then my step-grandmother, Katie, would be sitting up and she'd start telling those wonderful stories. During those evenings we really enjoyed ourselves. Us kids would lay there, and just listen to the stories. We were taught to be quiet. We were taught never to run around, never to make noise during the time they were telling stories. There was really no noise at all. So everyone would just lay around there, on those mats, and listen and listen, and one would say to the next, "Now it's your turn to tell what you know about Kwaati.* And each one of them would give the version of the stories that their parents had told them. But they were still all about Kwaati or Ishkus† or the Snot Boys or whales, or others. I bet the kids now would give anything to be able to understand Indian and listen to these stories, because sometimes there's hardly any meaning to it when you have to bring it out in English. It's hard; sometimes the story loses all its meaning. . . .

Sometimes they'd go on telling stories maybe two or three nights. Maybe they'd each bring something . . . maybe dried fish or fresh fish . . . whatever they had. Then the next day, they'd all get up and those that were close would go home and then come back at night. Those that had to paddle down from the river, some of them didn't go home. . . . They didn't stay around my grandpa's house during the day. They'd bring their lunch with them and then they'd be back in the evening again, to continue with the stories.

Ah, there were some *good* stories. *Really, really* good! But then, as part of it, after I thought back about it, thought back on those years, there was always a moral to the story. More or less, they were telling us how to live our lives.

From: Wright, Robin K., ed. *A Time of Gathering: Native Heritage in Washington State*. Seattle: Burke Museum/University of Washington Press, 1991.

---

*Kwaati, a major character who figures prominently in Makah stories, was a mischievous trickster.
†Ishkus was a mean ugly old woman who stole misbehaving children.

RETELLING NAVAJO STORIES

Luci Tapahonso

*Luci Tapahonso, a Navajo woman born in 1953 in Shiprock, New
Mexico, who has published four books of poetry, is a professor of English
at the University of Kansas. In this section of a paper she presented at a
1992 conference of state humanities councils, Tapahonso explains how the
retelling of an ancient story by a Navajo storyteller today is essentially the
same as it was told hundreds of years ago.*

In our cosmology, it is said that the present day Navajos were preceded in
three previous worlds by the Earth Surface People. The Earth Surface
People assumed human form in this world, which is referred to, in most stories, as the fourth world. Before this they had varying physical forms and
were often distinguished by colors. It is said that their journey through the
worlds was marked by encounters with danger, fear, and finally security. As
they left each previous world, they were guided by unseen spirits—the holy
people. Their emergence into this world and their survival thereafter
depended on the knowledge and wisdom they acquired during their journeys. The survival of the People in each world, including this one, depended
on what had happened in the first three worlds. This body of knowledge is
referred to as *saad*—which encompasses stories, songs, prayers, ritual oratories, and instructions or teachings. It is said that a person who is raised well
and taught this knowledge is wealthy. To Navajos, a person's worth is determined by the stories and songs she or he knows, because it is by this knowledge that an individual is directly linked to the history of the entire group.

The retelling of a story or the singing of a song is essentially the same
today across the Navajo Nation as it was many centuries ago. The elements
of these stories and songs include the proper use of rhythm, meter, symbolism, concrete diction, and imagery. Other aspects include a sense of place
and heavy use of repetition. The Navajo language lends itself well to rich,
connotative allusions to time, surrounding physical conditions, and historical
as well as spiritual imagery. For instance, to begin a story, one usually says,
alk'idaa' jini, which translates to "a long time ago, they said . . ." This phrase
serves an an opener or a signal for one to listen. The mental and emotional
participation of the audience is as crucial as the telling of the stories and the

153

A Navajo elder tells stories to school children at a reservation school in Arizona. Photograph by Paul Conklin.

singing of the songs. The phrase "they said" refers to people who told the story at some time long ago.

A Navajo audience is unlikely to doubt the storyteller's assertion that the events related did indeed occur. It is also understood that the stories or songs do not "belong" to the teller, but that her or his role is that of a transmitter. Thus an individual can't "own" a song or story in the same sense that one can "copyright" a work. *Alk'idaa* means that the story is ancient and has always been told in the same way. Sometimes there are slight variations and these differences depend on geography, dialects of the Navajo language, or the individual oration style of the storyteller. The essense of the story, though, retains the original format, cadence, repetition, imagery, and closing. Sometimes varying accounts of the same story are told in a single session with each storyteller starting with, "The way I heard it was . . ."—which doesn't discount other versions, but rather adds to the body of knowledge being exchanged.

From: Tapahonso, Luci. "Singing in Navajo, Writing in English: The Poetics of Four Navajo Writers." *Culturefront* 2, no. 2 (Summer 1993): 36–75.

COYOTE STORIES

~~~~~~~~~~~~~~~~

Janet Campbell Hale

Janet Campbell Hale, a member of the Coeur d'Alene tribe of northern Idaho, was born in 1946 in Los Angeles and grew up on the Coeur d'Alene Indian Reservation and Yakima Indian Reservation in Washington. The author of acclaimed novels, The Owl's Song *(1974) and* The Jailing of Cecelia Capture *(1985) as well as poetry, she told the story of her family and her own experiences in* Bloodlines: Odyssey of a Native Daughter. *In this passage, she writes about the time her father told Coyote stories.*

Every evening we would ask Dad and Uncle to tell Coyote stories, but they would refuse. Not until the temperature dropped to its lowest point, they said. Because telling Coyote stories could cause the weather to change drastically, and they didn't want to take a chance on its changing for the worse. When the temperature hit forty degrees below zero, they decided it couldn't get any colder. "Forty below," they said. "Forty below. That's it. Coyote stories tonight." Then they began. Every evening (I think there were only about three until the snowplows came and cleared the roads and freed us to go home) from then on we had a Coyote festival.

Coyote is an outrageous character that all Indian tribes of the West told stories about. No, not like in Road Runner cartoons. Not that stupid. And not that single-minded either. And not a failure, at least not always. He had no scruples, none at all. He would tell his kids, "Look at that!" and while their heads were turned, he would steal food from their plates. He lied and swindled and took advantage of everyone. Once, when he got tired of chasing rabbits, he pretended he was dying and wanted the rabbit chief and his people to come to his tepee so he could apologize to them for killing so many rabbits and making their lives miserable for so many years. He wanted to die with a clear conscience. So the rabbit chief came, and Coyote lay there all weak and pitiful and said how his soul was tortured because of the sort of life he'd lived. The rabbit chief forgave him—they all did—and told him he could die in peace. Coyote said, "Come closer, please. I want to tell you more." His voice was so weak. They drew closer. Then he signaled his kids with his eyes, and they closed the exit tight, and Coyote jumped up and clubbed the rabbits to death. He had enough food to last awhile. He wouldn't have to go chasing rabbits for weeks. Sometimes the stories were hilarious. Sometimes he got his just desserts. Like the time he believed the sun's job was easy and he got the sun to trade places for a day. As Coyote (now the sun) moved across the sky high above the earth, he looked down and saw all kinds of goings-on. He knew everyone's secrets and, being the sort of person he was, he was not about to keep his mouth shut. He ridiculed them and laughed at them and told all their secrets. But he did himself in because he saw himself and revealed his own embarrassing secrets and the next day had to take his own place again and live with being the butt of everyone's jokes for a very long time.

From: Hale, Janet Campbell. *Bloodlines: Odyssey of a Native Daughter*. New York: Random House, 1993.

HER STORIES TAUGHT US
A LESSON

Wilma Mankiller

Wilma Mankiller, a Cherokee woman born in 1945 at Mankiller Flats in rural Oklahoma, became Principal Chief of the Cherokee Nation in 1985, making her the first woman principal chief and the first Indian woman to hold such a position in any large tribe. In her autobiography, published in 1993, she describes her personal struggles, political work, and the history of her people. Here she tells about her Aunt Maggie, who told stories in the old Cherokee tradition.

The one relative who impressed me most was my father's Aunt Maggie Gourd. Dad stayed with her for a while when he was growing up. She lived only about a mile and a half from our house. We often visited her, and she spoke English well....We traded farm goods and produce with Aunt Maggie. My brother Johnny and I walked to her house with eggs to swap for fresh milk. If we were lucky, Aunt Maggie had a story to tell us. I didn't know it at the time, but Aunt Maggie told stories in the old Cherokee tradition. Some of these tales were frightening and others were not, but all of her stories taught us a lesson of some kind. . . .

Since Johnny and I were frequently asked to watch over our younger brothers and sisters while the older ones worked, Aunt Maggie tried to impress on our minds the importance of taking that task seriously. That is why one afternoon she told us the tale of the young Cherokee man and woman who took their baby into the woods. They stopped to make camp. They spread a blanket on the ground and put the baby on it to nap. While the child dozed, the parents moved some distance away so they would not disturb the child's dreams. They built a fire, and when it was going well and their campsite was prepared, they returned to the blanket for the baby. The infant was gone. Only the blanket remained. They searched and searched, but never found their child.

Aunt Maggie told us that the Little People, *Yunwi Tsunsdi*, who live in the woods wherever Cherokee live, had come across the baby. Believing it had been abandoned, they took it to raise as one of their own. Aunt Maggie's story had an impact. Johnny and I made a solemn vow to always keep a very close watch on our brothers and sisters and not allow them to be taken away by the Little People.

Stories of Little People have always been among the favorites of Cherokee children. The Little People look like Cherokees but are small, only about three feet tall. They speak our language. Cherokees always describe them "secondhand." It is said that if one sees the Little People and tells about it, that person will surely die. If anything is found in the forest, Cherokees assume that it belongs to the Little People.

. . . It is also said that Little People watch out for small children in the woods, like the baby in Aunt Maggie's story. But mostly, Little People are known to be mischievous.

I grew up loving Aunt Maggie's stories. They were a rich feast.

From: Mankiller, Wilma, and Michael Wallis. *Mankiller: A Chief and Her People.* New York: St. Martin's Press, 1993.

TRADITIONS

Anami'e-giizhigad	Nitam-anokii giizhigad	Niizho-giizhigad	Aabitose	Niiyo-giizhigad	Naano-giizhigad	Gizibiigisaginige-giizhigad

Page from Ojibwe Calender Unit *published by the Minnesota Chippewa Tribe. "Ode'imini-Giizis" means "Strawberry Moon" in the Ojibwe language and corresponds to the month of June. Courtesy of the Minnesota Chippewa Tribe.*

Among the several hundred separate native cultures in North America alone, there existed, and still exists, a pluralism of world views and lifeways probably unimaginable to those who still believe there are generic Indians belonging to generic tribes living in a generic place and time. The preconception of the generic Indian has overshadowed the reality of the social and political organizations, clothing styles, shelters and art forms, musical traditions, economic systems, languages, education, spiritual and philosophical beliefs, and adaptive mechanisms of countless native peoples. The selections in this section attest to the diversity of the cultural practices of Native American societies, which allowed them to maintain their uniqueness as indigenous peoples.

Herein Black Hawk (Sac) describes his people's national dance, during which warriors recounted heroic exploits. Martha Kreipe de Montaño (Potawatomi) discusses powwows. Deriving from nineteenth-century warrior traditions, these popular twentieth-century social gatherings include feasting, singing, and dancing. Chief Joseph (Nez Percé) explains the value his people placed on truth telling. Sarah Winnemucca Hopkins (Paiute) describes the rituals of the council-tent, where people went for advice. Luther Standing Bear (Lakota) describes the laws governing social behavior, while Jeff Jones (Nomlaki) tells about messengers, or runners, who carried news between villages. Belle Highwalking (Cheyenne) and John (Fire) Lame Deer (Lakota) talk about in-law avoidance.

Native peoples conceptualize time in a manner different from non-Indians, and there were, and are, differences in views of the cosmos even from tribe to tribe within close geographic areas. Carl Sweezy (Arapaho) explains the difference between Indian and Euro-American concepts of time. Nuligak (Eskimo) and James Larpenteur Long (Assiniboine) offer the many different names each of their peoples has for the moon.

Native people took great pride in personal appearance, traditionally ornamenting their heads and bodies with tattoos and piercing their ears. Louis Simpson (Wishram) describes ear-piercing rituals for babies, and Delfina Cuero (Diegueno) relates the ear-piercing rituals for boys at puberty as well as the custom of tattooing youngsters.

Native people have always been a generous and sharing people. They mount give-aways in memory of people, for men in the service, and on other occasions to show love and respect. Myrtle Lincoln (Arapaho) tells about her people's give-aways. Mark Tucker (Yupik Eskimo) and Lorraine Titus (Athabascan) describe potlatches at which hosts give away everything they own and Ignatia Broker (Ojibway) describes sharing her city apartment with other Ojibway people.

Native societies also emphasize sports and games in their traditional lives, as Joseph B. Oxendine (Lumbee) explains in his account. And finally, no discussion of Indian life would be complete without a look at native humor. Contrary to the image of the silent, stoic Indian, a sense of the comic has always suffused Indian life. Rayna Green (Cherokee) dishes out some of this characteristic humor, Joseph Medicine Crow (Crow) elaborates on the misconception many have of Indians being humorless people, and Marvin Cook (Navajo) supplies a cartoon illustrating Navajo humor.

NATIONAL DANCE

~~~~~~~~~~~~~~~~

Black Hawk

Black Hawk, a Sac* leader born in 1767 in the village of Saukenuk, now present-day Rock Island, Illinois, dictated the story of his life in 1833 to Antoine LeClaire, a government interpreter and trader. A warrior since the age of 17 but defeated by the U.S. Army in 1832 in the so-called Black Hawk War, Black Hawk describes the Sac national dance recounting exploits in battle.

When [the crane dance] is over, we feast again and have our national dance. The large square in the village is swept and prepared for the purpose. The chiefs and the old warriors take seats on mats, which have been spread on the upper end of the square, next come the drummers and singers, the braves and women form the sides, leaving a large space in the middle. The drums beat and the singing commences. A warrior enters the square keeping time with the music. He shows the manner he started on a war party, how he approached the enemy, he strikes and shows how he killed him. All join in the applause, and he then leaves the square and another takes his place. Such of our young men as have not been out in war parties and killed an enemy stand back ashamed, not being allowed to enter the square. . . . What pleasure it is to an old warrior, to see his son come forward and relate his exploits. It makes him feel young, induces him to enter the square and "fight his battles o'er again."

This national dance makes our warriors. When I was traveling last summer on a steamboat, on the river going from New York to Albany, I was shown the place where the Americans dance the war-dance, (West Point), where the old warriors recount to their young men what they have done to stimulate them to go and do likewise. This surprised me, as I did not think the whites understood our way of making braves.

From: LeClair, Antoine and John B. Patterson. *Life of Ma-ka-tai-me-she-kia-kiak, or Black Hawk.* Cincinnati, 1833.

---

*Formerly spelled *Sauk.*

IT IS A DISGRACE TO TELL A LIE

Chief Joseph

Chief Joseph, the Nez Percé leader, was born about 1840 in the Wallowa Valley of Oregon. In the summer of 1877, he led some 750 Nez Percé men, women, and children from Oregon toward Canada, seeking refuge and freedom. Pursued by 2,000 army troops, Chief Joseph eluded the soldiers until October 5, 1877, when exhaustion, freezing weather, and hunger forced him to surrender. In 1879, Chief Joseph told his story about the Nez Percé War to a reporter from North American Review. *Anxious to correct untruths about his people, Chief Joseph explains the value his people placed on telling the truth.*

M y friends, I have been asked to show you my heart. . . . I want the white people to understand my people. Some of you think an Indian is like a wild animal. This is a great mistake. I will tell you all about our people, and then you can judge whether an Indian is a man or not. I believe much trouble and blood would be saved if we opened our hearts more. I will tell you in my way how the Indian sees things. The white man has more words to tell you how they look to him, but it does not require many words to speak the truth. What I have to say will come from my heart, and I will speak with a straight tongue. Ah-cum-kin-i-ma-me-hut (Great Spirit) is looking at me, and will hear me. . . .

Our fathers gave us many laws, which they had learned from their fathers. These laws were good. They told us to treat all men as they treated us; that we should never be the first to break a bargain; that it was a disgrace to tell a lie; that we should speak only the truth; that it was a shame for one man to take from another his wife, or his property without paying for it. We were taught to believe that the Great Spirit sees and hears everything, and that he never forgets; that hereafter he will give every man a spirit-home according to his desserts: if he has been a good man, he will have a good home; if he has been a bad man, he will have a bad home.

From: "An Indian's Views on Indian Affairs." *North American Review* 269 (April 1879): 415–33.

THE COUNCIL-TENT IS
OUR CONGRESS

Sarah Winnemucca Hopkins

Sarah Winnemucca Hopkins, a Paiute woman born near Humbolt
Lake, Nevada sometime between 1844 and 1848, wrote a book published
in 1883 about the history of the Paiute bands of Nevada and the injus-
tices they suffered at the hands of the majority of Indian agents. In one
chapter she departs from her history and describes "Domestic and Social
Moralities," including a section on the traditional customs of men and
women in the chief's council tent, which she calls the Paiute version of the
United States Congress. She also slips in some thoroughly contemporary
opinions about women in general.*

The chief's tent is the largest tent, and it is the council-tent, where every
one goes who wants advice. In the evenings the head men go there to discuss everything with their people, as a father would in his family. Often they
sit up all night. They discuss the doings of all, if they need to be advised. If
a boy is not doing well they talk that over, and if the women are interested
they can share in the talks. If there is not room enough inside, they all go out-
of-doors, and make a great circle. The men are in the inner circle, for there
would be too much smoke for the women inside. The men never talk without smoking first. The women sit behind them in another circle, and if the
children wish to hear, they can be there too. The women know as much as
the men do, and their advice is often asked. We have a republic as well as
you. The council-tent is our Congress, and anybody can speak who has anything to say, women and all. They are always interested in what their husbands are doing and thinking about. And they take some part even in the
wars. They are always near at hand when fighting is going on, ready to snatch
their husbands up and carry them off if wounded or killed. One splendid
woman that my brother Lee married after his first wife died went out into
the battlefield after her uncle was killed, and went into the front ranks and
cheered the men on. Her uncle's horse was dressed in a splendid robe made

---

*Formerly spelled *Piute*.

of eagles' feathers and she snatched it off and swung it in the face of the enemy, who always carry off everything they find, as much as to say, "You can't have that—I have it safe;" and she staid [sic] and took her uncle's place, as brave as any of the men. It means something when the women promise their fathers to make their husbands *themselves*. They faithfully keep with them in all the dangers they can share. They not only take care of their children together, but they do everything together; and when they grow blind, which I am sorry to say is very common, for the smoke they live in destroys their eyes at last, they take sweet care of one another. Marriage is a sweet thing when people love each other. If women could go into Congress I think justice would soon be done to the Indians. I can't tell about all Indians; but I know my own people are kind to everybody that does not do them harm; but they will not be imposed upon, and when people are too bad they rise up and resist them. This seems to me all right. It is different from being revengeful. There is nothing cruel about our people. . . .

The chiefs do not live in idleness. They work with their people, and they are always poor for the following reason. It is the custom with my people to be very hospitable. When people visit them in their tents, they always set before them the best food they have, and if there is not enough for themselves they go without.

The chief's tent is the one always looked for when visitors come, and sometimes many come the same day. But they are all well received. I have often felt sorry for my brother, who is now a chief, when I saw him go without food for this reason. He would say, "We will wait and eat afterwards what is left." Perhaps little would be left, and when the agents did not give supplies and rations, he would have to go hungry.

At the council, one is always appointed to repeat at the time everything that is said on both sides, so that there may be no misunderstanding, and one person at least is present from every lodge, and after it is over, he goes and repeats what is decided upon at the door of the lodge, so all may be understood. For there is never any quarreling in the tribe, only friendly counsels. The subchiefs are appointed by the great chief for special duties. There is no quarreling about that, for neither subchief or great chief has any salary. It is this which makes the tribe so united and attached to each other, and makes it so dreadful to be parted. . . .

From: Hopkins, Sarah Winnemucca. *Life Among the Piutes: Their Wrongs and Claims*. New York: G. P. Putnam's Sons, 1883.

THE BABY HAS HIS
EARS PIERCED

Louis Simpson

Louis Simpson (ME'-nait), a Wishram man about 75 years old living on the Yakima Reservation in southern Washington State, described in July 1905 ear-piercing rituals for babies.

If now he should have a child, a baby, then the man [his father] would say: "Do you all now come! Now my son has a child, a little baby, and the ears of my son's child will have holes pierced into them." And then all the people get to be in the house. And then a little food is prepared. Now then the people eat, all eat. And then the baby is given to an old man. Now then he pierces holes into the child's ears,—five holes in one of his ears, again five holes in the other does the old man make, if he should know how to do it [one who is practiced in the operation is selected, not any one at random]. Now here a tanned elk-skin lies spread out, thereon the baby has his (ears) pierced. And then the tanned elk is cut up into pieces enough for one pair of moccasins (as gift) for each person. And then various (other) things are distributed: small baskets, and horse-hair rope, and twined basket-bags. Gifts would be made to the people, the old people. Now the boy or the girl has become good. Beads are strung through holes in the child's ears. If it did not have its (ears) pierced, it would be laughed at. And then a head-flattener is laid on its head, is put on its forehead. If its head should not have a flattened forehead, it would be laughed at. . . . Thus long ago the Wishram used to do.

From: Sapir, Edward. *Wishram Texts*. American Ethnological Society Publications, vol. 2. Leyden: E. J. Brill, 1909.

RULES OF POLITE BEHAVIOR

~~~~~~~~~~

Luther Standing Bear

Luther Standing Bear, an Oglala Lakota (Sioux) man born in South Dakota during the mid-1860s, wrote several books about his people because he wished to improve the image of Lakotas and Indians in general in the minds of white readers as well as educate them about the strengths of traditional Lakota culture. In his 1933 work, Land of the Spotted Eagle, *which Standing Bear considered his most important book, he describes "customs, manners, experiences, and traditions—the things that make all men what they are." He tells of the Lakotas' outward life and inner life, especially the "laws of conduct" governing social behavior.*

T he Lakotas were a social people, loving human companionship and association and admiring the use of manners and deportment that accompanied their social life.

The rules of polite behavior that formed Lakota etiquette were called *woyuonihan,* meaning "full of respect"; those failing to practice these rules were *waohola sni,* that is, "without respect," therefore rude and ill-bred.

A good deal of time was spent in merrymaking, with feasts, songs, dances, and social ceremonies, and anyone coming as a visitor, whether friend or stranger, was welcomed.

Such expressions of greeting as "How do you do?" or "How are you?" which imply questions, were never used. Men usually greeted a friend with "*Hohahe,*" which means "Welcome to my tipi." Very good friends often used an exclamation of pleasure and surprise, "*Hun-hun-he,*" and "*Kola,*" the Lakota word for friend. To a relative and to close friends the usual words of greeting were "*Hun-hun-he tahunsa.*" All relations, not of the immediate family, and all close friends were *tahunsa,* or cousins, since it was not customary to call anyone by name. For women a smile, and, if at home, the proffer of food was the genteel welcome, though two women of close friendship frequently greeted each other with the feminine usage of cousin, or "*Hun-hun-he-jepansi.*"

The tipi door was always open for anyone to enter and it was not polite to walk in without knocking and unannounced, for the phrase "Come in" was never used to bid one to enter, though when the visitor was in he was at once seated as a mark of hospitality. A stranger, however, coming into the village, especially at night, would call out the fact that he was a stranger and would state his business. The man of the tipi would meet the traveler and on finding him an acceptable visitor would say, "I'll ask my wife to cook you some food." The stranger then followed his host into the tipi, knowing that he would be received as a guest.

When the visitor departed, there were no effusive "Good-byes" and no urgent invitations regarding return visits on either side. The visitor, when ready to leave, would simply say, "It is now time for me to go," and having so spoken it would have been poor etiquette to beg him to stay longer.

Praise, flattery, exaggerated manners, and fine, high-sounding words were no part of Lakota politeness. Excessive manners were put down as insincere and the constant talker was considered rude and thoughtless. Conversation was never begun at once, nor in a hurried manner. No one was quick with a question, no matter how important, and no one was pressed for an answer. A pause giving time for thought was the truly courteous way of beginning and conducting a conversation. Silence was meaningful with the Lakota, and his granting a space of silence to the speech-maker and his own moment of silence before talking was done in the practice of true politeness and regardful of the rule that "thought comes before speech." Also in the midst of sorrow, sickness, death, or misfortune of any kind, and in the presence of the notable and great, silence was the mark of respect. More powerful than words was silence with the Lakota and his strict observance of this tenet of good behavior was the reason, no doubt, for his being given another fallacious characterization by the white man—that of being stoic. He has been adjudged dumb, stupid, indifferent, and unfeeling. As a matter of truth, he was the most sympathetic of men, but his emotions of depth and sincerity were tempered with control. Silence meant to the Lakota what it meant to Disraeli when he said, "Silence is the mother of truth," for the silent man was ever to be trusted, while the man ever ready with speech was never taken seriously.

Children were taught the rules of *woyuonihan* and that true politeness was to be defined in actions rather than in words. They were never allowed to pass between the fire and an older person or a visitor, to speak while others were speaking, or to make fun of a crippled or disfigured one. If a child thoughtlessly tried to do so, a parent, in a quiet voice, immediately set him right. Expressions such as "excuse me," "do pardon me," and "so sorry," now so often lightly and unnecessarily used are not in the Lakota language. If one chanced to injure or discommode another, the word *wanunhecun* or "mistake" was spoken. This was sufficient to indicate that no discourtesy was intended and that an untoward happening was accidental.

Young Indian folk, raised under the old courtesy rules, never indulged in the present habit of talking incessantly and all at the same time. To do so would have been not only impolite, but foolish; for poise, so much admired as a social grace, could not be accompanied by restlessness. Pauses were acknowledged gracefully and did not cause lack of ease or embarrassment.

A woman of correct social manner was modest, low-voiced, and reserved. She sat quietly on the tipi floor, never flouncing herself about nor talking loudly and harshly. A woman who laughed loudly in order to attract attention was put down as common and immoral and was at once discredited and shunned. . . .

Men, in the presence of women, were very deferent. The freedom and ease of the Tipi Iyokihe [community hall for men] was dropped for a more circumspect manner. The taboos of speaking directly to sisters and cousins were strictly observed and one unacquainted with the rules of polite conduct would be led to think the men cold and indifferent toward their women, though actually their attitude and intent were of extreme respect. . . .

From: Standing Bear, Luther. *Land of the Spotted Eagle*. Boston: Houghton Mifflin Co., 1933.

MESSENGERS

~~~~~~~~~~~~~~~~~~~~

Jeff Jones

Jeff Jones, a Nomlaki man born about 1865 near Paskenta, California, narrated information in 1936 to an anthropologist about messengers who announced dances to neighboring villages. These runners, chosen because they could run long distances, also possessed well-developed memories.

Newsboys [messengers] can carry news from Paskenta to Tehama and back between evening and dawn. It is about thirty miles each way. They trot. They have free passage into enemy territory. It is necessary that they eat special kinds of food which is more preserving to the Indian body. The runners have to be careful of their diet. They are from twenty-five to forty years old, for they can't do this work when they are too young. They have to keep their wind. Special ones are picked for this—not just anyone. . . .

The runner is in a dangerous position. He does no other work, for he must always be ready to go. When he isn't running, he practices. He doesn't hunt or fish, but is well taken care of. He gets paid for his trips wherever he goes.

Old blind Martin has been a newsboy. He made trips from Paskenta to Tehama. He said he never shot at a man in his life. He carried news over and back and had to remember every word he heard. After the runner comes back, after he catches his breath, he tells everything that was said. Two fellows repeat what he said, so that everything is heard three times. Everyone listens, and when they are all through they discuss the matter. . . .

The messenger who announces the *tami* (dance-feast) to neighboring villages and invites the people has strings with knots in them—one for each day until the dance is to start. One string is given to each headman of a village, and every day he unties one knot until they are all untied. The first knot is untied on the day that the messenger delivers it. The people come on the day the last knot is untied. The Indians used to laugh about this custom because now they can just say, "Next Saturday."

From: Goldschmidt, Walter. *Nomlaki Ethnography*. University of California Publications in American Archaeology and Ethnography, vol. 42, no. 4. Berkeley: 1951.

THE ASSINIBOINES' TWELVE-MOON CALENDAR

James Larpenteur Long

James Larpenteur Long, or First Boy, an Assiniboine man born in 1888 near Oswego, Montana, collected the stories of 25 of the oldest Assiniboines living in the 1930s. The Assiniboines, *the result of his interviews, also includes his remarks about the Assiniboine calendar.*

January was *Wicogandu*, Center Moon, because October to April was allotted to the winter season. Therefore, January was the halfway mark and considered the Big Moon. It was also called *Witehi*. This meant Hard Moon or Hard Time Moon, on account of the severe cold weather during that period.

On account of the sap's freezing, cottonwood trees burst with loud reports in that moon, which was a sign the Center Moon was on duty.

There was always a question at that time of the year as to the correct count of the moon. Groups were pitted against each other in argument; and even a man and wife would disagree and take sides.

Those that counted in error never admitted it, even after signs in that moon were brought to their attention.

That sort of gentle family argument continued through the winter moons until spring, when it gradually died away only to come up again the next winter.

February was *Amhanska*, Long Dry Moon. The days lengthened in that moon.

March was *Wicinstayazan*, Sore Eye Moon. Snow blindness was common during that period.

April, *Tabehatawi*, Frog's Moon. The croaking of the frogs was heard in that moon.

May, *Induwiga*, Idle Moon. The winter season was over and there was a pause before summer began.

June, *Waheqosmewi*, Full Leaf Moon. All leaves reached their full growth in that moon.

July, *Wasasa*, Red Berries Moon.

August, *Capasapsaba*, Black Cherries Moon. Chokecherries ripened in that moon.

September, *Wahpegiwi*, Yellow Leaf Moon.

October, *Tasnaheja-hagikta*, The Striped Gopher Looks Back. There were summerlike days in that moon. The supposition was that the gopher, although in its hibernation, came out to have a last look at the fine weather. That animal was often seen out after the full moon. It was also called *Anukope*, Joins Both Sides, which meant part summer and part winter, because there was warm and cold weather in that moon. So the moon was a dividing line between summer and winter.

November, *Cuhotgawi*, Frost Moon. In that moon the heavy frost covered the leafless trees, bushes and the landscape; the early morning air glistened as the sun rose. November was rightly named.

December, *Wicogandu-sungagu*, Center Moon's Young Brother. Because January was considered the Big Moon, December was a young brother who clung to his older brother.

Old men kept account of the days in a moon by notching on their pipe cleaners, one notch for one day. These pipe cleaners were made from a small willow the size of a pencil and about a foot long. A row of notches the length of a pipe cleaner would constitute a moon period, or a month. One of these sticks notched down four sides counted four months, and three fully notched sticks made a full year.

From: Long, James Larpenteur. *The Assiniboines: From the Accounts of the Old Ones Told to First Boy.* Edited by Stephen Kennedy. Norman: University of Oklahoma Press, 1961.

WE COUNTED TIME BY SLEEPS

Carl Sweezy

Carl Sweezy, an Arapaho man born around 1881, grew up on the Oklahoma Cheyenne-Arapaho Reservation in the "old ways" of his people. A painter who captured his people's dances, hunts, games, dress, and ceremony on canvas before he died in 1953, he told what he knew about his people's cultural ways to author Althea Bass, who later published his account. Sweezy goes to some length to explain the difference between Indian and Euro-American concepts of time.

Every white man seemed to have a great concern about time. We had our own names for the seasons and for the months that made up the year, but they were not the same as those the white man used. And we did not know how he counted time, by minutes and hours and days of the week, or why he divided the day into such small parts. And we found that there were two ways of counting it, for the Quakers spoke of First-day, Second-day, Third-day, and of First-month, Second month, and Third-month, while others spoke of Sunday and Monday and Tuesday, and of January and February and March. . . . It was a long time before we knew what the figures on the face of a clock meant, or why people looked at them before they ate their meals or started off to church. We had to learn that clocks had something to do with the hours and minutes that the white people mentioned so often. Hours, minutes, and seconds were such small divisions of time that we had never thought of them. When the sun rose, when it was high in the sky, and when it set were all the divisions of the day that we had ever found necessary when we followed the old Arapaho road. When we went on a hunting trip or to a sun dance, we counted time by sleeps.

White people who did not try so hard to understand the ways of Cheyenne and the Arapaho as we did to understand their ways, thought we were all lazy. That was because we took a different attitude toward time from theirs. We enjoyed time; they measured it. Our women did not say, on Monday (or on Second-day, as the Quakers put it) we wash our clothes; on Tuesday we iron them; on Saturday we bake and clean; on Sunday we do not work and we go to church. Our men did not say, after breakfast, at eight o'clock I go to my schoolroom, or to my office, or to the commissary; at twelve I go home to my dinner; at one I go back to work all afternoon. They did not say, this week we break sod and plough; next week we plant our corn or our potatoes and melons and cabbage.

For hundreds of years we had gone on a long hunt twice a year, whenever our scouts had come in to report that buffalo were plenty out on the Plains; we had held our buffalo dance before we left, and had set out with our best bows and arrows, our shields and lances for protection from our enemies if we should meet with any of them, and pemmican for food to eat until we killed meat. We had taken our women and children along because they too loved to move over the prairies, making camp where grass was green and water fresh, and because our women must skin the animals and dress the hides and dry the meat where we killed it. No Sundays could be set aside for church or rest, or Mondays for washing, when we followed the buffalo road. And we had no set date for coming back, for that depended on the buffalo and on the weather. When we had meat enough and the skins were dry enough to pack, we started back to the home camp.

But we were not an idle nation of people. If we had been idlers, we would have been wiped out by our enemies, or by bad weather and starvation long ago. Before our Reservation days, we had hunted and traded over the land that makes up many states now—the Dakotas and Utah and Wyoming and Nebraska and Kansas and Colorado. . . . Those were brave, free days. We had no time, and no need, to plant crops or raise corn and hogs and chickens, or build houses and barns like the white man's then. But when we followed the buffalo road we worked hard, just as white people who followed the corn road worked hard. No people who get their living from Mother Earth as she provides it for them, and who fight off other tribes wanting to hunt and graze their horses over the same land, can be lazy.

From: Sweezy, Carl. *The Arapaho Way: A Memoir of an Indian Boyhood.* Edited by Althea Bass. New York: Clarkson Potter, 1966.

ESKIMO MOON NAMES

Nuligak

Nuligak, an Inuit (Eskimo) man born in 1895 in the Mackenzie Delta, spent his life along the Arctic Ocean. Around 1960, after Maurice Metayer asked him to write his memoirs, he put his story down in Eskimo, and Metayer translated the results. In his autobiography, Nuligak wrote that when he was 14 years old, his grandfather taught him the Eskimo names of the moon, admonishing him: "You, remember them."

Naoyavak, my grandfather, said to me one day, "I will teach you how to recognize the different moons; I am getting old and many do not know the Eskimo names of the moons. They have forgotten. You, remember them." Then Grandfather took little sticks and stood them up in the snow. There were twelve of them. We were then in midwinter. It was the new moon. From what I can judge now, the month corresponding to that new moon must have been January.

This is what I retained of what he taught me in that month of January, 1909.

The January moon is called *Avunniviayuk* in Eskimo. It is during this month that the dwarf seals produce their little ones. Premature young of the ordinary seals freeze and do not survive.

The February moon is *Avunnivik*. The true seals bring forth their young. These develop and become the seals we hunt.

March is *Amaolikkervik*. The little snow birds (*amaolikat*) arrive from the south.

The April moon receives the name of *Kriblalikvik* because the sun has melted the top of the snow, and as we stare at it, it sparkles with whiteness.

Tigmiyikvik is our month of May, the time when ducks and geese return from the south.

June is called *Nuertorvik*; in our kayaks we go after muskrats swimming in the rivers and lakes—we hurl harpoons.

To the July moon we give the name *Padlersersivik* because everything dries up during this month, even the earth.

August becomes *Krugyuat Tingiviat* in Eskimo—the young swans take their flight.

In September the Inuit of the Arctic Ocean leave in their kayaks to harpoon seals, using a special harpoon, the *aklikat.* Therefore the moon is called *Aklikarniarvik.*

In the month of October one of the first signs of cold is the forming of thin ice on the sandy shores of the ocean. This ice is called *tuglu,* and the moon *Tugluvik.*

In November it is cold and when we open the door white mist fills the igloo; this is the mist of the freezing days. That is the reason why this moon is called *Itartoryuk.*

We call the December moon *Kaitvitjuitk* because during this month of darkness the Inuit assemble, forget their worries, rejoice, dance, perform with puppets, and the like.

Today the Inuit do not know these names in their language; I am almost the only one who knows these words.

From: Nuligak. *I, Nuligak.* Edited by Maurice Metayer. Toronto: Peter Martin Associates, 1966.

TATTOOING AND NOSE PIERCING

Delfina Cuero

Delfina Cuero, a Diegueno woman born about 1900 in the San Diego, California, coastal area, told the story of her life to Florence Shipek, a researcher for the Mission Indian Claims Case, in 1965. Gifted with a remarkable memory of places, plants, and activities, Cuero explains the reasons for the then-defunct Diegueno traditions of tattooing youngsters and piercing the noses of boys at the age of puberty. Circumstances beyond their control forced the Dieguenos to make radical changes in these customs, along with many others.

My grandmother told me about what they did to girls as they were about to become women. But I'm not that old! They had already stopped doing it when I became a woman. Grandma told me they dug a hole, filled it with warm sand and kept the girl in there. They tattooed her all around her mouth and chin. . . .

My grandmother was only at the Mission under a priest for a little while and the Indians still did it then away from the Mission. My grandmother was tattooed all over her face but not my mother or father. My husband came from the mountains around Campo and he had a tattoo on his forehead. It was real pretty, blue-green and real round, like the moon and about the size of a half dollar. He had been through the boys' ceremony. The people who stayed always in the mountains did these things longer than the people who lived closer to the coast.

They used to take the boys to a special place where they taught the way to be good men. They sang special songs at these ceremonies and teased the boys too, like they used to do for the girls. Some things were done differently for the boys. They made a tu•nak [a hole in their nose] with a sharp stick. It was to make the boys clean. The men used to put a stick or a shell through the hole, or a button of some sort. They used things that we don't know now. My grandfather had a hole through his nose. He was never taught at the Mission, even though he had always lived in the valley until he was old. Some men and women put holes in their ears for ornaments but no one in my family ever did that. The tu•nak was not for ornament.

The reason a young man or woman was tattooed or the man had his nose pierced was that it was needed when you died. It helps you to go on the straight road. If you don't have it, you might turn into a stink bug with its end up in the air and you can't get near the straight road when you die. Now as I am getting old, I wonder if I should have a few lines tattooed so I won't have that happen to me when I die.

From: Cuero, Delfina. *The Autobiography of Delfina Cuero.* As told to Florence Shipek. Los Angeles: Dawson's Book Shop, 1968.

THEY GIVE AWAY

Myrtle Lincoln

Myrtle Lincoln was an Arapaho woman born on June 25, 1888, at Cantonment, Oklahoma. When she was interviewed on August 5, 1970, by the Duke Oral History Project, she explained the tradition of give aways and how it has changed over the years.

They have got a respect for this child and a love for him. That's why they give away for him. They give away things, you know. And them that you give away to—it's up to them. Next, when they have their own powwow—why if they give her things, she—just like they change gifts. That's the way it is. Now look at all these people that always be giving away—having special. And then a person passing away, they give away for them because they had a love for him or her . . . and they give away for them to show their love and respect for this person. . . . Long time ago people used to give away, you know, when anybody dies or anybody is dancing. They didn't give away— they used to give away horses. They'd have good bundles and load this horse with blankets and give them away to their friends, you know. To show their love and respect for whoever they had special for. That's been that way all, as long as I could think back. . . . And like these boys in the service—they got respect for them. They always start getting ready, you know—start saving stuff. When he comes home, they're going to have special for him and give away. And they always give a feed. You know—feed people. So that them people will help this boy that way. But this other way—this old Indian way—they used to not have dinners. They used to not give dinners. They used to have dance and boy, you'd see horses come in from every direction— But now what we give away is just cloth. . . . And you give away to people— your friends. . . . Some of them, they look around and see a poor person over there, and they give away to them. If they don't give back, it's all right. When you give away things, you just give it. But it's Indian way they turn around and give you things. . . .

From: Duke Indian Oral History Collection. University of Oklahoma Western History Collections, vol.2, fiche 6–7: 1–2 (T–615).

AVOIDING IN-LAWS

Belle Highwalking

Belle Highwalking, a Northern Cheyenne woman born in 1892 on the Northern Cheyenne Reservation in Montana, recorded her life history in 1970 and 1971 so her grandchildren would remember her. In her narrative, spoken in Cheyenne and translated by her daughter-in-law, she briefly talked about the practice of mother-in-law and father-in-law avoidance.

When a couple first married, they put up their own tent separate from their parents. A mother-in-law was very bashful toward her son-in-law and never talked or looked at him. The girls would feed their husbands. I know this because we had a separate tent and my stepmother was bashful towards Floyd [Belle's husband]. But she treated him good and would even cut up his food for him. This was how well they treated their sons and daughters-in-law. Even today this is true. When I am sitting right across from my son-in-law at the table, I don't talk to him even though many of these old ways are gone now. . . .

One night a man came to visit who was Floyd's uncle and whom I called "father-in-law." You weren't supposed to talk to your father-in-law and so I didn't speak to him. He used to be my brother-in-law before I married Floyd and then he used to tease me a lot. After he became my father-in-law, he became very bashful and wouldn't speak to me. One time we were in the tent and my sons wanted to go out. This man, who was very fat with a very big belly, was standing at the tent entrance. I was going to say, "Hurry up and go out so someone can come in." That was what I meant to say but I got all confused and said, "Get out of the way, Big Belly." I got very scared and my family thought I said it on purpose. Floyd laughed loudly and the boys and their friends laughed and ran out, yelling and hollering. I was very embarrassed because he was my father-in-law. Floyd told the different ones that teased me what I had said. They asked me, "Did you really tell your father-in-law that?" I denied it but I really did say it. I just denied it.

From: Highwalking, Belle. *Belle Highwalking: The Narrative of a Northern Cheyenne Woman.* Edited by Katherine M. Weist. Billings, Montana: Montana Council for Indian Education, 1979.

MALE AND FEMALE RELATIVES

~~~~~~~~~~~~~~~

John (Fire) Lame Deer

John (Fire) Lame Deer (Tahca Ushte), a Lakota (Sioux) born about 1900 on the Rosebud Reservation in South Dakota, told the story of his life to Richard Erdoes in Lame Deer, Seeker of Visions: The Life Story of a Sioux Medicine Man. *In it he recounts his life as a rodeo clown, soldier, sign painter, spud picker, jail prisoner, tribal policeman, sheepherder, and a* wicasa wakan, *a holy man of the Lakotas. In the following discussion of "men-women business," he explains the traditions governing behavior between male and female relations, especially in-laws.*

We have a special word to express our shyness in sex—*wistel-kiya*. That's a bashfulness between male and female relatives. It means that you don't pronounce the names of certain relations, look them in the face, or talk to them directly. It's not because we are shamed of the sex act but because of our fear of what you call incest. This for us was a most evil thing, so bad you didn't even want to think or hear about it.

Therefore you could josh your sister-in-law, be playful with her, tell her jokes, and she would do the same with you. If you ever stepped out of line with her—well, that could cause a big row, lead to a hell of a fight with her husband, if she was married, but it wouldn't be anything terribly shameful or unnatural. It would just be misbehaving.

But it was different with a man's own relatives, his sisters or female cousins. You don't look them straight in the eye, kid around or touch them. And a girl has to be very reserved with her brothers and male cousins. But between a man and his mother-in-law, a woman and her father-in-law—why, it is just as if there was a brick wall between them. They avoid each other completely. That is because your in-laws are looked upon as real parents. Cutting up with your mother-in-law would be like sleeping with your own ma; you can't even imagine such a thing.

I know of a young man who was friendly with an old lady. He liked to drop in on her for a chat and piece of pie. Those two really liked each other. After a while the young man fell in love with the old lady's daughter. He lived with her as man and wife and they had kids together, but he would not marry her, because that would have made the old woman he loved so much into his mother-in-law. Then he couldn't have been friends with her anymore.

It's hard to avoid your mother-in-law altogether. If they happen to be in the same room the son-in-law sits in one corner and she in another, fidgety, as far apart as possible. He is hungry and muttering to himself, loud enough for her to hear, "I wish somebody would cook a meal for me." He isn't talking to her, mind you; he's just thinking aloud. But she suddenly gets the idea of putting the kettle on her old wood burner. She is talking to herself, too: "Those lazy so-and-so's; nobody cut wood for me today. I wish somebody had." Well, the young man suddenly gets it into his head to go out and do some chopping. That's one way of communicating. My dad was very old-fashioned. He never talked to his mother-in-law. If he wanted to tell her something, he told his wife, and she told her.

Lame Deer, John (Fire) and Richard Erdoes. *Lame Deer, Seeker of Visions*. New York: Simon and Schuster, 1972.

THE MUSEUM OF THE PLAINS
WHITE PERSON

~~~~~~~~~~~~~~~~~~~~

Rayna Green

*Rayna Green, a Cherokee woman born in 1942 in Dallas, Texas, is direc-
tor of the American Indian Program at the Smithsonian Institution's
National Museum of American History. A folklorist, scholar, poet, and
essayist, she also knows how to dish out the legendary humor so characteristic of native peoples. In an "after feast speech" she gave before hundreds of native women at a 1981 conference on educational equity in
Tahlequah, Oklahoma, she targeted museum policies regarding collecting
native sacred objects and bones. Her comments were made nine years
before President George Bush signed landmark legislation protecting
Indian grave sites on federal lands from looting and making it easier for
tribes to repatriate culturally identifiable remains, funerary objects, and
sacred objects found on federal (not state or private) lands.*

... the thing I'm most excited about recently is the grand project. This is a
multimillion-dollar project, it's been funded by all the major foundations in
the country. It's very exciting. As you know, all over the country, the
Cherokee Nation and many of the Indian nations all over the country have
established their own museums. I've done a great deal of museum consulting for the National Endowment and for the tribal museums, for the Indian
Museum Association. But I had found a real lack of a particular kind of
museum that I really feel we need. And this is going to be a major cultural
institution. I want to tell you about it because I am so thrilled to be part of
this. This idea, I have to give credit, was originally hatched up by the ex-
chairman of the Winnebago Tribe, Louis LaRose, and myself, late one night
in a serious scholarly discussion in Albuquerque. Basically what we want to
develop is a unique, cultural institution. I know you will be thrilled. This is
an institution that is meant for Indian people. It is something we've been
needing for a long time. It's something that is particularly needed to meet a
very special critical need. The museum is called THE MUSEUM OF THE PLAINS
WHITE PERSON. It meets this critical need that I spoke of. It's very serious.
You see, we began to be very worried. As you know their (White people's)

184

culture is dying out. Very soon, very soon there will be very few surviving White persons. We worry about this. What will the last surviving White persons do when they have no one to ask what their language was like, what their customs and clothes were like. So, we began to worry about this and we came up with the idea of the the MUSEUM OF THE PLAINS WHITE PERSON. As I said, it's been met with great reception all over the country. Foundations have rushed to pour money in. Indian people have given money for it. I can't tell you how many shawl and blanket raffles have gone on to pay for this museum. And I want to tell you something about the museum and perhaps this will inspire some of you to go to those few White people that you know are living out there and quickly acquire artifacts from them before they disappear. Because, you know, they don't know how to take care of them. We worry about this. It's quite serious.

The first big collection that we are working on, and this is really inspiring, is the bone collection. As you know, all museums have to have a bone collection. We have begun a national campaign to acquire the bones of famous White people. We want little Indian children to be able to come in and study these and Indian scholars want to pore over them, the different skull shapes and so forth. And, of course, when we do acquire them we will acquire them permanently. As you know, they cannot be given back once they have been handled. We do need to study them for years. And so we are acquiring these. We have just acquired, I think, what is a quite moving find. One of the most important ones. We have just acquired the bones of John Wayne. As you realize what great significance this can have for the scholars, what a study of his bones will tell us about these people and what their lives were like. Well, so that's very important.

There are a number of other famous bones that we want to acquire and I am sure you can begin to guess whose we have our sights on. It's going to be thrilling. The collection will be quite large, of course. We have planned to make the collection as large as it needs to be with as many samples. So, we are going to begin a massive grave excavation all over the country. We have, through our legal offices, which have become very sophisticated, as you know, acquired clear title to at least eighty percent of all the graves in White cemeteries all over the country. We plan to move in with steam shovels right away. We've acquired Mr. Peabody's big coal shovel which did strip mining up at Northern Cheyenne in order to begin and it's going to be an amazing project.

I'll tell you a few things about some of the other collections that I think are quite exciting. We are going to have collections of their food, for example—their food ways. We are going to reconstruct a McDonald's in its entirety. In that we're going to have true-to-life plastic exhibits of white bread, mayonnaise, iceberg lettuce and peanut butter which will be everywhere—

smeared all over everything. Primarily stuck to the roof of everyone's mouth. We are going to have several exhibits about their customs. We want to have some performing arts there and we have found the last of a number of White people who know their dances and songs and who have preserved these intact and we are going to have everyday, living exhibits of the two-step, the fox-trot, the disco and other dances. This is going to be very exciting when children come to visit, particularly.

We have acquired exhibits of their costumes. In fact, in the condominium that we are going to reconstruct in its entirety, inside the museum, there will be a typical little family with the gentleman in the three-piece suit and a briefcase and all the other artifacts of their civilization.

We have found one very unusual thing that I do want to tell you about. It's an archaeological remain that we have found somewhat in the vicinity of what used to be called "Los Angeles." It's very interesting. It proves that their culture was very flighty. They seemed to change rulers quite regularly. It's kind of interesting. In fact, we found an archaeological artifact that indicates that they changed rulers regularly. It's a big thing they used to call a neon sign—and it says QUEEN FOR A DAY. We are going to do some more excavation to determine just how they did depose their rulers and how they transferred power.

Well, I think you'll agree that this is one of the most exciting things that Indian people have done—one of the most exciting contributions that we could make. As young Indian scholars we are deeply pleased to be able to make this. . .

From: Green, Rayna. "After-Feast Speech: Contemporary Indian Humor." In *Words of Today's American Indian Women: OHOYO MAKACHI.* Compiled by Ohoyo Resource Center Staff. Wichita Falls, Texas: Ohoyo Resource Center, 1981.

Going to T.P. [Trading Post]

The drawing shows humor operating within a Navajo context. The wagon, very much in demand for transportation and work on the Navajo Reservation, carries a father, mother, and son to the local trading post. During summer months, canvas covers like the one pictured on the wagon are used. The trips to the trading post are exciting for the young ones, a time for a soda pop or piece of candy as a reward for helping out at home. If there is more than one sister or brother, only the best-behaved get to go. So the boy who gets to go is making faces at the ones left behind.

Drawing by Marvin Cook, a Navajo cartoonist who grew up on the Navajo Reservation.

Date of cartoon: July 6, 1994

WE WERE A SHARING PEOPLE

Ignatia Broker

*Ignatia Broker, an Ojibway (Chippewa) born in 1919 on the White
Earth Reservation in northern Minnesota, was a storyteller, teacher,
author, and respected leader working for both civil and human rights.
Honored in 1984 by the New York–based Wonder Woman Foundation
that annually gave awards to women over age 40 whose accomplishments
inspired others, she won in the category "striving for peace and equality."
The following excerpt about the native tradition of sharing came from
Broker's* Night Flying Woman: An Ojibway Narrative *(1983), a
book about her great-great-grandmother, Oona.*

I remember living in a room with six others. It was a housekeeping room,
nine by twelve feet in size, and meant for one person. It was listed with the
price agency at five dollars a week, but the good landlady collected five dollars from each of us each week. However, she did put in a bunk bed and a
rollaway which I suppose was all right because we were on different shifts
and slept different times anyway. It was cramped and crowded but we had a
mutual respect. We sometimes shared our one room with others who had no
place, so that there might be nine or ten of us. We could not let friends be
out on the street without bed or board. As long as our landlady did not mind,
we helped and gave a place of rest to other Ojibway people.

Our paydays were on different days and so whoever had money lent car-
fare and bought meat and vegetables. Stew was our daily fare because we
had only a hot plate and one large kettle.

I mention this practice because I know other Indian people did the same
thing, and sometimes whole families evolved from it. This was how we got a
toehold in the urban areas—by helping each other. Perhaps this is the way
nonmaterialistic people do. We were a sharing people and our tribal traits are
still within us.

From: Broker, Ignatia. *Night Flying Woman: An Ojibway Narrative.* St. Paul: Minnesota Historical
Society Press, 1983.

POTLATCHES

~~~~~~~~~~

Lorraine (Felix) Titus

In 1984, Lorraine (Felix) Titus, an Athabascan woman interviewed her grandfather, Walter Northway, a traditional Athabascan man born in 1876 in the village of Northway located on the Nabesna River in Alaska. In the course of their conversation, he explains the different kinds of potlatches and the reasons for giving them. Lorraine published this information in a book named after her grandfather, who lived to be 117 years old.

We have different kinds of potlatches. Some are in honor of children and some are for adults. My son was named after my grandpa's father, Taiy-tah. . . . We named him—put it on his birth certificate and everything—but we never actually used that name for about a year until we could have a potlatch. In a way the potlatch was to show the people that he will be using that name. So we had to have a potlatch. It was like buying the name.

At that time, I bought a whole bunch of snowshoes and bow and arrows that my grandpa made. He did them just like they did in the old days. And I got bear spears he carved out of bone. I kept buying those things and putting them aside. He never knew what I was doing with them.

Usually people would get together and do bunch of potlatches together so everybody can help share with the food and work. I waited for that and did a potlatch on my son to get his name when he was a year and a half. We gave out all those gifts.

Another time for a potlatch was when my son had his first haircut. We never cut his hair till he was five years old. Then my grandpa made a potlatch over him. We had to pick someone who wasn't related to my son in our culture. James Gallen did it. He bought new scissors to cut Taiy-tah's hair. Then we took the hair back to my grandfather. Grandpa put a pair of snowshoes, five blankets, and fifty dollars with the hair and gave it back to James. James had to burn the hair.

They'd do things, too, if one of your sons or daughters picked their first berries. They'd give all the berries away. Or, if they kill their first moose, they'd give all the moose away and do a big potlatch on it. If someone gets hurt and nearly dies, they'd do something for that escape, too, later on. We do potlatch in honor of something or in thanks of something. And in memory, too.

The same time I made a potlatch for my son, there was quite a few different ones going on. I think one was in memory of my grandpa's grandson that drowned up in Birch Creek. I think they were having a memory potlatch over him. See, we have a death potlatch during funeral. Then maybe couple years down the road or a year later, it depends on when the family could get ready, we bring back the memory and have another potlatch to put the dead person away.

I found a lot of people here think that potlatch is a waste of time and waste of money. But I remember my first potlatch that I held . . . it seems like it takes all the hurt and frustration out of you. Making a potlatch may be expensive but when you do it from deep down in your heart, it takes all that sad feeling out of you. . . .

During death it's the same thing. It makes you feel good to give away gifts to the people that are with you. A lot of times that's why they have a second potlatch to bring back the dead and completely put the person away. I mean you'll still remember the person, but the potlatch helps to get rid of the rest of the feeling. That's one thing Grandpa spent a lot of time explaining to me.

From: *Walter Northway*. Fairbanks: Alaska Native Language Center, University of Alaska, 1987.

TRADITIONAL INDIAN SPORTS

Joseph B. Oxendine

Joseph B. Oxendine, a Lumbee man raised in an Indian community in Pembroke, North Carolina, received his doctorate in physical education and psychology from Boston University. A three-sport athlete in high school and college and a professional baseball player with the Pittsburgh Pirates, in 1988 Oxendine published American Indian Sports Heritage, *which studies Indian sports traditions before and after contact with non-Indian cultures. Here he explains how traditional Indian games and sports meshed with ritual and ceremony.*

Games were an integral part of the culture of all tribes. They were evident in ceremonies and festivals relating to war, hunting, harvest, birth, death, and other important community events. The characteristic of *play* was universal, although the nature and variety of games differed from tribe to tribe. . . .

Games among traditional American Indians ranged from the seemingly trivial activities primarily for the amusement of children to major sporting events of significance for persons of all ages. The latter activities often commanded the interest and participation of whole communities. . . .

In most of the traditional Indian societies, games of skill or dexterity were rarely played by adults for mere amusement or fun. Rather, they were played for some purpose that was a matter of importance to the community. To a considerable extent, sports were enjoyed in the same manner as are popular sports today; in addition, however, they were interrelated with social issues. The particular significance varied with the tribes, the sport, and the community need at the time. Although it may not be apparent in most of today's Indian communities, sports were originally meshed in tradition, ritual, and ceremony. . . .

Reports from Indian groups ranging from the northeast to the southwest and from Canada to Mississippi show that the religious significance of sport enhanced its status in the lives of Indians. This spiritual connection, along with the inherent value of sport itself, ensured that it would be more than frivolous activity. . . .

Sometimes the game was focused toward a specific goal, such as the bringing of rain in a time of drought, celebrating success in hunting or in battle, healing the sick, or encouraging fertility for one or more persons. At other times the motivation was more general—perhaps simply to please the gods or to establish the superiority of one god over another. It is significant that many early commentators, particularly those writing prior to 1800, would include an explanation of a contest's cultural or religious significance along with the description of the game itself. In addition, the widespread practice of wagering on the outcome of games added to their significance.

One can argue that today's sports and games among non-Indian groups are likewise more than idle amusement because they are rarely played exclusively for the physical values to be derived. For example, golf matches among friends may be played for a soda, for a dollar a hole, or for higher stakes. High school athletic contests or evening bowling matches have league championships, trophies, and recognition at stake. Certainly, professional athletes play for money and recognition. Even neighborhood pickup softball games often involve bragging rights or other benefits. In comparison, however, Indian games were more deeply rooted in ceremony and practically all contests involved betting. Preparation for Indian sports included spiritual as well as physical exercises, and the outcome was assumed to be influenced by a power beyond the control of the participants.

Although it has become less clearly defined, the ceremonial significance of Indian sport has continued into the 20th century. However, the quality of participation in sports with no cultural connection to Indian life appears to be affected. For example, when Indians began participating in popular non-Indian sports, it was often suggested that they did not perform to their maximum capacity. . . . In a situation devoid of the traditional Indian ritual, many Indians seemed to lack interest in performing beyond the obvious requirements of a particular task. Long and rigorous training schedules in preparation for subsequent events outside the total cultural context were often foreign to their concept of sport. For instance, while playing major league baseball with the New York Giants, Jim Thorpe was accused of being lazy by manager John McGraw. . . . Thorpe was never so characterized, however, when surrounded by fellow Indians at the Carlisle School. . . . Furthermore, many Indians in recent years have dropped out of sports participation altogether. Perhaps the artificiality of the sports climate contributes to this loss of interest and involvement.

From: Oxendine, Joseph B. *American Indian Sports Heritage*. Champaign, Illinois: Human Kinetics Books, 1988.

CONTEMPORARY POTLATCHES

Mark Tucker

Mark Tucker, a Yupik Eskimo, was born in Emmonak, Alaska, where he was a bilingual instructor in the local school when he wrote the following piece in 1990. He grew up in a family of five children, who with their parents lived off the land as their ancestors did for thousands of years. Tucker's piece and other Alaska native student writings from Chukchi College, a Kotzebue-based campus of the University of Alaska, have won state and national media prizes, including the Robert F. Kennedy Journalism Award.

The word *potlatch* comes from the Indian word, *pat shotl*, which means "giving." At a potlatch, one village invites another village to watch some dancing and to accept gifts.

Alaska native villages have sponsored this kind of potlatch as far back as anyone can remember. The Indians of the Northwest Coast also hold potlatches to celebrate the completion of a new totem pole or to celebrate the building of a new house by a member of the clan.

In the past at some potlatches the host and their relatives would give away everything they owned just to impress their guests. Then, the village that received all the gifts at the first potlatch would reciprocate by holding a second one. This village often gave everything back to the first village, in addition to many other gifts.

Years ago, wood carvers created different types of animal masks for dancers to wear during the potlatch. Prior to the celebration, the carvers would lay the masks out in the *qasgig* (sod house) and a man (usually a shaman) chosen by the village would shout at each mask as if he were that animal. For example, if the mask were a seal, he would scream like a seal, or if it were a fox, he would howl like a fox.

Many Yup'ik Eskimo villages still present potlatches. Potlatches here in Emmonak occur twice every winter.

During the potlatch, people believe that the spirits of the dead float around in the room where the guests come and gather. The guests consume the food distributed to them and sip on a cup of water. This way, the spirits of the dead are relieved from their thirst and hunger.

At the potlatch, the performers sing between sixteen and twenty songs; it all depends on how many new songs the elders compose. Some elders introduce four songs, others fewer. Some songs have been sung as long as anyone in the village can remember, but if a song was sung by a shaman in the past people are afraid to sing it after the shaman has died.

Nowadays, when all the songs and dances are completed, the guests go to their relatives' homes to rest for the night. The next morning the potlatch continues, and a man selected by the elders hosting the potlatch inquires of the guests which song or dance they would like to have performed. In this morning dance, everyone just enjoys themselves, knowing that the spirits of the dead have been relieved from hunger and thirst.

Later that afternoon, the men from the other villages gather in the dance hall to receive gifts to take back home. The following evening there is a dance called *tukriaq*, meaning "to knock," to send the spirits of the dead back wherever they came from.

Once a child attains a certain age, the parents and grandparents prepare a "first dance" (like a debut) for that child. The mother and grandmothers make such gifts as yarn gloves, socks, mittens, hot plate holders and aprons. The father and grandfathers make things like spears, spear throwers, harpoons, ice picks, fish traps and ulus.

When the child is ready to dance, his family hands out these gifts to the family of the person whose name was handed down to the child. It is a Yup'ik custom that a newborn child is named after the last elder in the village to die.

After the potlatch, the child is allowed to dance as many songs as he or she wants at any social event.

I first danced in a potlatch when I was about eight years old. Things have changed since then, but I remember the place where we practiced Eskimo dancing; it was a *qasgiq*. Gatherings in *qasgiqs* back then often got crowded rapidly when large amounts of guests arrived to be entertained. The shaman of the hosting village would use his powers to make enough room in the *qasgiq* so that all the guests had room to come in and watch the performance. A gas lantern lighted the room then. To heat the *qasgiq*, the men took fire baths in them, then danced after taking the bath. Electricity has replaced gas lighting, and an oil stove heats the gathering place now.

The potlatch cannot be compared to square dance, rock'n'roll dance, Irish dance or even folk dance. Rather, potlatches are an integral part of Alaska native culture. Even though modern Western ways have altered the native culture, our traditional values live on through contemporary potlatches.

From: Tucker, Mark. "Potlatches Are Integral Part of Culture." *Tundra Times* September 24, 1990.

INDIAN HUMOR

Joseph Medicine Crow

Joseph Medicine Crow, a Crow man, was born in Lodge Grass, Montana, in 1913. Designated tribal historian and anthropologist by the Crow Tribal Council in 1948, he began recording stories and collecting data about his tribal culture and history in 1932. In his 1992 book, From the Heart of the Crow Country, *he devotes a chapter to "Crow Indian Humor," regaling readers with stories Indians tell about one another.*

Contrary to the general impression that Indians are stoical, unsmiling, and stone-faced, Indians are, in fact, full of humor and hilarity among themselves. At powwows men from different tribes visit and exchange new jokes and funny stories, and before long the same joke is told all over the Indian country.

In the old pre-reservation days, the main form of Crow Indian humor was the singing of jesting songs. Rival warrior societies would compose songs about each other's anecdotes, eccentricities, and breaking certain clan taboos, such as a man's mentioning the name of his mother-in-law.

Today, this form of humor has been replaced by what is called "telling about one's ways." This particular form of humor is not used indiscriminately. Only the Opposites (children of patrilineal clans) may use it to tease, ridicule, and castigate one another publicly. The Opposites, sometimes called "teasing clans," have the license to watch one another, and they are quick to fabricate outrageous tales about one another's ways. People enjoy these humorous tales, and before long these incredible stories become true.

Today tribal people tell jokes and humorous stories about themselves and laugh at themselves. Life on reservations, with high unemployment, alcoholism, and poor health, is often harsh. Indian humor stories provide an outlet for frustrations. People "roll with the punch" with these grin-and-laugh-provoking stories. There are, however, some militant and activist Indians who object to these stories as "racial jokes," but as a whole the reservation Indians not only tolerate but enjoy listening to and telling these stories. . . .

After World War II rodeo became a great pastime on the various reservations throughout the Indian country. In between the so-called all-Indian

195

rodeo, many Indian rodeo cowboys would go to country-fair rodeos and other off-reservation rodeos.

The story goes that several boys from a reservation in South Dakota formed a team and would go rodeoing all summer. One day after the rodeo the boys sat around and talked about their performance. Then one of them said to the bareback rider Joe Stinks: "Joe, you just gotta change your name. The rodeo announcers joke about your name, sometimes saying that your ride was a 'stinker' and all that. As it is, the whites like to make fun of our names and tend to look down at us."

One day they practically forced Joe to go to the county courthouse and have his name changed legally. Soon he was on the road hitchhiking. But before long he was back, saying that it would take twenty-five bucks to make a name change.

After a good day at a rodeo the boys chipped in and gave Joe twenty-five dollars. He left and came back the next day all smiles. The boys surrounded him, curious to know if he had selected a good white-man's name, like Jones, Smith, or Johnson. He just smiled and told them to listen to the announcer. They would hear his new name just before he was to come out of the chute on the horse called W. O. Grey.

Finally there was only one more rider to come out. The announcer cleared his throat and boomed over the sound system: "Ladies and gentlemen, we have a real treat for you! The bucking horse of the year, W.O. Grey, is now in chute number six. And the cowboy on him will be JOE STINKS NO MORE!"

The audience howled, but the group of Indian cowboys standing against the arena fence moaned, "Oh no."

From: Medicine Crow, Joseph. *From the Heart of the Crow Country*. New York: Orion Books, 1992.

POWWOWS

Martha Kreipe de Montaño

Martha Kreipe de Montaño, a member of the Prairie Band of Potawatomi from Kansas, has a master of arts in the ethnohistory of North American Indians and has curated exhibitions at the University of Kansas's Museum of Anthropology, the Museum of the American Indian, and elsewhere. Currently the manager of the Resource Center of the Smithsonian National Museum of the American Indian, in 1993 she wrote about the powwow, a popular twentieth-century tradition that is a "way of sharing, reinforcing, and expressing Indian heritage."

The word *powwow* came into the English language from an eastern Algonquian language. In the Massachuset language, *pauwau* literally means "he uses divination." It refers to a shaman or medicine man, who could divine the future from information and power received while dreaming. . . . Today "powwow" is sometimes used to refer to an important meeting, but to Native Americans it refers to a gathering of Indian people to visit, feast, sing, and dance together.

Powwows, in the Native American sense of the word, probably started in the last decades of the nineteenth century as Indian people adapted to new conditions. The majority of powwow dances were war dances, which originated with the warrior societies of the Plains. When Indian people were confined to reservations, the war dances became social dances. But they did not lose their connection to warriors. People who are in the armed service today or are veterans are today's equivalent of the warriors of old, and powwows often recognize and honor them. In addition, much of the powwow clothing for men has evolved from insignia worn by warriors. The roach headdress, feathered bustles, and eagle feathers worn by men in powwows were once worn only by proven warriors. Today they are worn by Indian men and boys as a symbol of Indian identity. Women's powwow clothing are contemporary versions of traditional clothing, usually made from buckskin or cloth.

Powwows are held outside in grassy areas or inside, often in gymnasiums, when weather dictates. The center of the powwow is the drum, which refers to the instrument and to the singers who play the drum and sing at the same time. On the northern and southern Plains, some powwow traditions differ. For example, on the southern Plains, a single drum is placed in the center of the dance arena, while in the north, one or more drums are placed at the edge. Spectators sit in bleachers or on folding chairs. Participants dance either sunwise (clockwise) or counterclockwise around the drum. In the northern tradition, men and women usually dance in opposite directions.

Powwows are not so much a performance for an audience as they are a way of sharing, reinforcing, and expressing Indian heritage. Since many pow-wows are held every year, and most are open to the public, a powwow is a good way to learn about American Indian heritage. The details of the pow-wow vary with the location, but in general, they begin with the Grand Entry, in which all dancers, dressed in their finest regalia, enter the powwow arena dancing slowly in a parade around the drum. Intertribal War dances follow, interspersed with Honor dances and other special dances such as the Two-step, Round dance, or Crow Hop.

Contests draw dancers from far away to compete for prize money. Dancers compete in gender and in age groups. For example, there are often junior and senior divisions as well as "tiny tots." Within age groups, there are cate-gories based on styles of dancing and types of regalia worn while dancing. Dancers are judged for their dancing, their regalia, and the extent of their participation. In general, men compete in "traditional," "fancy dance," and "grass dance" categories. Popular women's dance categories are "tradition-al," "northern shawl," and "jingle dress."

Each dancer interprets the dance individually within the canons of their particular dance category. Most dances do not have coordinated choreogra-phy, every dancer chooses steps as a way to express his or her own Indian identity. As the dancers circle the drum, from communities far and near, with different customs, each one dancing a personal interpretation, all are united by the heartbeat of Mother Earth expressed through the drum.

From: Hirschfelder, Arlene and Martha Kreipe de Montaño. *Native American Almanac: A Portrait of Native America Today*. New York: Prentice-Hall General Reference, 1993.

WORSHIP

A girl's parents bless their daughter and her sponsor with sacred pollen during this Western Apache puberty ceremony. Photograph by Helga Teiwes. Arizona State Museum, University of Arizona.

Indian country in North America is home to hundreds of religious traditions that have endured despite a long history of persecution and suppression by the early missionaries and the U.S. government. These traditions are as dignified, profound, and richly faceted as those of other faiths practiced throughout the world. They deserve the respect, status, and recognition accorded other great spiritual traditions.

Each tribe performs ceremonies according to instructions given in sacred stories. Some of the most important ceremonies need to be conducted at certain sacred places at specific times of the year. Some ceremonies mark important life-cycle events in a person's life and take place at important times, such as solstices and equinoxes. There are ceremonies to heal the sick, renew relationships with spiritual beings, initiate people into religious societies, ensure success in hunting and growing crops, pray for rain, and give thanks for harvests of food. Some ceremonies must be performed in order to ensure the survival of the earth and all forms of life. Today, as in the past, native peoples also worship by dancing. Many Indians continue to dance to keep ancient ways alive and to connect themselves to the past.

The speakers in this section share information about various aspects of native spirituality. Barney Old Coyote (Crow) explains how native worship was integrated into the Indian way of life, and Irene Stewart (Navajo) stresses the importance Navajos place on prayers of gratitude. Joe S. Sando (Jemez Pueblo) provides an insider's view into ancient Pueblo religious beliefs. Joseph Medicine Crow (Crow) describes native healing, and John (Fire) Lame Deer (Lakota) talks about being a medicine man.

Each native tribe had its own distinct ceremonies. John Cummings (Crow) explains the Sun Dance, one of the best-known but least understood religious ceremonies of native North America. Thomas Wildcat Alford (Shawnee) describes the Bread Dance, and Andy Fernando (Upper Skagit) talks about the First Salmon Ceremony, a centuries-old observance held to honor the year's first catch. Julian Lang (Karuk) describes the role baskets play in the Jump Dance, and Linda Hogan (Chickasaw) discusses the sweat lodge ceremony, a spiritual cleansing universal to native people throughout the United States.

The ritual and ceremony surrounding life-cycle events are discussed in Captain John V. Satterlee's (Menominee) account of the puberty fast for children. Mourning Dove (Colville) describes the spiritual training boys and girls received that enabled them to find a guardian spirit. Yoimut (Yokuts) describes the Lonewis, the mourning ceremony for the dead. Wolf-Chief (Hidatsa) speaks of the sacred bundles of medicine men, while Tyon (Lakota) talks about the sacredness of the number four and the circle.

SACRED BUNDLES

~~~~~~~~~

Wolf-Chief

Wolf-Chief, a Hidatsa man born in 1849 on the Fort Berthold Reservation in North Dakota, provided Gilbert L. Wilson, an anthropologist, with information about his people's religious beliefs. His narrative, which targets similarities between the honor Indians gave sacred bundles and the honor Europeans gave certain sacred materials, was issued in 1914 as part of chapter four of Goodbird the Indian: His Story, *a book designed to teach Christian youngsters about other cultures.*

Many medicine men added to their mystery power by owning sacred bundles, neatly bound bundles of skin or cloth, containing sacred objects or relics that had been handed down from old times. Every bundle had its history, telling how the bundle began. . . .

The owner of a sacred bundle was called its keeper; he usually kept it hung on his medicine post, in the back part of his lodge. A sacred bundle was looked upon as a kind of shrine, and in some lodges strangers were forbidden to walk between it and the fire.

When a keeper became old, he sold his sacred bundle to some younger man, that its rites might not die with him. The young man paid a hundred tanned buffalo skins and a gun or pony, and made a feast for the keeper; at this feast, the young man received the bundle with the rites and songs that went with it. This was called "making a ceremony."

White men think it strange that we Indians honored these sacred bundles; but I have heard that in Europe men once honored relics, the skull, or a bone, or a bit of hair of some saint, or a nail from Jesus' cross; that they did not pray to the relic, but thought that the spirit of the saint was near; or that he was more willing to hear their prayers when they knelt before the relic.

In much the same way, we Indians honored our sacred bundles. They contained sacred objects, or relics, that had belonged to some god—his scalp, or skull, the pipe he smoked, or his robe. We did not pray to the object, but to the god or spirit to whom it had belonged, and we thought these sacred objects had wonderful power, just as white men once thought they could be cured of sickness by touching the bone of some saint.

A medicine man's influence was greater if he owned a sacred bundle. Men then came to him not only because the spirits answered him when he fasted, but because, as its keeper, he had power from the gods of the sacred bundle.

From: Goodbird, Edward. *Goodbird the Indian: His Story.* Told to Gilbert L. Wilson. New York: Fleming H. Revell Co., 1914.

THE NUMBER FOUR
AND THE CIRCLE

Tyon

*In 1917, Tyon, an Oglala Lakota man who was a professional story-
teller, also served as a valuable interpreter for J. R. Walker, a physician
who cultivated the friendship of "shamans." Tyon, who knew Lakota customs, ceremonials, and language and understood most of the information
given him by Lakota sacred practitioners, shared the following information with Walker, who lived among the Oglala, about the importance of
the number four and the circle.*

In former times the Lakota grouped all their activities by fours. This was
because they recognized four directions: the west, the north, the east, and
the south; four divisions of time: the day, the night, the moon, and the year;
four parts in everything that grew from the ground: the roots, the stem, the
leaves, and the fruit; four kinds of things that breathe: those that crawl, those
that fly, those that walk on four legs, and those that walk on two legs; four
things above the world: the sun, the moon, the sky, and the stars; four kinds
of gods: the great, the associates of the great, the gods below them, and the
spiritkind; four periods of human life: babyhood, childhood, adulthood, and
old age; and finally, mankind has four fingers on each hand, four toes on each
foot and the thumbs and the great toes taken together form four. Since the
Great Spirit caused everything to be in fours, mankind should do everything
possible in fours.

The Oglala believe the circle to be sacred because the Great Spirit caused
everything in nature to be round except stone. Stone is the implement of
destruction. The sun and the sky, the earth and the moon, are round like a
shield, though the sky is deep like a bowl. Everything that breathes is round
like the body of a man. Everything that grows from the ground is round like
the stem of a plant. Since the Great Spirit has caused everything to be round
mankind should look upon the circle as sacred, for it is the symbol of all
things in nature except stone. It is also the symbol of the circle that marks
the edge of the world and therefore of the four winds that travel there.
Consequently it is also the symbol of the year. The day, the night, and the
moon go in a circle above the sky. Therefore the circle is a symbol of these
divisions of time and hence the symbol of all time.

For these reasons the Oglala make their tipis circular, their camp-circle
circular, and sit in a circle in all ceremonies. The circle is also the symbol

of the tipi and of shelter. If one makes a circle for an ornament and it is divided in any way, it should be understood as the symbol of the world and of time. If, however, the circle be filled with red, it is the symbol of the sun; if filled with blue, it is the symbol of the sky. If the circle is divided into four parts, it is the symbol of the four winds; if it is divided into more than four parts, it is the symbol of a vision of some kind. If a half circle is filled with red it represents the day; filled with black, the night; filled with yellow, a moon or month. On the other hand, if a half circle is filled with many colors, it symbolizes the rainbow.

One may paint or otherwise represent a circle on his tipi or his shield or his robe. The mouth of a pipe should always be moved in a circle before the pipe is formally smoked.

From: Walker, J. R. *The Sun Dance and Other Ceremonies of the Oglala Division of the Teton Dakota.* American Museum of Natural History Anthropological Papers, vol. 16, part 2. 1917.

PUBERTY FAST

Captain John V. Satterlee

Captain John V. Satterlee ("Little Doctor"), a Menominee man, was for many years a mediator between his people and those who studied them. In the summer of 1920, speaking in the language of the Menominee Indians of Wisconsin, he dictated information about the puberty fast.

Long ago in the ancient time our ancestors . . . used to have supernatural power, for the spirits took pity on them and blessed them, giving them help. This was the rite they always performed: they fasted, afflicting their own souls. They ate nothing and drank nothing. Parents made their children fast so that they might therefrom gain a continuance of mortal life. This was what the faster was to get as a blessing from the spirits: he was to see an evil vision or else to see a good vision; this was what the faster gained, if he was really helped by the spirits. And it was through this that a person succeeded in prolonging and assuring his life.

At the beginning of the fast the father of the family handed him a bowl filled with food, and some charcoal. And then the one who was performing the puberty-fast chose what he wanted to do for himself. Well then,—if he had a good foreboding, he took the charcoal and painted his face, that he might be favorably observed by all the spirits that dwell above, as well as those underneath, inside the earth. And this alone was what he desired, whoever performed the puberty-fast, that he might see a good vision, that he might be given a supernatural blessing, having earned it for himself. And as a matter of fact, those who properly performed this rite lived quite a while, as did also their descendants down to their great-grandchildren.

Today, however, this custom no longer exists: it has by this time entirely sunk into disuse. The white-skinned American has headed it off and disturbed it; likewise, in fact, all things are now of strange seeming. But so much I remember: and the reason I tell of it is that it may be known to people, how things used to be in the olden time.

If this person in his fast was deceived by an evil underground spirit, that was when he saw an evil vision, and if he accepted it, that was then the

205

reason why he would turn bad, be of evil character, and not lead a good life. That was what he had by mischance gained for himself.

When a young person began to fast, his body was really clean, as was symbolized by his painting his face with charcoal. And this was why he was able to see a vision, because there was nothing in his stomach. The father, when he arranged his child's fast, would ask him from time to time what sort of vision he had seen. If the faster related an evil vision, then the father would need to tell his son to eat. He did this so that the latter should reject that bad dream.

Now, on the other hand, if this puberty-faster saw a proper vision, because a good spirit was disposed to bless him, then the father would tell his son to keep on fasting, so that he might reach a greater number of days. In this way he was able to bring it about that good thing was firmly placed, that blessing which he was seeing in dreams.

This puberty-faster would do this; that was the way he was made to do: somewhere on clean ground a little hut was built for him. There that faster would stay, lying there and desiring as he fasted to see a good vision. In that way he would endure a large number of days. Then finally he would burn with hunger and be parched with thirst. After a while, when he became too thirsty, he was helped by being made to put a piece of lead into his mouth, so that his tongue and throat would not be too dry. This was, along with other things, a reason why he was able to endure many days; some (fasters) ten days and some fifteen days. A person like this was one who properly and in all forms succeeded in making the fast.

If, however, a faster by mishap set foot on something dirty or on the ground where it had been defiled, then he was not for a long time able to be blessed by the spirits.

From: Bloomfield, Leonard. *Menomini Texts.* American Ethnological Society Publications, no. 12. 1928.

SPIRITUAL TRAINING

Mourning Dove [Christine Quintasket]

Christine Quintasket, a woman from the Colville Confederated Tribes of Washington State and born about 1885, was the first native woman to publish a novel, Cogewa *(1927). Additionally, she wrote a manuscript about her life among her people on the Colville Reservation in the late nineteenth and early twentieth centuries. Writing during the 1930s under the pen name Mourning Dove, or sometimes* Hu-mi-shu-ma, *her spelling of the Okanogan name of the bird, she describes the spiritual training of six- or seven-year-old boys and girls.*

Children, at the early age of six or seven, were continually sent out each night to hunt for a guardian spirit to enable them to be shamans. Both boys and girls were obliged to undertake this search.

First a child was sent out for water to a spring or a creek close to the tipi. He or she was given a little basket and was expected to return with water for the parents or the spiritual teacher to prove that the destination was reached and the child was not playing "hooky." This first lesson was intended to make the child familiar with darkness and brave enough to overcome a fear of ghosts.

As children grew older they were sent a little farther away each night until they graduated from short to long distances, when the teacher or parent gave them something special to take along on these night journeys. The article might be a small piece of fur from the medicine bag of a shaman or a bone from some animal that was the guiding spirit of a shaman. The child took this to some designated spot chosen by the tutor and left it there or had to sleep with it there all night. Sometimes the place was a sweat house or the skeleton of a dead animal, in the hope that the child would receive a vision of the animal spirit associated with the entrusted skin or bone. On some occasions this exercise, directed by a tutor, was intended to prepare the child to inherit the guide of the shaman after his death. The child was always instructed never to run away from any [apparition in] animal form that chose to speak to him or her while on these expeditions hunting for knowledge.

It was supposed that lost spirits were roving about everywhere in the invisible air, waiting for children to find them if they searched long and patiently enough. The Sweatlodge spirit was the most powerful for someone to find, as traditional teachings specify that "it" is part of the Great Spirit, who changed his wife and mate into this ribbed conical shape. No other guiding spirit could ever overcome this power because "it" had five special strengths: wood for ribs, fire for heat, stones for stamina, earth for support, and water for cleansing. In all, it was a symbol of combined strengths, much more than the abode of any animal or spirit. The power of any individual supernatural could be easily found and devoured by Sweatlodge, according to Indian theory.

A child might find these supernatural powers almost anyplace: water, cliffs, forest, mountains, remains of lightning-struck trees, animal carcasses, old campfires, or the sweat lodge itself. The spirits were supposed to appear to a child when they were impressed by the dedication and lured by the purity of the persistent seeker.

[The spirit's] appearance came to a child in a vision, in the form of an animal or an object that spoke about how the spirit would help him or her in future life, especially when needed during times of distress. It sang its spiritual song for the child to memorize and use when calling upon the spirit guardian as an adult. Such a vision did not always come to a child while awake. Sometimes it came while the child was asleep beside the token he or she had been given.

Parents usually knew when children had found a spirit because they acted in a dreamy, hazy mood upon their return to the tipi. They did not play, preferring to sit around in deep thought. The visionary was not questioned by the elders, because children were not supposed to tell the secret or it would break the charm of their connection with some form of power and the spirit would be lost. If a child attempted to tell a parent or tutor, the adult quickly reminded the youngster of the duty not to reveal what was found or heard on the hunt [quest].

Finding a spirit gave a child a future career in medicine, with the ability to cure the sick or to foresee things that would happen to others, like accident, sickness, or death in the family. The power included the ability to keep such an accident from happening, since the guardian spirit warned him or her during sleep before such a thing could happen. It also specified in dreams and visions what to do to overcome personal sickness or how to protect against an attempt by another shaman to kill you to get your spirit powers. Such death and alienation of powers could occur only if the rival had stronger power to begin with. Thus, if a child found only one spirit, he or she was much more easily overcome by another, more experienced shaman. The more spirits a child found, the greater future success, influence, and importance that person would have, and the greater his or her resistance against other shamans.

He or she could better protect self and family, cure others, and acquire many riches and ponies as compensation.

Indian theory holds that each spirit has the same strengths as its animal counterpart, as judged by close observation of nature and the outcome of actual fights, in "real" life, between such animals or shamans with their powers.

Parents always impressed on their children the motto: "Obedience in listening to the words of wise elders makes a successful medicine person." While the power and the guidance for a career came from a spirit, it was the elders, learned in these tribal traditions, who provided the fine points of usage and established the social context for approved practice.

Another warning often repeated with the advice of a tutor emphasized the importance of the family for an individual. Elders said: "The orphan has no education, schooling, or advice to become a great person."

It was thus only a natural necessity that parents should send their children out into the night to hunt for this secret knowledge to make themselves great and powerful. This training, for all its hardships, continued until puberty, when particularly strenuous work was added to the regime to give the child energy and stamina for a long life.

From: [Quintasket, Christine]. *Mourning Dove: A Salishan Autobiography.* Edited by Jay Miller. Lincoln: University of Nebraska Press, 1990.

BREAD DANCE

Thomas Wildcat Alford

*Thomas Wildcat Alford, a Shawnee born in 1860 in Indian Territory
[now Oklahoma], who was believed to be the great-grandson of Tekamthi
(Tecumseh), famous for his oratorical skills and for organizing a native
confederation that ultimately failed, narrated to Florence Drake the story
of Shawnee culture and history. Published in 1936, Alford's narration
includes a description of the Shawnee people's sacred Bread Dance.*

One of the most sacred rites of our people was called *Tak-u-wha Nag-a-way*
(Bread Dance), and I am glad to say that the custom still is followed though now
with the sincerity and faith that characterized the dances I remember in my
youth. Our people believed that before they planted a crop or started the important work of the new year they should hold a Bread Dance when the Great Spirit
would be implored to bless the people and give them a bounteous crop and a
prosperous, peaceful year. Contrary to the white man's idea of religion—which
seems to require a gloomy countenance when praying for a blessing—the
Shawnees believed that in order to obtain a blessing they should show a merry
spirit and a contented countenance. Therefore when we sought a blessing it
required an occasion when all were gay and cheerful, and we looked forward to
the spring Bread Dance, as to our most festive occasions. The Bread Dance really opened the festivities of spring and summer, when all nature seemed to be
rejoicing and happy. Not until after this important ceremony would anyone ven-
ture to plant a crop of corn or undertake any important work.

The time for celebrating the Bread Dance was determined as follows: Early in
the spring when the buds began to swell on the trees, the birds began to sing and
chatter to their mates, the wild ducks and geese departed for their northern
homes, the air became soft and warm, the sun rose earlier, the days grew longer.
Reciting all these evidences of the passing of winter, the chief gave orders to his
people to make preparations for their festival of the Bread Dance. *But even then the
dance could not be held until after the full of the moon.*

From: Alford, Thomas Wildcat. *Civilization, as told to Florence Drake*. Norman: University of
Oklahoma Press, 1936.

LONEWIS (CRYING DANCE)

〜〜〜〜〜〜〜〜

Yoimut

Yoimut, an 85-year-old woman who believed herself to be the last sur-vivor of the Chunut Yokuts tribe that once occupied the northeast shore of Tule Lake in California, was interviewed in 1949. The historian of her tribe, she described the rituals of the Lonewis *(or crying dance), a mourning ceremony for the dead. Clothes stuffed like the dead people, plus their possessions and baskets were burned on the fifth night of* Lonewis.

I was about six years old when we moved . . . to the "Fish" Rice Rancheria. My father died about two weeks after we went there. My mother washed for Mrs. Rice and for Mrs. Blankenship for a long time to get money enough to have the *Lonewis* (Lo-ne'-wis) for the dead people. At the *Lonewis* we have a big meeting and cry and dance for the dead people once a year. The *Lonewis* was at Sulawlahne, the "Fish" Rice Rancheria. Lots of people were there; I think five or six hundred. Many of our people had died and there were lots of dead people to cry and sing for. . . .

Our *Chumlus* (Choom'-loos) had all of our clothes to put on us after we washed. My mother had painted her cheeks with black paint and had cut her hair off when my father died. We got the black paint [graphite] from a hill by the place you call Stokes Mountain. . . . We cried almost all of the time until the *Lonewis*. All of the time after my father died we did not eat any meat until after the *Lonewis* was over.

My mother had paid our *Chumlus* the money for the clothes. Mother had not changed clothes since my father died. We had not spoken my father's name. After the *Lonewis* was over the *Chumlus* had to wash us and put our clean new clothes on us. Then we could all be happy again.

As soon as we camped, my mother began fixing the man to burn in the fire at the *Lonewis*. She had saved her money for a year and had bought a good suit of clothes at Mr. Sweet's store in Visalia. . . . She had a good hat, shoes, socks, and underwear.

Mother stuffed the clothes with tules and fastened them together so they looked like a man. She painted the face. Then she got out the fine baskets she had made to burn, and all of father's things she had saved. Then she was ready for the *Lonewis*.

211

If some man lost a wife they fixed some clothes like a woman and burned it. If they lost a little boy or a girl they dressed it up like a boy or girl. For a baby they fixed it on a baby cradle and burned it. . . .

The morning of the second day the *Teah* (chief of the village) sent his *Win-at'-un* (messenger) to tell all the people to come together. He talked to them for a long time. Then the people from each tribe talked. They told about their dead people that they had been crying for. . . . They ate acorn mush and talked until about four o'clock. Then they all went back to their own shades and sat down.

Soon the *Winatun* came around to tell them to build their fires and get ready for the dancing and singing. . . . Then they all got ready. They built fires and got ready to dance all night.

The *Winatun* built a big fire in the middle of all the fires. It . . . burned until the *Lonewis* was over. It was about twenty feet across.

At sundown everybody was ready. Nobody talked. Everything was quiet. When we could just see *Ne'-waw Chi'-tus* [the evening star], Tepwuhtra, the *Teah*, stood up in front of his fire. We all watched him. He called in a loud voice . . . "we are ready." In a little while everyone was crying. Then they began to dance. . . . All of the time until the *Lonewis* was over, all day and all night, someone was singing, someone was crying, someone was dancing. . . .

The fourth night was when we came out with the clothes stuffed like the dead people. About midnight they were brought out and carried around and pointed at the big fire for two or three hours. . . . They took the stuffed clothes back into the house this fourth night. They did not burn them. Then some of the people sang and cried and danced until the next night.

The fifth night about midnight they brought out the same stuffed clothes and marched around and around the fire singing the same song. But this time they threw everything in the fire. . . . Then the chief called ["we are ready"] and they threw everything in the fire, almost all at once. The fire was almost covered up with stuffed clothes, baskets, and things that had belonged to the dead people. . . .

My mother worked hard to get the money to buy the clothes to burn in the fire for my father. . . . But you white people do the same thing. You save money and dress dead people in good clothes. You spend lots of money for coffin. Then you bury your father, mother, maybe your wife. You put everything in ground and all decay. We *burn* good clothes and they *do not* decay. They go to *Tih-pik'-bits Pahn* [the hereafter] so our dead person always has good clothes to wear. What do you think?

On the sixth morning everyone was dancing when *Tow-ahn'-itch*, the morning star, was beginning to fade and it was getting daylight. The *Teah* called ["we are ready,"] and everyone ran to the creek to be washed. The dancing and singing and crying of the *Lonewis* was over. We could be washed and dressed in our new clothes and have a big feast of meat and let our hair grow again. . . .

Everyone is tired and happy and feels good until someone else dies in the family. When I was a little girl our people died so fast that we were getting ready for *Lonewis* all of the time. That is why I remember it so much.

From: Latta, Frank Forrest. *Handbook of Yokuts Indians*. Oildale, California: Bear State Books, 1949.

DINE'E RITUALS

Irene Stewart

Irene Stewart, a Navajo woman born in 1907 in Canyon de Chelly, Arizona, began to write the story of her life in 1965. Educated at Haskell Institute in Oklahoma, hundreds of miles away from her homeland, she found that her hard years of study of Euro-American culture and religion finally enabled her to live in both Navajo and Euro-American societies. Despite being Christian, she maintained a deep respect for Navajo spiritual ways. In her general description of Navajo religious beliefs, she laments the fact that some Navajos no longer observe the ancient prayers and rituals and some medicine men do not know correct ceremonial procedures.

When our great *Hozhooji* Way is not being used anymore, *Sa'a Naaghaii* will take it away from us forever. Our people no longer observe even the smallest beliefs, such as daily rituals by which all the hogan tasks and habitual ways were done. I recall how the women got up before sunrise and took out the ashes, saying a prayer as they did so. When they finished cooking, the charcoal was poked back into the fire with a prayer of gratitude and abundant blessings were asked that all the household members would walk the Blessing Way.

Stirring sticks used to stir mush were objects of prayer; each time they were used the user offered up a prayer. Even children were taught rituals. When a child lost a milk tooth he ran outside with it, closed his eyes, turned his face away and threw the tooth over his right shoulder toward the east with these words, "May I eat a fat gopher with the new one." This was done so he would grow a strong tooth that would last to old age.

In early times *Dine'e* [Navajos] were very religious; they were zealous with all their rituals. They went out before sunrise with their pollen to pray, especially after a bad dream. *Dine'e* religion is for healing the sick of body and mind. Intricate chants to drive out evil spirits and resist witches and ghosts, numerous sandpaintings, prayers, and blessings to please the gods—all these are part of the ritual for the many different ceremonies that make up the *Hozhooji* Way.

The People believe in one great divine supreme being and in a good universe, so *Dine'e* want to live a good life. They also believe there are forms of witchcraft and sorcery. . . .

Dine'e religion is big, filled with reverence for the great spirit who has control over all. *Dine'e* found everlasting peace in some things they did; their findings confirmed their customs. So we should say little or nothing against their religion. Many present-day medicine men practice the ceremonies to heal those sick in body and mind. To me it is like having first the light of fire, then the candle, oil, gas, and finally electricity to shed an even broader light.

Long ago, *Dine'e* learned to associate material beauty with the beauty of holiness. Their prayer for this is:

> *White Shell Woman, Changing Woman, Mother Earth,*
> *Father Sky, everlasting and peaceful,*
> *Turquoise Woman, Changing Woman, everlasting and*
> *peaceful,*
> *With beauty before me I walk*
> *With beauty behind me I walk*
> *With beauty above me I walk*
> *With beauty under me I walk*
> *With beauty beside me I walk.*

. . . When our Blessing Way is forgotten, our elders say the earth will be destroyed by fire. Already, in these days, our medicine men do not know the correct procedures for our ceremonies. Of the fifty or more of our big and little ceremonies, many have been forgotten. Now we know the few that can be remembered, but they are not performed skillfully the way they were by the old-time medicine men.

These days some of our medicine men have become unscrupulous; they have cast off some of the ancient beliefs and are using parts of the ceremonies for public shows to gain profits instead of for healing purposes. Our elders used to say, "There will come a time when the People will desert the old ways." It was said that women and girls would wear trousers instead of skirts, bob hair, pluck eyebrows, wear red stuff on their lips. That time is here. I see it all around.

From: Stewart, Irene. *A Voice in Her Tribe: A Navajo Woman's Own Story*. Socorro, New Mexico: Ballena Press, 1980.

CROW SUN DANCE

~~~~~~~~~~~~~~~~

John Cummings

John Cummings, a former Crow tribal chairman and one of the most experienced Sun Dancers of the Crow Tribe of Montana, was interviewed when he was in his seventies by Stuart Connor in October 1970. His oral interview about the sacred Sun Dance of his people [along with more than 800 other oral histories] is in the University of South Dakota's archives.

Q: **(Stuart Connor):** How many Sun Dances have you danced in?

A: (John Cummings): Forty-three. I've been in forty-three of them.

Q: Can you tell me about the physical part of the Sun Dance—the cutting of the trees, the building of the lodge, and the various songs and dances that go on through the whole thing?

A: The belief of the Indian is that everything on the earth that is created was created by one person. Now you take the trees and the grass and the sagebrush and anything that grows and has a root and that grows on the ground was made or created by this one person which has a meaning of life, and that's the root of the Indian religion. . . . The tree represents life. The leaves represent life. I mean that they cure certain diseases, certain sicknesses. And when a man uses these things, he believes in this creator. He believes that these things could be done by believing. The white man says faith and hope. The Sun Dance is the same way.

When you go into a Sun Dance, you go out and pray with the center pole, center post; it's a forked post. I was told way back, thousands of years ago, there was a man that was sacrificed to a forked tree in order to live and in order to pray. When a man prays he should pray from the bottom of his heart, soul, body, and mind. You've got to sacrifice the water and the food. You might say you have to do penance; you suffer in there—you get dry and you get hungry, you get tired, you get sleepy. And sometimes a man has visions of the good things that are needed in life, or his people's needs. Now you take all these . . . the white people call them the medicine men—in former days they went out and they fasted. What visions they saw were brought home to help their people, not to ruin the people but to help the people to live, and support their people, and that still exists today—that's what the Sun Dance is for.

When I first went in, I had a son in the Marine Corps, and I had about sixteen nephews in the armed forces. So I made up my mind I'd go in there and I'd pray for these—my son and my nephews—they can go through this war and come home to their homes. And it all come true. I didn't lose a son.

Q: Does the cutting of the center pole and the cutting of the upright poles which go into the walls of the Sun Dance lodge go through a certain ritual or procedure?

A: The center pole, when a man goes out—a man that's putting on the Sun Dance—he goes out and looks for this tree, that's the center tree. When he finds one and says this is it, this is the one I'm going to use, then they go after the tree. Before they cut the tree they will pray with a pipe—pray to the Great Spirit that they want to use this tree to pray with, to fast with, and they want their prayers to come true—that's why they are using this tree. Wood was created for the betterment of a human being. Then they take this tree to where they are going to have the lodge. After digging the hollow, they pray again and they set up the center pole. The rest don't go through all that ceremony. That's just that one tree.

From: "John Cummings." In *To Be an Indian: An Oral History.* Edited by Joseph H. Cash and Herbert T. Hoover. New York: Holt, Rinehart and Winston, 1971.

MEDICINE MAN

John (Fire) Lame Deer

John (Fire) Lame Deer (Tahca Ushte), a Lakota (Sioux) man born about 1900 on the Rosebud Reservation in South Dakota, was among many other things a wicasa wakan, *a holy man or medicine man of the Lakotas. His autobiography,* Lame Deer, Seeker of Visions: The Life Story of a Sioux Medicine Man, *is laced with wit and humor. In it he describes his many occupations as well as his time in prison. In the following excerpt, he spells out his beliefs about being a holy person.*

I believe that being a medicine man, more than anything else, is a state of mind, a way of looking at and understanding this earth, a sense of what it is all about. Am I a *wicasa wakan?* I guess so. What else can or would I be? Seeing me in my patched-up, faded shirt, with my down-at-the-heels cow-boy boots, the hearing aid whistling in my ear, looking at the flimsy shack with its bad-smelling outhouse which I call home—it all doesn't add up to a white man's idea of a holy man. You've seen me drunk and broke. You've heard me curse or tell a sexy joke. You know I'm not better and wiser than other men. But I've been up on the hilltop, got my vision and my power; the rest is just trimmings. That vision never leaves me—not in jail, not while I'm painting funny signs advertising some hashhouse, not when I am in a saloon, not while I am with a woman, especially not then.

I am a medicine man because a dream told me to be one, because I am commanded to be one, because the old holy men—Chest, Thunderhawk, Chips, Good Lance—helped me to be one. There is nothing I can, or want, to do about it. I could cure you of a sickness just with a drink of pure cold water and the workings of my vision. Not always, but often enough. I want to be a *wicasa wakan*, a man who feels the grief of others. A death anywhere makes me feel poorer. A young woman and her child were killed the other night on the highway. I feel so deeply about them. At sundown I will talk to the Great Spirit for them. I will fill my pipe and offer it on their behalf. I do this always. Would you believe it, that when Robert Kennedy was assassi-nated shortly after he had come here to talk to us Indians, I went into my sweat lodge and made an offering for him. Could you imagine a white man praying for Crazy Horse?

... I also think that it is [a] very wise sort of Indian psychology that a medicine man doesn't dress up fancy with feathers and war bonnets when he performs a ceremony. You have seen me praying, performing a wedding, or running a ceremony in an old sweatshirt and patched pants. There's a purpose in this, a certain humbleness in the presence of the spirits, but not of men. It means a medicine man should be stripped down to the bare essentials when he does these things. It's not the package and the wrapping which counts but what is inside, underneath the clothes and the skin.

As I get older I do less and less curing and ceremonies and more and more thinking. I pass from one stage to another, trying to get a little higher up, praying for enough gas to make it up there.

I haven't told you all I know about the herbs and about the ways of our holy men. You understand that there are certain things one should not talk about, things that must remain hidden. If all was told, supposing there lived a person who could tell all, there would be no mysteries left, and that would be very bad. Man cannot live without mystery. He has great need of it.

From: Lame Deer, John (Fire) and Richard Erdoes. *Lame Deer, Seeker of Visions*. New York: Simon and Schuster, 1972.

ONENESS: WORSHIP AND LIFESTYLE

Barney Old Coyote

Barney Old Coyote, a member of the Crow Tribe of Montana, testified in support of Senate Joint Resolution 102, a landmark measure on American Indian religious freedom. At the February 24, 1978, hearing, he explained how native worship was integrated into every aspect of the Indian way of life.

American Indian culture, tradition, and history are the basis for Indian identity, values, and uniqueness in the United States of America. There is a common background for Indian culture, tradition, and values, particularly in the area of worship, lifestyles and the perception of the Indian to his environment. This to the extent that it has been correctly represented that the "American Indian lived in harmony with nature." This was and continues to be true with the Indian in his manner and style of worship, which manner extends into practically every facet of the Indian way, including culture, social, economic and other areas of the Indian lifestyle. The area of worship cannot be delineated from social, political, culture, and other areas of Indian lifestyle, including his general outlook upon economic and resource development.

Similarly, Indian worship is not readily divided among many forms as it is with Christianity and other religions. The separation of church and state generally does not apply to Indian situations, although there is exception to this as with any rule. . . . The Northern Plains Indians were unique in that they hunted the bison as an integral part of their way of life. Another unique facet of Northern Plains culture are the sites, mediums and method of worship. The Indian uses permanent sites, semipermanent and almost every location for his worship. He uses every form of nature, including animals, plants, birds, fishes, and every form of living and nonliving things in his worship, which practices frequently extend to other areas of the Indian lifestyle.

In spite of common backgrounds and similarities, there is a great variety of methods of worship among Indians. There is no orthodoxy which can be applied in total across Indian peoples or even among tribes. This variety and difference in orthodoxy does not lessen the authenticity nor the peace of mind it brings to tribal and individual practitioners of Indian worship. This worship is mentioned in that it is an integral part of the Indian way of life and culture which cannot be separated from the whole. This oneness of Indian life seems to be the basic difference between the Indians and non-Indians of a dominant society.

From: "Statement of Barney Old Coyote." U.S. Congress. Senate Select Committee on Indian Affairs. *American Indian Religious Freedom: Hearings.* 95th Cong., 2d sess., 1978.

THE FIRST SALMON CEREMONY

Andy Fernando

Andy Fernando, the former chairman of the Upper Skagit Tribal Community in Sedro Woolley, Washington, wrote the introduction to a book published in 1986 about Northwest Coast Indian treaty fishing rights. In it, he describes the First Salmon Ceremony, a centuries-old observance held during the spring by his people as well as other tribes living along river valleys throughout western Oregon and Washington. Each tribe, according to its own pattern, gives the first catch of the year, taken from important fishing places, elaborate and ceremonious welcome and honor so that salmon beings will continue to favor the humans who fish there.

According to a centuries-old Northwest coastal Indian tradition . . . this first salmon will neither be sold nor traded nor even preserved for eating later in the year. The many generations born before the girl's grandfathers and great-grandparents had each celebrated the same first catch in the late spring of the year. During the long winter months, Indian families mostly remained indoors in their great cedar longhouses along the banks of the river, subsisting on stores of dried salmon, berries, roots, and game. Fresh food, particularly their staple diet of salmon, was scarce during these months. By the spring months of *pedhweywats*—the time of robins whistling—the stocks of food were depleted or spoiled, well-fed game was scarce, and edible plants and berries were not yet ready to harvest. But in those spring months king salmon would return to the river, completing their four-year cycle from river-hatched eggs to ocean-dwelling juveniles to mature adults ready to spawn their progeny. The spring salmon were few in number, but they returned earlier than other salmon to seek the colder snow-fed streams, and their larger size and firmer flesh made them a fine prize. The entire village would gather together and appoint fishermen to each catch one salmon—no more.

In fine regalia, accompanied by a fanfare of deerskin drum and special village songs, the first salmon caught would be carried from the riverbank to the gathered villagers. A village leader, or shaman, would carefully clean and save the salmon's entrails, then carve away the meat until a carcass of head, bones, and tail was left, still connected. The entrails would be placed in the skelton, and the framework of bones from the flashing bright salmon laid on

222

The Tulalip First Salmon Ceremony, Tulalip Reservation, Marysville, Washington.
Photograph by Natalie B. Fobes.

a mat of fresh, spring-green ferns. Meanwhile, the villagers would have
raised a fire of alderwood, the smoke thick from the new sap filling the wood.
The wood's low blaze would cook the salmon slowly, and leave a mild smoke
taste in the meat. The pieces of salmon meat would then be skewered on
thin sticks carved from small ironwood trees growing along the riverbank; the
end of each stick had been sharpened so it could be staked into the ground
near the fire. Nearly an hour would pass before the salmon was fully cooked,
but the villagers would gladly wait, perhaps speculating to each other about
the upcoming season; or talking of where and how they would set their nets,
or build their fish traps, or spear their salmon; or reminiscing over the generations before who had gathered in the same campsite to perform the first
salmon ceremony.

When the salmon was cooked, everyone would gather to eat. It mattered
not whether there were ten villagers or a hundred: each would share equally
in the fruit of the first catch. The meal finished, leaders would recount the
village stories of great fishermen and hunters of fact, legend, and myth—
or all three combined. The headmen and women would speak of the
importance of the first salmon ceremony, of sharing the first catch, harvest,
or kill, of the high status bestowed to those villagers who were given the gift
and the power to provide food for the village.

In the end, the headmen would lift the fern mat cradling the remains of
the salmon, and, followed by the villagers, walk to the riverbank. The drums
would sound and songs ring around the valley, echoes from the steep slopes
above singing praise back to the gathering. Placing the fern mat on the water

with the salmon's head pointed downstream, the headman would release the mat to float on the river toward the sea, signifying the completion of the salmon cycle. The villagers and the salmon had fulfilled their duty, prescribed by the Great Spirit. The salmon had returned to the appointed time and place; the villagers had faithfully honored the salmon in sharing and ceremony. The people thereby assured themselves of a good season, and the harvest would begin.

From: Fernando, Andy. "Introduction." In *Treaties on Trial: The Continuing Controversy over Northwest Indian Fishing Rights*, by Fay G. Cohen. Seattle: University of Washington Press, 1986.

BASKETS ARE LIKE JEWELS

Julian Lang

Julian Lang, a Karuk from northwestern California, describes, in the August 1991 issue of Parabola, *the crucial role baskets play in the Jump Dance, one of the world renewal ceremonies to "fix the world." Himself a singer and dancer in the sacred dances of his people, Lang conveys the belief of the Karuk, Hupa, and Yurok people that these baskets are alive and need to dance.*

By today's standards the task of weaving a basket must seem silly to some, compared to deep space exploration or the transmittal of data concerning the origin of the universe. After all, a basket consists of woven sticks, plaited together into containers. Some of us put our dirty clothes into a basket, but for the most part, basketry has fallen into disuse if not obsolescence. It seems the time has passed when basketry was marveled at for its utility and perfected design. In northwestern California, however, a uniquely shaped, nonutilitarian basket is still essential to three local Indian tribes for conducting their ceremonies to "fix the world." Without the baskets the Hupa, Karuk, and Yurok would not be able to perform the highly important Jump Dance without solving extremely difficult spiritual problems and taking drastic measures.

I am a Karuk Indian and have held these dance baskets in my hands many times. Each possesses its own weight, shape, and danceability. Some of these baskets display the innovative mark of the artists, while others suggest strict adherence to traditional proportion and construction. Whatever the sensibility of the weaver, the baskets are known to the Karuk people as *víkapuhich;* the Yurok call them *e'gor;* the Hupa say *na'wech.* Their cylindrical shape suggests the feminine; their decoration, the sublime. These little baskets are found nowhere else in the world. Within our traditional culture and psyche, the baskets are like jewels.

In order for us to fully appreciate the role that baskets play in our ceremonies and life, it is necessary to look at our *pikva,* our creation stories, and also to the voices of our oldest generations. The stories give us a glimpse of the foundation of our cultural identity. When we saw the high regard in which the white man held the Bible, we translated it into our language as *apxantinihichpikva,* or "white man's creation stories."

One of many stories about basket weaving takes place during the *pikva-hahirak* ("creation story-time-and-place"), when the *Ikxaréeyav* family (the *Ikxaréeyav* are the Spirit-beings of the *pikva* time) lived in a good way until the father abandoned them in favor of a new wife, and their family life was disrupted. The jilted mother told the children they were going "a different way." They were going to be transformed. The father knew this was about to happen and returned to the house of his first wife, but it had already been abandoned. He caught up with his family on the hillside above the village and killed them in a fit of blind rage. Before dying, the wife cursed him, "You will be nothing once Human has arrived! We will be sitting in front of Human (at the annual World Renewal ceremonies). We will be beauty!" The slain family then metamorphosed into the materials used to weave a basket: hazel, willow, bull pine, maidenhair fern, and woodwardia fern. Thus, basketry materials are to us not just natural fibers, but gifts of divine origin.

The three local tribes perform the Jump Dance as part of the ceremony to fix the world. This dance is a ten-day ceremony that is held to help rid the earth of sickness and other potential natural catastrophes. It is solemn, ecstatic, and beautiful in its simplicity. The songs are slow and sonorous. Each song begins quietly but is repeated at a higher pitch and intensity as it continues. In steady cadence a line of male dancers stamps the earth to rid it of sickness and all bad thoughts, to set the world back on its axis. Each stamp is followed by the swift lifting heavenward of a smallish, cylindrical basket that we call a *vikapuhich*. The body of the basket is decorated with bold, shiny black designs on a creamy ground. It has been split lengthwise and attached to a hazel stick handle that is wrapped in finely tanned buckskin. A small bunch of yellowhammer flicker feathers is attached at one end.

A popular symbolic interpretation of this basket is that of family, home, and village. The *vikapuhich* contains a prayer for the world to be in balance. The basket is lifted to heaven and then retracted, bringing with it the spirit world's acknowledgment and luck. In unison the line of dancers then stamp out all that is bad. Over and over again the basket is raised, then retracted, followed by the stamping out of sickness. Accompanied by songs originally inspired by the wind, the dance soon brings on a collective illumination: the elders cry, the young yearn.

From: Lang, Julian. "The Basket and World Renewal." *Parabola: The Magazine of Myth and Tradition* 16, no 3 (August 1991):83–85.

SWEAT LODGE CEREMONY

Linda Hogan

Linda Hogan, a Chickasaw woman born in 1947 in Denver, Colorado, has published numerous volumes of poetry and the acclaimed novel Mean Spirit. *In the February 1992 issue of* Parabola, *she describes, in poetic terms, a sweat lodge ceremony in which she participated. Nearly universal among native peoples throughout the United States, the sweat lodge ceremony serves several purposes including purifying the body, curing ailments, and maintaining good health.*

I am sent home to prepare. I tie fifty tobacco ties, green. This I do with Bull Durham tobacco, squares of cotton which are tied with twine and left strung together. These are called prayer ties. I spend the time preparing in silence and alone. Each tie has a prayer in it. I will also need wood for the fire, meat, and bread for food. . . .

In the background, the sweat lodge structure stands. Birds are on it. It is still skeletal. A woman and man are beginning to place old rugs and blankets over the bent cottonwood frame. A great fire is already burning and the lava stones that will be the source of heat for the sweat are being fired in it.

A few people sit outside on lawn chairs and cast-off couches that have the stuffing coming out. We sip coffee and talk about food, about recent events. A man tells us that a friend gave him money for a new car. The creek sounds restful. Another man falls asleep. My young daughter splashes in the water. Heat waves rise up behind us from the fire that is preparing the stones. My tobacco ties are placed inside, on the framework of the lodge.

By late afternoon we are ready, one at a time, to enter the enclosure. The hot lava stones are placed inside. They remind us of earth's red and fiery core, and of the spark inside all life. After the flap, which serves as a door, is closed, water is poured over the stones and the hot steam rises around us. In a sweat lodge ceremony, the entire world is brought inside the enclosure. The soft odor of smoking cedar accompanies this arrival of everything. It is all called in. The animals come from the warm and sunny distances. Water from dark lakes is there. Wind. Young, lithe willow branches bent overhead remember their lives rooted in ground, the sun their leaves took in. They remember that minerals and water rose up their trunks, and birds nested in their leaves, and that planets turned above their brief, slender lives. The thunderclouds travel in from far regions of earth. Wind arrives from the four directions. It has moved through caves and breathed through our bodies. It is the same air elk have inhaled, air that passed through the lungs of a grizzly bear. The sky is there, with all the stars whose lights we see long after the stars themselves have gone back to nothing. It is a place of immense community and of humbled solitude; we sit together in our aloneness and speak, one at a time, our deepest language of need, hope, loss, and survival. We remember that all things are connected.

Remembering this is the purpose of the ceremony. It is part of a healing and restoration. It is the mending of a broken connection between us and the rest. The participants in a ceremony say the words, "All my relations," before and after we pray; those words create a relationship with other people, with animals, with the land. To have health it is necessary to keep all these relations in mind.

From: Hogan, Linda. "All My Relations." *Parabola: The Magazine of Myth and Tradition* 17, no. 1 (February 1992): 33–35.

INDIAN HEALING ARTS

Joseph Medicine Crow

Joseph Medicine Crow, a Crow man, was born in Lodge Grass, Montana, in 1913. Designated tribal historian and anthropologist by the Crow Tribal Council in 1948, he began recording stories and collecting data about his tribal culture and history in 1932. In his 1992 book, From the Heart of the Crow Country, *he addresses the subject of Indian healing arts.*

The central and formal aspects of Indian medicine were ceremonial in nature. As such, then, the healing arts of the Indian were, and still are, an integral part of his religion. To the Indian, medicine and religion are closely interwoven and knitted together. One is an integral part of the other; one cannot function without the other. It is almost impossible to tell where practical healing ends and ceremonial healing begins. . . .

There was . . . one thing that tribes held, more or less, in common. This concerned the attitude, concept, and philosophy of the *cause* and *cure* of diseases. In general, North American tribes classed disease by cause rather than by symptom, the part of the body affected, or any other characteristic. It seemed that they were primarily concerned with *why* a person was sick or hurt rather than with what the sickness or injury was all about.

These causes were identified and listed under two categories: the natural and the supernatural. Naturally caused diseases and illnesses were such things as complications from childbirth, broken bones, wounds from warfare or encounters with animals, and accidents; death in early childhood and death from old age were also considered natural. Supernaturally caused diseases and afflictions were such things as bad luck due to breaking taboos, loss of soul, possession by evil spirits, intrusion of a foreign object into the body, and effects of witchcraft or black magic.

The method of treating and curing the sick, injured, and afflicted depended on the type of cause diagnosed. The treatment of naturally caused ailments involved practical knowledge of physical manipulations and techniques such as heat treatments, cauterization, bone setting, sutures, poultices, and so on, and also the use of time-proven and usually dependable medicinal herbs. The treatment of supernaturally caused ailments and afflictions was a much more serious and complicated affair. Any one of the causes already mentioned could create a large number of symptoms and complications, to use a modern medical term; thus, professional diagnosis was necessary.

And this brings us face-to-face with the so-called medicine man. So we ask again who and what was this individual called "medicine man" by the white man, *Wicasa Wakan* by the Sioux, *Batce Baxbe* by the Crow, and other names by other tribes? To be sure, he was not always an Indian. Primitive men of all races, ages, and parts of the world had them. This medicine man, or better, man of medicine, was both born and made. He was born of supernatural circumstances and made of natural circumstances.

First, we ask how was he made? He was made over thousands of centuries of gastronomical experimentation with unknown plants. Some killed him and some cured him, of course, but then he came through with good and practical knowledge of herbs that were best suited for relieving and curing his aches and pains. This was the practitioner who generally first handled the common ailments and injuries diagnosed to be caused by natural things and circumstances. He was the specialist who knew by training what herbs to prescribe for toothaches, skin troubles, insect and snake bites, broken ankles, wounds, and other common and external ailments.

Next, we ask how was he born to be a medicine man? There comes a time in the lives of people (family group, clan, band, tribe) when an event, or a series of happenings, disrupts the ordinary, routine, and usual ways of doing things and living. The people are not able to explain it; they can't straighten things out, or they are powerless to do anything about it all. This, then, is the time when the people start wondering, guessing, and finally blaming the bad state of affairs on an outside cause, some big force or forces beyond the realm of the natural. Here—as men seek and attempt to influence, guard, regulate, and control the supernatural force or power causing all the troubles and to establish a better working relationship—the medicine man is born!

With his innate intelligence and other capabilities, which are perhaps more acute, sensitive, and responsive than in other people, the medicine man comes up with a definition of the situation and a solution. To be sure, he does not come up with an instant answer. He must go through a period of soul searching, propitiation, and vision seeking; ultimately he must experience a holy communion with the Great Power and gain spiritual insight and wisdom in the ways of the Great Spirit. It is then known that this man can receive power and use it to help his people in sickness and distress.

Thus, he becomes the man, the special one, who can use supernatural powers to diagnose the cause of serious ailments, injuries, and wounds, and he is able to prescribe the right treatment and cure. He becomes the man who is able to diagnose the cause of a great tribulation threatening his people and to invoke the appropriate ceremonial procedure to solve or otherwise relieve and release the people from the situation. He can look into the future and foretell or prophesy coming events, good or bad. If bad, he is able to avoid or circumvent the impending threat.

There were medicine men and medicine men, which is to say there were divisions, classes, and ranks in this profession. These were, of course, arranged differently from tribe to tribe, and from culture area to culture area, but they were basically the same.

One thing is sure. This unusual and interesting individual was more than just the white man's stereotyped image of a character in weirdo costumes and paraphernalia, brandishing rattles and feathers, muttering unintelligible grunts, chanting invocations, and jumping and hovering over a poor sick and scared person. More often he is depicted as deceiving his patient or subject with trickery and sleight of hand. It is said that he lived and thrived by imposing on the credulity of those who depended on him and by asking exorbitant fees.

On the contrary, the average Indian medical or holy man was a decent sort, hardworking, sincere, aware of the seriousness of his responsibilities, and dedicated to the individual well-being and general welfare of his people and community. It is indeed unfortunate that the true image of this indispensable man of the tribe and his genuine and great contributions have been so long belittled, tarnished, and obscured by the ethnocentric white man.

From: Medicine Crow, Joseph. *From the Heart of the Crow Country*. New York: Orion Books, 1992.

THE PUEBLOS HAVE NO WORD
FOR "RELIGION"

Joe S. Sando

Joe S. Sando, born into the Sun Clan at Jemez Pueblo, New Mexico, in 1923, has authored several books on Indian history and taught Pueblo history at the University of New Mexico. Currently Director of Archives at the Pueblo Indian Cultural Center in Albuquerque, he gives an insider's view of Pueblo religion in an excerpt from his book Pueblo Nations: Eight Centuries of Pueblo Indian History, *published in 1992.*

The Pueblos have no word that translates as "religion." The knowledge of a spiritual life is part of the person twenty-four hours a day, every day of the year. In describing the beliefs and practices of today, the traditional religion may also be understood. There is little basic change. The tradition of religious belief permeates every aspect of the people's life; it determines man's relation with the natural world and with his fellow man. Its basic concern is continuity of a harmonious relationship with the world in which man lives. To maintain such a relationship between the people and the spiritual world, various societies exist, with particular responsibilities for weather, fertility, curing, hunting, and pleasure or entertainment. Even today, most Pueblo people belong to a religious society, and have an important place in pueblo religious activities. The traditional calendar of religious events is so full that there is no time left for any new or innovative religious practices as is sometimes possible with non-Pueblo Indians who accept, as one example, the Peyote Way. . . .

The religious rituals and ceremonials themselves, maintained by the Pueblos today, are the same ones they have practiced since their ancestors lived in pit houses. The oratories, prayers, and songs are the same. These observances are not spontaneous outpourings, nor outbursts of the troubled heart. They are carefully memorized prayerful requests for an orderly life, rain, good crops, plentiful game, pleasant days, and protection from the violence and the vicissitudes of nature. To appease or pledge their faith to God, they often went on sacrificial retreats, often doing without food and water as penance or cleansing of body and soul for the benefit of man throughout the world. . . .

Pueblo religion does not proselytize. It is not written, but is enshrined in the heart of the individual. Although most Pueblo people have been nominally Roman Catholic for more than three hundred years, the native religion is the basis of their system of belief. . . .

Some observers have said that the Pueblos "dance all the year round." This may be true, and was more the case in the past, since their ceremonial calendar covers the whole year. Through dance and song one can realize a sense of rebirth and rejuvenation. The great summer Corn Dances of the Pueblos have caused many non-Indians to rejoice over the wonderful feeling of spiritual rebirth they have experienced.

The Pueblos believe that the Great One is omnipresent. They ask for permission to use the physical form of an animal before it is killed. They believe that animals have an inner spiritual component. This is the spiritual life they invoke with a short prayer. It is not a new idea; other natives throughout the Americas have this ritual. In taking branches from the sacred Douglas fir tree, the Pueblo men will inform the Creator that the intent is not to mutilate the tree, but to decorate the human being in the performance of a sacred ritual or dance in His honor. In Pueblo religion, the Douglas fir is used to adorn most dancers, male and female. It is also used to decorate the altar and shrine, where a likeness of a patron saint is kept during the day of the feast. For many years Pueblo families did not have Christmas trees. An unsold fir on a sales lot is a sad sight indeed, and is considered sacrilegious. This tree is not used to decorate a front yard either, since tradition has it that one is changing nature when a fir tree is dug up and moved to the yard in a pueblo or a village.

After a fir branch has been used during a dance, ceremonial or social, the branches are taken away and disposed of in the river. Often some are kept in the home until dry. They are then burned in the open fireplace to produce the fresh smell of the fir tree in the room, or taken to the garden or farm where they will decompose and thus serve as fertilizer while returning to Mother Earth.

Sando, Joe S. *Pueblo Nations: Eight Centuries of Pueblo Indian History.* Santa Fe: Clear Light Publishers, 1992.

DISCRIMINATION

Manufactured Indian images found throughout the world. Photograph by John C. Goodwin.

*E*very day, we are presented with inauthentic, unrealistic, and offensive images of Indians—in films, outdated textbooks, and other forms of communication. In spite of recent efforts on the part of many to correct these stereotypes, this steady diet of distorted imagery and information about native cultures still exists. Native peoples must also deal with the legacy of compulsory federal boarding school policies that tried to eradicate their cultural and spiritual practices, languages, and traditional stories.

Stereotypes and misinformation deny the dignity and dynamism of native cultural practices and the distinctiveness of their multiple traditions. As the following excerpts show, individual Indian people as well as their cultures have been subjected to monumental discrimination and gross injustice. The more contemporary excerpts show ways in which native people themselves are now working to create realistic images of the vitality and variety of native peoples today.

Schooling imposed on native peoples ranks high as a destructive force. Tulto (Taos Pueblo) describes how his boarding school education painfully stripped him of his culture. Joseph H. Suina (Cochiti Pueblo) reveals why school, with its leave-your-Indian-language-at-home attitude, was a bitter experience, as it was for both James R. Gooden (Inupiaq Eskimo), who recounts his teacher's cruel bigotry, young Amera Ingnacio (Ute-Wampanoag), who protests her teacher's insensitivity, and William Penseno (Ponca), who exposes Euro-American school practices that were based upon a view of Indian students as inferior.

Other institutions ostensibly devoted to knowledge also discriminate against native peoples. Howard Rock (Inupiaq) shows this in his piece on scholarly conference organizers who did not include native peoples—the subjects of the conference—as participants. Bea Medicine (Lakota) faults anthropologists who ignore or belittle native women in their studies, Mary Gloyne Byler (Eastern Band of Cherokee) criticizes certain book publishers for offensive characterizations of native peoples, and Tim Giago (Lakota) criticizes the mainstream press for biased reporting.

Jeannie Blatchford Greene (Eskimo) and Ivan Star Comes Out (Oglala Lakota) describe how non-Indians routinely view native people as objects. Woody Kipp (Blackfeet) writes about the ignorance about native religious rites, while Trudie Lamb-Richmond (Schaghticoke) decries the marketing of Indian spiritual traditions by "plastic medicine men." Elias Johnson (Tuscarora) brilliantly takes to task those who characterize native people as savage barbarians. So does Arthur Caswell Parker (Seneca), who blasts government agencies and U.S. citizens for robbing native people of seven essential rights. Beverly Singer (Santa Clara Pueblo) zeroes in on Hollywood stereotypes of American Indians, while Charlene Teters (Spokane) battles stereotyping and the use and abuse of Indians as mascots.

THE IROQUOIS ARE NOT SAVAGES

Chief Elias Johnson

Elias Johnson, a Tuscarora chief born and brought up by Tuscarora parents on their New York reservation, was bothered by history books for schoolchildren that filled young minds with "imperfect ideas" about Indians. Fueled by the desire for a "kinder feeling" between white people and Indians, he wrote a history of Tuscarora Indians that was published in 1881. In it he responded to "the slanders . . . which the historians have wont to spread concerning us" by showing how Christians were no strangers to barbaric behavior themselves.

In all the early histories of the American colonies, in the stories of Indian life and the delineations of Indian character, these children of nature are represented as savages and barbarians, and in the minds of a large portion of the community the sentiment still prevails that they were bloodthirsty, revengeful, and merciless, justly a terror to both friends and foes. Children are impressed with the idea that an Indian is scarcely human, and as much to be feared as the most ferocious animal of the forest.

Novelists have now and then clothed a few with a garb which excites your imagination, but seldom has one been invested with qualities which you would love, unless it were also said that through some captive taken in distant war, he inherited a whiter skin and a paler blood.

But I am inclined to think that Indians are not alone in being savage—not alone barbarous, heartless, and merciless.

It is said they were exterminating each other by aggressive and devastating wars, before the white people came among them. But wars, aggressive and exterminating wars, certainly, are not proofs of barbarity. The bravest warrior was the most honored, and this has been ever true of Christian nations, and those who call themselves christians have not yet ceased to look upon him who would plan most successfully the wholesale slaughter of human beings, as the most deserving his king's or his country's laurels. How long since the paeon died away in praise of the Duke of Wellington? What have been the wars in which all Europe, or of America, has been engaged, that there has been no records of her history? For what are civilized and Christian nations drenching their fields with blood?

At the very time that the Indians were using the tomahawk and scalping knife to avenge their wrongs, peaceful citizens in every country of Europe, where the Pope was the man of authority, were incarcerated for no crime whatever, and such refinement of torture invented and practiced, as never entered in the heart of the fiercest Indian warrior that roamed the wilderness to inflict upon man or beast.

We know very little of the secrets of the Inquisition, and this little chills our blood with horror. Yet these things were done in the name of Christ, the Savior of the World, the Prince of Peace, and not savage, but civilized. Christian men looked on, not coldly, but rejoicingly, while women and children writhed in flames and weltered in blood. Were the atrocities committed in the vale of Wyoming and Cherry Valley unprecedented among the Waldensian fastness and the mountains of Auvergne? Who has read Fox's book of Martyrs, and found anything to parallel it in all the records of Indian warfare? The slaughter of St. Bartholomew's days, the destruction of the Jews in Spain, and the Scotch Covenanters, were in obedience to the mandates of Christian princes,—aye, and some of them devised by Christian women who professed to be serving God, and to make the Bible the man of their counsel. . . .

To come down to the more decidedly christian times, it is not so very long since, in Protestant England, hanging was the punishment of a petty thief, long and hopeless imprisonment of a slight misdemeanor, when men were set up to be stoned and spit upon by those who claimed the exclusive right to be called humane and merciful.

Again, it is said, the Indian mode of warfare is, without exception, the most inhuman and revolting. But I do not know that those who die by the barbed and poisoned arrow linger in any more unendurable torment than those who are mangled with powder and lead balls, and the custom of scalping among Christian murderers would save thousands from groaning days, and perhaps weeks, among heaps that cover victorious fields and fill hospitals with the wounded and dying. But scalping is not an invention exclusively Indian. "It claims," says Prescott, "high authority, or, at least, antiquity." And, further history, Herodotus, gives an account of it among the Scythians, showing that they performed the operation, and wore the scalp of their enemies taken in battle, as trophies, in the same manner as the North American Indian. Traces of the custom are also found in the laws of the Visigoths, among the Franks, and even the Anglo-Saxons. The Northern Indians did not scalp, but they had a system of slavery, of which there are no traces to be found among the customs, laws, or legends of the Iroquois.

Again, it is said, "They carried away women and children captive, and in their long journey through the wilderness, they were subjected to heartrending trials."

The wars of Christian men throw hundreds and thousands of women and children helpless upon the cold world, to toil, to beg, and to starve.

This is not so bright a picture as is usually given of people who have written laws and have stores of learning, but people cannot see in any place that the coloring is too dark! There is no danger of painting Indians so they will become attractive to the civilized people.

There is a bright and pleasing side to the Indian character, and thinking that there has been enough written of their wars and cruelties, of the hunter's and fisherman's life, I have sat down at their fireside, listened to their legends, and am acquainted with their domestic habits, understand their finer feelings and the truly noble traits of their character.

It is so long now since they were the lords of this country, and formidable as your enemies, and they are so utterly wasted away and melted like snow under the meridian sun, and helpless, that you can sit down and afford to listen to the truth, and to believe that even your enemies had their virtues. Man was created in the image of God, and it cannot be that anything human is utterly vile and contemptible.

Those who have thought of Indians as roaming about in the forests hunting and fishing, or at war, will laugh perhaps, at the idea of Indian homes, and domestic happiness. Yet there are no people of which we have any knowledge, among whom . . . family ties and relationship were more distinctly defined, or more religiously respected than the Iroquois.

The treatment which they received from the white people, whom they always considered as intruders, aroused, and kept in exercise all their ferocious passions, so that none except those who associated with them as missionaries, or as captives, saw them in their true character, as they were to each other.

Almost any portrait that we see of an Indian, he is represented with tomahawk and scalping knife in hand, as if they possessed no other but a barbarous nature. Christian nations might with equal justice be always represented with cannon and balls, swords and pistols, as the emblems of their employment and their prevailing tastes. . . .

In the picture which I have given, I have confined myself principally to the Iroquois, or Six Nations, a people who no more deserve the term savage than the whites do that of heathen, because they have still lingering among them heathen superstitions, and many opinions and practices which deserve no better name.

From: Johnson, Chief Elias. *Legends, Traditions, and Laws of the Iroquois, or Six Nations, and History of the Tuscarora Indians.* Lockport, New York: Union Publishing Co., 1881.

SEVEN STOLEN RIGHTS

Arthur Caswell Parker

Arthur Caswell Parker, or Gawaso Wanneh, a Seneca man, was born in 1881 on the Cattaraugus Seneca Indian Reservation in New York. An archaeologist at the New York State Museum from 1906 to 1924, he also edited a journal published by the Society of American Indians, a reform organization. In an article published by the American Journal of Sociology *in 1916, he blasts the people of the United States and governmental agencies for stealing seven rights from Indian peoples.*

The people of the United States through their governmental agencies, and through the aggression of their citizens have: (1) robbed the American Indian of freedom of action; (2) robbed the American Indian of economic independence; (3) robbed the American Indian of social organization; (4) robbed a race of men—the American Indian—of intellectual life; (5) robbed the American Indian of moral standards and of racial ideals; (6) robbed the American Indian of a good name among the peoples of the earth; (7) robbed the American Indian of a definitive civic status.

Each of the factors we have named is an essential of the life of a man or a nation. Picture a citizen of this republic without freedom, intellectual or social life, with limited ability to provide his own food and clothing, having no sure belief in an Almighty Being, no hero to admire, and no ideals to foster, with no legal status, and without a reputable name among men. Picture a nation or a people so unhappy. Yet civilization has conspired to produce in varying degrees all these conditions for the American Indians.

So much for the seven great robberies of the race. We have not even cared to mention the minor loss of territory and of resources—these are small things indeed compared with the greater losses that we have named.

But though the robbery has been committed, the government and great citizens will exclaim, "We have given much to atone for your loss, brother red men!"

Let us examine then the nature of these gifts. The federal government and the kind hearts of friends have (1) given reserved tracts of land where the Indians may live unmolested (but are they unmolested?); (2) given agents and superintendents as guardians, and constituted a division of the Department of the Interior as a special bureau for the protection of the red race (but is the Indian protected?); (3) given schools with splendid mechanical equipment (but is the Indian educated in any adequate degree?); (4) given the ignorant and poor clerks who will think and act for them, and handle their money (does this develop manhood, ability, and good citizenship?); (5) given food, clothing, and peace (has the ration system been honest and adequate?); (6) given a new civilization (and with it a host of alluring evils); (7) given a great religion (but in the light of hypocrisy and a commercial conscience how could the Indian absorb it or be absorbed by it?).

So great and good gifts must have a price, the conqueror thought, for men cannot have these boons without suffering some diability. Measures are necessary to protect the givers and even government itself from the results of its own charity and leniency to a people but lately regarded as enemies. The government therefore as a price has denied the Indians the real benefits of civilization and placed them in a position where they have become the prey of every moral, social, and commercial evil. The Indians have been made the material for exploitation.

The Indians were not at once denied the fundamental rights of human beings, living in an organized, civilized community. It was only as the seven great robberies became more or less complete and the reservation system grew that the great denials took effect. The robberies and the denials are of a subtle psychological character and many there are who will ingeniously argue that the Indians still have all the things we have mentioned, or may have them if they will to, and that the seven gifts are but the gratuities of a charitable government.

But the men who so argue are devoid of finer spiritual perceptions or, perchance, they are unable to see from another man's viewpoint when they have one of their own. They are not wanting men and women who are unable to realize that another man can be hungry when their own stomachs are full. There are men having considerable mental endowments and a knowledge of the world who say, "If I were in his place, I would do thus and so. I would seize opportunity and soon all would be well." Men of this character are still mentally blind and spiritually dull and are the first to deny that any great wrong has been done after all. They are insensible to the fact that the red man has felt his debasement and that his soul and his children's souls are bitter with a grief they cannot express and which they cannot cast out.

The result of such denials of basic human rights to proud men and women is definite and deep. Whether he can express his thoughts in words or not, whether the turmoil in his heart finds voice or not, every American Indian who has suffered the oppression that is worse than death feels that civilization has (1) made him a man without a country; (2) usurped his responsibility; (3) demeaned his manhood; (4) destroyed his ideals; (5) broken faith with him; (6) humiliated his spirit; (7) refused to listen to his petitions. . . .

If these statements seem to tinge of satire and of bitter invective to the civilized man, they are nevertheless very real things to the Indian who knows wherein he is wounded. To him this analysis will seem mild indeed, for it says nothing of a thousand deeds that made the four centuries of contact years of cruel misunderstanding. Yet to him these earlier years were better years than now, for he was then a free man who could boast a nation, who could speak his thought, and who bowed to no being save God, his superior and guardian. Now will we here mention the awful wars against women and children, the treacherous onslaughts on sleeping Indian villages, the murders of the old and helpless, the broken promises, the stolen lands, the robbed orphans and widows—for all of which men professing civilization and religion are responsible—for this is aside from our argument. We mention what is more awful than the robbery of lands, more hideous than the scalping and burning of Indian women and babies, more harrowing than tortures at the stake—we mean the crushing of a noble people's spirit and the usurpation of its right to be responsible and self-supporting:

Let it be affirmed as a deep conviction that until the American Indian is given back the right of assuming responsibility for his own acts and until his spirit is roused to action that awakened ideals will give him, all effort, all governmental protection, all gifts are of small value to him.

The Indian must be given back the things of which he has been robbed, with the natural accumulation of interest that the world's progress has earned. American civilization and Christianity must return the seven stolen rights without which no race or community of men can live.

From: Parker, Arthur Caswell. "The Social Elements of the Indian Problem." *American Journal of Sociology*, 22 (September 1916) 252–267.

THEY TOLD US THAT INDIAN
WAYS WERE BAD

~~~~~~~~~~~~~~~~~~~~~~~~~~~~

Tulto

*Tulto, or Sun Elk, born about 1870 in Taos Pueblo in New Mexico, was
the first from the pueblo to go to Carlisle Indian School in Pennsylvania,
where he lived for seven years. In conversations with historian Edwin
Embree, published in 1939, he describes how seven years' worth of
"lessons" teaching him that Indian ways were "bad" and "uncivilized"
resulted in the leaders of Taos Pueblo rejecting him after his return.*

Seven years I was there. I set little letters together in the printing shop and
we printed papers. For the rest we had lessons. . . .

They told us that Indian ways were bad. They said we must get civilized.
I remember that word too. It means "be like the white man." I am willing to
be like the white man, but I did not believe Indian ways were wrong. But
they kept teaching us for seven years. And the books told how bad the
Indians had been to the white man—burning their towns and killing their
women and children. But I had seen white men do that to Indians. We all
wore whiteman's clothes and ate whiteman's food and went to whiteman's
churches and spoke whiteman's talk. And so after a while we also began to
say Indians were bad. We laughed at our own people and their blankets and
cooking pots and sacred societies and dances. I tried to learn the lessons—
and after seven years I came home. . . .

It was a warm summer evening when I got off the train at Taos station.
The first Indian I met, I asked him to run out to the pueblo and tell my family I was home. The Indian couldn't speak English, and I had forgotten all
my Pueblo language. But after a while he learned what I meant and started
running to tell my father "Tulto is back."

I started walking out to the pueblo and as I got to the brook, about halfway
to the pueblo, here came my father and my mother and many brothers and
cousins. They all began hugging me, and we all cried and were very happy.

I have not thought about all this for many years. . . . I guess I was happier at
the little brook than I have ever been since. My family loved me and I was
at home. We chattered and cried, and I began to remember many Indian
words, and they told me about an uncle, Tha-a-ba, who had just died, and
how Turkano, my old friend, had finished his year's fast and was joining the

Black-eyes to become a priest and delight maker. Two little sisters and many little cousins had come along with the family to meet me. All these children liked me and kept running up and feeling my whiteman's clothes and then running away laughing. The children tried to repeat the English words I said, and everyone was busy teaching me Pueblo words again. We sat down on the grass and talked until it became dark. . . .

The chiefs did not want me in the pueblo. I went home with my family. And next morning the governor of the pueblo and the two war chiefs and many of the priest chiefs came into my father's house. They did not talk to me; they did not even look at me. When they were all assembled they talked to my father.

The chiefs said to my father, "Your son who calls himself Rafael has lived with the white men. He has been far away from the pueblo. He has not lived in the kiva nor learned the things that Indian boys should learn. He has no hair. He has no blankets. He cannot even speak our language and he has a strange smell. He is not one of us."

The chiefs got up and walked out. My father was very sad. I wanted him to be angry, but he was only sad. So, I would not be sad and was very angry instead. And I walked out of my father's house and out of the pueblo. I did not speak. My mother was in the other room cooking. She stayed in the other room but she made much noise rattling her pots. Some children were on the plaza and they stared at me, keeping very still as I walked away.

I walked until I came to the whiteman's town, Fernandez de Taos. I found work setting type in a printing shop there. Later I went to Durango and other towns in Wyoming and Colorado, printing and making a good living. But this indoor work was bad for me. It made me slight of health. So then I went outside to the fields. I worked in some blacksmith shops and on farms.

All this time I was a white man. I wore whiteman's clothes and kept my hair cut. I was not very happy. I made money and I kept a little of it and after many years I came back to Taos.

My father gave me some land from the pueblo fields. He could do this because now the land did not belong to all the people, as it did in the old days; the white man had cut it up and given it in little pieces to each family, so my father gave me a part of his, and I took my money and bought some more land and some cattle. I built a house just outside the pueblo. I would not live in the pueblo. . . .

From: Embree, Edwin. *Indians of the Americas: Historical Pageant.* Boston: Houghton Mifflin Co., 1939.

SCHOOL IS THE ENEMY

William Penseno

William Penseno, a Ponca man from Oklahoma and a member of the National Indian Youth Council organized in 1961 mostly by college students, testified on February 24, 1969 before the Senate Special Subcommittee on Indian Education, 91st Congress, chaired by Edward Kennedy. Testimony from the hearings filled seven volumes. In his lengthy testimony, a portion of which appears here, Penseno blasted public and government Indian schools as the "enemy" because they both perceived Indians as inferior, culturally deprived underachievers.

The school is the enemy. Public and Indian education are teaching us not to survive in a healthy community but how to be disintegrated. Embalming is a recent addition to Indian school curriculums. They are planning our funeral with a premature death certificate called termination.

Let it be heard here we are not people of a romantic past or irrelevant present. We intend to live until the end of time. Indians are a different people; different, not wrong; different, not opposing; different, not inferior; different, not anomalous. We are not culturally deprived, disadvantaged, or under-achievers. We do not take this in an ideological vacuum.

Tribalism is no hindrance to us but support. We have a basic confidence about our affairs that has been developed over thousands of years. It takes imagination and cohesion to survive the way we did for the past hundred years or so.

The school is the enemy. It attacks the very roots of the existence of an Indian student. May I quote from some of the teachers at these schools: "Just because you are Indian, don't be lazy." "Don't be so much an Indian." "I would rather have a spoon than a horse"—as if they were different.

A student in Ponca City asks if she has to sit by an Indian. The teacher says, "No, I know what you mean." Our girls are called squaws. We are greeted with, "How." If it rains, we are asked if we have been dancing. If we get a haircut, we are asked if they can scalp us. Everything we know and cherish is derided and made a butt of jokes.

We are given etiquette lessons in Indian schools as if we didn't know how to express our feelings properly. One boarding school has lessons in dating, as if we could not be trusted in courtship, as if we weren't taught right, as if what our folks tell us and show us is wrong or at least backward. . . .

The school is the enemy. It attacks the existence of an Indian student. Simply stated, the problem with Indians is that they are Indians as seen by others. This is stated in a myriad of sophisticated ways to excuse the miserable performance of those charged with teaching Indian students.

The fact that a graduate class at a federal boarding school had a median level of ninth grade in a battery test was described as something wrong with the students. The structure of school administrators interpret all of this reality in the defense of their schools. Never does the administration even fear that something could be wrong with the school. . . .

Indian education is an alien system designed not to meet Indian needs and goals but to minimize the havoc and embarrassment caused by the disruption of Indian institutions by outside influences. Social disorganization is the name of the game, and a chief contributor over the years has been the federal education program. The chief effort toward helping Indians has been through education. The result of the federal participation is cultural deprivation. The Indian community is deprived of its most energetic and creative members with their period of bondage as a planned, permanent condition.

The success is measured in terms of how permanently the Indians become removed from their families. In other words, he does not go back to the blanket. Indians send their children to schools with mixed emotion. They want them to eat, but they send them off to school at the dire risk of losing them.

Each time I go to college, my grandfolks all come over for dinner and pray that I will come back to them. It is not just my physical presence they want. Having Indian blood is not a necessary good. Having an all-Indian staff at boarding school does not necessarily help.

Who killed Sitting Bull? Who captured Geronimo? Who betrayed Chief Joseph? Indians did.

Indian schools deprive the student of the teaching experience and counsel of his elders. This sickness cult called social aspiration is actually rewarded in the school systems. . . .

It is frequently said that the hope of the Indians is in their youth. They are less contaminated and have more of a chance to get out of the cultural trap. It is then, that the Indian hope is that their youth and education will be their salvation. To accomplish this, all the values that the Indians hold must be invalidated in the schools. Their behavior must become most like the whites see themselves as acting. In other words, it is the aping of what Indians think whites expect of them, a caricature of what society demands.

Those who do not follow this behavior are soon ousted as being troublemakers and unprogressive. It is not that there is something per se wrong with these problems. It is that it works a destructive effort on individual human beings who think they have to become something different in order to learn a task.

Students who show promise are told: "You are not like other Indians. You are exceptional." These definitions that have been cast about us are not true. This is not what Indian people consist of. We are proud people and people of many talents. It is absurd to consider that these definitions are what Indian nature is.

The schools further contribute to socialization by teaching a student an experience that cannot be shared with their parents. This further widens the gap between members of families. It reminds me of the last summer I spent at a boarding school. The local superintendent came to speak to us about why Indians did not achieve. He said Indians were not achievement oriented and that Indian parents had too much grip on their children. The children not being able to put up with the school cannot adjust and drop out.

The blame was then placed on the parents. They did not make the children go to school. There was never a moment when the question was presented about the school. The schools are the process through which a student gains intellectual eyes to view the world. The power of the school as a defining agency becomes obvious. School cannot be separated from the community in which it is situated or from the genesis of the perspective that is presented by the school. . . .

I was visiting an Indian school last month. Movies are being shown in the auditorium about cavalry and Indians. The army was outnumbered and holding an impossible position. The Indians attempting to sneak up on the army were being killed, one every shot.

When it finally appeared that the Indians were going to overrun the army, the cavalry appeared over the horizon with their bugles blowing. The whole auditorium full of Indian students cheered. This is what I mean. How better could the effects be stated? This is Indian education. It is neither Indian nor education.

From: *Indian Education*, part 1. U.S. Congress. Senate Special Subcommittee On Indian Education. *Hearings*. 91st Cong., 1st sess., 1969.

TOO MANY SCIENTISTS, NOT ENOUGH CHIEFS

~~~~~~~~~~~~~~~

Howard Rock

Howard Rock, an Inupiaq [Eskimo] man born in 1911 at Point Hope, Alaska, founded in 1962 and edited The Tundra Times, a Fairbanks newspaper, that kept native people in 203 villages and subscribers in the "lower forty-eight" informed about their culture. Rock was nominated for a Pulitzer Prize in 1975, a year before he died. Here he criticizes a conference on native peoples that failed to include natives as participants.

The highly publicized science conference at the University of Alaska this week discussed the native people and their social changes. As [with] any high-level confab, there was little room for the natives to take any appreciable part in it. This might be viewed as a face-saving effort by the conferees after some static developed based on a sore thumb that spelled that there were too many scientists and not enough chiefs.

Such conferences should always have a good cross-section of the people being discussed. We believe sciences developed, on peoples especially, don't always get to the bottom of things because scientists who study a race don't always reach the real depth of the philosophies of life of those they study. As far as we know, scientists, such as anthropologists, have had no working knowledge of the languages of their subjects, which are a key to the understanding of the intricacies of life of a particular people. Man is not like a piece of stone, whoever he is. He is a complex piece of machinery or mechanism. Based on this, we believe that no foolproof evaluation of any people, especially Eskimos and other races, has been produced to date.

Under this situation, then, conferences such as the one held at the university this week should always include people being evaluated. Through this manner of doing things, scientists, especially those who delve into human behavior, can perhaps learn a lot more than they know now because there are native people who can enlighten them.

From: Rock, Howard. "Too Many Scientists and Not Enough Chiefs." *Tundra Times*, 29 August 1969.

TOO MANY CHILDREN'S BOOKS

Mary Gloyne Byler

Mary Gloyne Byler, a member of the Eastern Band of Cherokee Indians of North Carolina, was for many years editor of Indian Affairs, *the newsletter of the New York–based Association on American Indian Affairs. In 1973, she wrote a long introduction to her bibliography of American Indian authors for young readers, in which she cites the abuses of publishers turning out books filled with offensive contents or illustrations, subtle stereotypes, misconceptions, and clichés.*

American Indians have had to struggle for more than their physical survival. It is not only land that has been appropriated; it has also been a fight to keep mind and soul together, for along with the United States Cavalry, missionaries, educators and the "Americanizers," have come the writers of books about Indians.

Down through the years the publishing industry has produced thousands of books about American Indians—a subject that fascinates many. Fact and fiction—it is not always possible to tell which is which—have rolled off the presses since "frontier" days. But American Indians in literature, today, as in the past, are merely images projected by non-Indian writers.

Most minority groups in this country have been, and are still, largely ignored by the nation's major publishing houses—particularly in the field of children's books. American Indians, on the other hand, contend with a mass of material about themselves. If anything, there are too many children's books about American Indians.

There are too many books featuring painted, whooping, befeathered Indians closing in on too many forts, maliciously attacking "peaceful" settlers or simply leering menacingly from the background; too many books in which white benevolence is the only thing that saves the day for the incompetent, childlike Indian; too many stories setting forth what is "best" for American Indians.

There are too many stories for very young children about little boys running around in feathers and headbands, wearing fringed buckskin clothing, moccasins and (especially) carrying little bows and arrows. The majority of these books deal with the unidentified past. The characters are from unidentified tribes and they are often not even afforded the courtesy of personal names. In fact, the only thing identifiable is the stereotyped image of the befeathered Indian. . . .

Non-Indian writers have created an image of American Indians that is almost sheer fantasy. It is an image that is not authentic and one that has little value except that of sustaining the illusion that the original inhabitants deserved to lose their land because they were so barbaric and uncivilized.

This fantasy does not take into account the rich diversity of cultures that did, and do, exist. Violence is glorified over gentleness and love of peace. The humanistic aspects of American Indian societies are ignored in the standard book. . . .

A more direct assault is made upon the humanity of American Indians by the use of key words and phrases which trigger negative and derogatory images. Words such as savage, buck, squaw and papoose do not bring to mind the same images as do the words man, boy, woman and baby.

Descriptions of half-naked, hideously painted creatures brandishing tomahawks or scalping knives, yelping, howling, grunting, jabbering, or snarling are hardly conducive to a sympathetic reaction to the people so described. Ethnocentric bias is translated into absurdities, that is, making a point of the fact that American Indians could not read or write English when the Pilgrims arrived; they did not have clocks; they had no schools. . . .

It has been well established by sociologists and psychologists that the effect on children of negative stereotypes and derogatory images is to engender and perpetuate undemocratic and unhealthy attitudes that will plague our society for years to come.

It is time for American publishing houses, schools, and libraries to take another look at the books they are offering children and seriously set out to offset some of the damage they have done.

From: Byler, Mary Gloyne. "Introduction." In *American Indian Authors for Young Readers*, compiled by Mary Gloyne Byler. New York: Association on American Indian Affairs, 1973.

ABOUT "SLUM TA"

~~~~~~~~~~~

Charlene Teters

Charlene Teters, a member of the Spokane tribe in Washington, an artist, and mother of two children, has spent years battling through her installations, the stereotyping, trivialization, and commercialization of Native American cultures. A member of the National Coalition on Racism in Sports and the Media, she has used her art to protest the use and abuse of Indians as mascots. She is also a teacher and Director of Placement and Alumni Affairs at the Santa Fe–based Institute of American Indian Arts. In "Slum Ta," a portion of her 1994 "What We Know About Indians" installation, Teters has combined a photographic portrait of one of her children, labeled with her name and Bureau of Indian Affairs census number, with a cartoon Indian image. Viewers must look around or through the cartoon image to see the real child. By juxtaposing these images, Teters hopes to force viewers to confront the way false images hide the true identity of native people.

"Images of noble savages, warriors, braves, and Indian princesses are non-Indians' perceptions of what is Indian, created by authors and writers, and encouraged by the white establishment. These manufactured images are used to sell everything from butter to cars, and are powerful in their impact on non-Indian people. But this is not the American Indians' perception of themselves."— Charlene Teters, 1994

Piece by Charlene Teters
"Slum Ta"—from the installation "What We Know About Indians" by Charlene
Teters. Photograph by Don Messec.

NATIVE AMERICANS AND
ANTHROPOLOGY

Bea Medicine [Hinsha-waste-agli-win]

Bea Medicine, Hinsha-waste-agli-win or Returns Victorious with a Red Horse Woman, a Hunkpapa-sihasapa Lakota woman and an anthropologist, has taught at Dartmouth College, Stanford University, and the University of Wisconsin, and has authored numerous articles and papers. Her long-standing interest in native women led her to her book on Native American women, which was published in 1978. In it, Medicine argues that Indian women have been ignored by both male and female anthropologists.

The anthropologist and the Native American have had a long history of interaction. Indeed, it has been suggested that American anthropology was built upon the backs of the Native American. Native American cultures have certainly been the focus of ethnological study for many generations, and interest in the "vanishing Americans" has been a potent force in the collection of cultural fact and artifact from the beginnings of American anthropology. . . .

Despite American anthropology's long-standing relationship with Native American societies, it has not been without its deficiencies. Materials have been few and scattered, and what has been gathered deals largely with the Indian male. If information from the past is scanty, the present accounts leave even more to be desired, for there are few contemporary studies of Indian females. . . . One must simply set about examining a great many ethnological studies of Indian tribes to glean information about the diverse role of women in native cultures.

This leads to another deficiency which becomes very apparent in any investigation of the anthropological studies of Native American societies. Early anthropological data regarding the Indian tribes of North America reveal the pervasive endocentric bias of nineteenth-century male academe. It is as if each Native American society were viewed as a "company of native men" and, as reported by male anthropologists, the female component of these societies was seriously shortchanged or cast in an unfavorable light. . . .

This has led to the charge, particularly in papers presented by Native American women, that anthropologists have always presented Indian women as "drudges." Shirley Hill Witt explicitly faults the "Anthros" for the perpetuation of this image. I share this view. In anthropological literature, native women have been referred to as drudges, beasts of burden, and other demoralizing terms. Native men have also not been reluctant to characterize Indian women in this manner. They are fond of pointing out that Indian women walked ten paces behind them. To this statement, I have replied, "Of course, we walked ten paces behind you. That's documented. And the reason that we did was to tell you where to go."

. . . Despite the fact that the "father of American anthropology," Franz Boas, encouraged women to enter the field, the work they produced did not focus specifically on the women's role in the native cultures of North America. For the most part, like the men, they seemed to be caught up in the fervor of collecting information before the tribes disappeared into the sunset, with the women ten paces behind them. Women students, in training as anthropologists, seemed tied to the same analytical tools and rubrics as their male counterparts.

Treatises on kinship, language, art, folklore, religion, and material culture were the result. But to say that the role of women was totally neglected would be a half-truth. They appeared in kinship charts or as adjuncts to men, in the various economic pursuits of indigenous cultures, and from these ethnographic accounts can be teased images of women. . . .

Therefore, in spite of all the limitations, deficiencies, and scarcities, it is to anthropological writings, whatever the quality and nature of the interaction, that one must go for information about Native American female prototypes. As accounts, these are to be preferred to historical writings, for the latter are often more derogatory and biased than the former concerning the status and role of the Native American female in North America.

From: Medicine, Bea. *The Native American Woman: A Perspective.* Austin, Texas: National Educational Laboratory Publishers, 1978.

ESKIMOS WILL ALWAYS
BE "DIFFERENT"

Jeannie Blatchford Greene

Jeannie Blatchford Greene, an Eskimo woman born in 1952, became fully aware of her identity, that is, that she was "different," when she moved from Sitka, Alaska. In a 1982 Tundra Times *column, she writes about the ignorance she encountered both in Seward, Alaska, and in California.*

I first discovered that I was native in 1963 when we moved from Sitka.

At the age of eleven years I was thrust into the reality of white vs. native. In Sitka, at that time, Caucasian, Indians and Eskimos lived together in harmony. I can remember white people and Tlingits visiting our home.

There were some in Seward who were not receptive to having another native family move in but we stayed and lived there anyway. I was suddenly "different." That was many years ago.

I experienced this again when in 1972 I visited my sister in Susanville, California. One evening at a local restaurant, some local people heard that I was Eskimo. I immediately became very well-known. My celebrity status was not based on the fact that I was bright or beautiful, but because I was an Eskimo who could actually use a telephone and ate white people's food. Alaska to them was a huge glacier and Eskimos were funny brown people who inhabited the area in a harmless but interesting fashion, not unlike penguins.

I sat in wonder as these people asked me questions that were so incredibly ignorant that I would more often than not explode in laughter. It was then that again I felt "different" . . . somewhat mysterious.

My trip to California was enlightening in other ways, too. Throughout my visit the local people would sit for hours talking about the beauty of this area or that area. I would anticipate visits to these places with high hopes only to be disappointed when I arrived there. The beauty I knew was of such grand scale that to talk about it—the water, the smells, the land—would only make me sound like a liar or perhaps trying to "out-do" their state.

When I finally arrived back in Alaska, after two months, I experienced something I will never forget. Driving from Anchorage to Seward my eyes opened for the first time to majestic splendor and grandeur.

My mind is full of stories told to me by my mother and father and grandmother. Experiences shared by people who lived here much longer than I. People who lived in villages and walked the tundra and hunted seal and walrus. Eskimo people who are not funny or "different." Eskimo people who are proud, geniuses in their art of survival . . . people who love deeply, hurt deeply, and who are friends of their provider, the land.

We don't have to explain why we are the way we are. We don't have to display our traditions. Yet we do . . . we share because who else will deal with the misconceptions that people have about us? Outsiders have put the welcome mat in front of OUR door and set OUR table for their nourishment.

Because we are here, because we are us and they are not us, Eskimos will always be "different" when all we want to be is here.

> *I'm people with you . . . be people with me*
> *Let's share those things that are warm*
> *Open your eyes, look closely at me*
> *I'm different but I mean you no harm.*
>
> *I'm proud to be Eskimo and different from you*
> *Will you accept my outstretched hand?*
> *You walk on the same ground that I do*
> *And we're one in our love for this land.*

From: Greene, Jeannie Blatchford "Outside Trip Showed Beauty of State." *Tundra Times*, 17, March 1982.

SCHOOL WAS A PAINFUL EXPERIENCE

~~~~~~~~~~

Joseph H. Suina

Joseph H. Suina, from Cochiti Pueblo in New Mexico, lived with his grandmother in a one-room house in the early 1950s. Now at the University of New Mexico in the Department of Educational Administration, he tells about his first-day school experiences in this excerpt from the essay: "Epilogue: And Then I Went to School."

At age six, like the rest of the Cochiti 6-year-olds that year, I had to begin my schooling. It was a new and bewildering experience. One I will not forget. The strange surroundings, new concepts about time and expectations, and a foreign tongue were overwhelming to us beginners. It took some effort to return the second day and many times thereafter.

To begin with, unlike my grandmother, the teacher did not have pretty brown skin and a colorful dress. She was not plump and friendly. Her clothes were one color and drab. Her pale and skinny form made me worry that she was very ill. I thought that explained why she did not have time just for me and the disappointed looks and orders she seemed always to direct my way. I didn't think she was so smart because she couldn't understand my language. "Surely that was why we had to leave our 'Indian' at home." But then I did not feel so bright either. All I could say in her language was "Yes, teacher," "My name is Joseph Henry," and "When is lunchtime?" The teacher's odor took some getting used to also. In fact, many times it made me sick right before lunch. Later, I learned from the girls that this odor was something she wore called perfume.

The classroom too had its odd characteristics. It was terribly huge and smelled of medicine like the village clinic I feared so much. The walls and ceiling were artificial and uncaring. They were too far from me and I felt naked. The fluorescent light tubes were eerie and blinked suspiciously at me. This was quite a contrast to the fire and sunlight that my eyes were accustomed to. I thought maybe the lighting did not seem right because it was man-made, and it was not natural. Our confinement to rows of desks was another unnatural demand from our active little bodies. We had to sit at these hard things for what seemed like forever before relief (recess) came midway through the morning and afternoon. Running carefree in the village and fields was but a sweet memory of days gone by. We all went home for lunch because we lived within walking distance of the school. It took coaxing and sometimes bribing to get me to return and complete the remainder of the school day.

School was a painful experience during those early years. The English language and the new set of values caused me much anxiety and embarrassment. I could not comprehend everything that was happening but yet I could understand very well when I messed up or was not doing so well. The negative aspect was communicated too effectively and I became unsure of myself more and more. How I wished I could understand other things just as well in school.

. . . My language . . . was questionable from the beginning of my school career. "Leave your Indian (language) at home" was the trademark of school. Speaking it accidentally or otherwise was a sure reprimand in the form of a dirty look or a whack of a ruler. This punishment was for speaking the language of my people which meant so much to me. It was the language of my grandmother and I spoke it well. With it, I sang beautiful songs and prayed from my heart. At that young and tender age, comprehending why I had to part with it was most difficult for me. And yet at home I was encouraged to attend school so that I might have a better life in the future. I knew I had a good village life already but this was communicated less and less each day I was in school.

As the weeks turned to months, I learned English more and more. It would appear comprehension would be easier. It got easier to understand all right. I understood that everything I had and was a part of was not nearly as good as the white man's. School was determined to undo me in everything from my sheepskin bedding to the dances and ceremonies that I learned to believe in and cherish. One day I fell asleep in class after a sacred all-night ceremony. I was startled to awakening by a sharp jerk on my ear and informed coldly, "That ought to teach you not to attend 'those things' again." Later, all alone I cried. I could not understand why or what I was caught up in. I was receiving two very different messages; both intending to be for my welfare.

From: Suina, Joseph H. "Epilogue: And Then I Went to School." In *Linguistic and Cultural Influences on Learning Mathematics*, edited by Rodney R. Cocking and Jose P. Mestre. Hillsdale, New Jersey: Lawrence Erlbaum Associates, Publishers, 1988.

DON'T STARE AT PEOPLE

Ivan Star Comes Out

Ivan Star Comes Out, an Oglala Lakota, wrote a column in Lakota and English for Indian Country Today, *formerly* The Lakota Times, *an award-winning weekly from Rapid City, South Dakota. An incident in a South Dakota restaurant was the subject of the 1989 column excerpted here. Countless Indians can relate to his experience because so many non-Indian people treat Indians as curiosities.*

Recently, my wife and I took our kids to town to eat out.

Every now and then they too want certain foods so we take them to a restaurant and let them go.

They order whatever they want and have a good time while eating together.

. . . Now, it was on such an occasion that we entered a restaurant and found the white people inside turning around and staring at us shamelessly. I thought they would get up and approach us.

Ignoring them we walked across the room and sat down at a table but they were still staring at us. I was reminded of a burrowing owl who would turn its head almost completely around without moving its body.

Each time we looked their way they would look away quickly but would soon be staring again when we were not looking.

My wife has often become angry and would start a verbal attack or stare just as blatantly back at them.

My grandmother of long ago told me, "Don't stare at people because it is disrespectful."

My grandmother was a person who never got past the second grade yet she knew that much. She knew respect for others.

. . . I don't want my kids to grow up seeing these things but each time we go on an outing we run into this.

Maybe they want to know more about us as Native Americans but all they seem to be doing so far is staring and not asking questions which makes it bad for everyone.

From: Star Comes Out, Ivan. "A Common Experience Among Indians." *Lakota Times**, 7 February 1989.

*Renamed *Indian Country Today* in 1992.

THE NEW TEACHER

James R. Gooden

James R. Gooden, Inupiaq Eskimo from Kiana, Alaska wrote the following for a writing class delivered to his remote village by satellite-assisted audioconference from Chukchi College, a branch of the University of Alaska at Kotzebue. Chukchi students are published through Chukchi News and Information Services, a student project founded in 1988 to create a rural and Alaska native voice in the media. In addition to capturing the state's highest media award from the Alaska Press Club, Chukchi students have won three national awards. Gooden's piece describes his experiences at a Fairbanks elementary school in the late 1950s.

I was instructed by the new teacher to occupy the last desk at the back of the room. Students filled about nine other desks in front of me. I felt strange, lost in this new setting: sixth grade in Fairbanks, 1959.

Each student had to stand and introduce himself. Then came my turn. A silence crept into the room as Miss Thompson, the teacher, strolled over to the large classroom window.

"My name is Ronald Gooden," I began.

"What kind of name is 'Ronnie Gooden'?" Miss Thompson asked.

I didn't respond. I didn't know. I just stood there.

"Okay," she continued. "Can you speak English?"

"Yes," I replied, puzzled by the slight grin on her face.

"What race do you belong to, Ronnie?" she asked, looking at the other students.

I looked into the faces of some of the students. I cleared my throat.

"I'm an Eskimo," I said.

"Do you live in an igloo?" Miss Thompson asked.

"No," I replied. I was beginning to choke up, afraid she would ask yet another question.

"Do your kind still eat raw meat?" she asked.

Miss Thompson walked toward me. I began to stiffen, pinching the seams along the sides of my pant legs.

"Yes, sometimes," I replied.

Some of the students began to giggle.

"Well, Ronnie, tell me this, do you still rub noses when you make love?" Miss Thompson asked.

"No, not that I know of," I replied. I began to shake a little, almost to the point of wanting to cry. Fortunately, I remained in control. The moment passed.

Miss Thompson went on with her student orientation about school operations. She explained the rules: on the class, on the school, on the playground, on rest room use. She thumbtacked the gym schedule to the bulletin board indicating the days and times it was to be used. She explained the school lunch program, the cost for the lunch, and the weekly menu.

Schoolbooks were handed out and properly marked. Textbook arrangement in the desk, she commanded, was not to be changed.

Despite all this, I was determined to do well.

At first, I earned fairly good grades, which surprised the teacher. I had always tried my best, as my mother and father had told me. I became the class artist, drawing head figures of presidents. Lincoln, Adams and Jefferson were my favorites. I played basketball, becoming center for the school team, the Hunter Hornets.

The change in Miss Thompson barely showed on the surface at first, except perhaps in her interrogation of me on that first day. Soon, though, we noticed Miss Thompson had indisputably begun to change. She began to carry a ruler in one hand, rapping it against the palm of the other. If she was displeased about anything, she would let us know by hitting the top of our desks without warning.

As we worked, she would pick papers from the desks. She picked mine more often than others. Mine always seemed to have the most mistakes, which she always would make sure the rest of the class knew.

When she spoke to me, her voice seemed to get a little higher than usual, while one foot tapped the floor.

My friend, Ronald Sheppard, and I, sensing unfairness, devised a plan to find out if she was grading my papers properly. Doing identical work, we decided to copy, but change the wording around just a little. On the average, Ronald was a B-plus student. We used American History, in which I had always received lower grades than Ronald. So we switched papers. I had Ronald's and he took mine. Surprise! I received a low grade, only it was really Ronald's paper. Was he shocked. I got my paper from Ronald. I received a B. I wasn't shocked.

Ronald and I took our papers to our basketball coach, Mr. Donowick. Mr. Donowick brought it to the principal's attention. Miss Thompson was notified.

We both got in trouble for playing a trick on the teacher and received zeroes for that paper. Ronald was then moved to the front of the class. I was to remain in the same spot. My grades improved, but essentially remained at the C– to D range.

Despite the odds, I would try extra hard to improve or correct my work, even though I knew that when Miss Thompson approached my desk with her fists resting on her hips, I would lose. Her piercing eyes would glare at me through those wire-rimmed glasses as she stood slightly bent over my desk.

"What are you doing?" she would ask.

"I'm doing my work over again," I would reply.

"No, you've already gotten a zero on the one I threw away in the trash can, and there is no make-up for sloppy work," she would say.

Time passed. I bore through the ordeal as best I could. In fact, Miss Thompson's throwing of my papers into the trash even went down to twice a week. During reading, though, others could either sit or stand when they read to the class. I was to stand and remain standing after the reading.

I hated Fridays. That was the day that test papers were graded and placed on top of the teacher's desk. My paper always seemed to be on top. Red slashes marked my whole sheet.

Some of the students began to dislike Miss Thompson. We gave her a nickname: "Old Lady Thompson." She reminded us of the cartoon character of the nice little old lady in "Sylvester and Tweetie," only the opposite.

Miss Thompson wore the same black dress, or at least it appeared so. She also wore a black hat, never taking it off. She wore those high, thick-heeled, below-the-ankle shoes of the mid-1940s.

I started to play hooky. Some days I played sick so as not to go to school. My absences kept increasing. Finally, report card day at the end of the school year arrived. I read mine: "TO BE RETAINED IN THE SIXTH GRADE NEXT YEAR." I sat in silence, not looking at anyone. The bell rang and then the dash for the door. I headed for the first trash can on the playground, where I watched the torn pieces of green paper hit the bottom of the barrel.

Summer passed. Back to the same school. I was assigned to the classroom across the hall from the one the previous year: a different classroom, a different teacher. I wasn't assigned to the back row anymore, and I began earning good grades. When I was called upon to do something in class, the teacher encouraged me with a smile. I grew a lot that year.

Mrs. Danforth, in her midforties, was very pretty with a pleasant personality. Her shoulder-length light brown hair, mixed with some gray, complemented her light complexion. She always wore pretty dresses and skirts with colorful blouses. A scent of flowers filled the room when she entered the classroom or passed by our desks. Thanks to Mrs. Danforth, I walked a little taller. I can still say a few of the French words she taught me. I will never forget her.

From: Gooden, James, R. "Miss Thompson's Bigotry Really Hurt." *Tundra Times*, July 26, 1989.

MAINSTREAM PRESS AND
INDIAN COUNTRY

Tim Giago

Tim Giago, an Oglala Lakota, was born in 1934 on the Pine Ridge Reservation in South Dakota. A business and journalism major at the University of Nevada, in 1981 he founded The Lakota Times *(renamed* Indian Country Today *in 1992), published independently in Rapid City, South Dakota. As editor of the paper, Giago writes a syndicated column,"Notes from Indian Country," that appears in over twenty U.S. papers. Giago has been given the Lakota name Nawica Kjici, which literally translates "He Stands Up for Them," usually shortened to "Defender." In a February 1990 column, Giago challenges mainstream press reporting about Indian people.*

At one time in my newspaper career I believed the only way for American Indians to bring an end to the racial stereotyping, the misconceptions, and the absolute lack of knowledge about the indigenous people was to join the mainstream press.

The mainstream press has fed upon the ignorance of the general population when reporting upon events happening in Indian country for generations simply because they are reporting to an audience as ignorant of Indians as themselves.

They have been able to do this with relative impunity because we are a small minority without the political or economic clout of the Black or Hispanic populations.

Many articles written about Indians are so full of holes, at least to those of us with a semblance of knowledge about the Indian situation in America, that these stories would have been challenged in an instant had they been written about a more vocal minority.

My personal experience with the mainstream press has been almost entirely of a negative nature, even with some of those newspapers that carry this column, or have carried it in the past.

When I worked as a newswriter for the mainstream press I soon discovered the attempts by management to treat me like all of the other reporters so as not to show preferential treatment was so intense that it had just the opposite effect. I ended up being discriminated against in the name of fair play.

When I was considering joining the mainstream press one large newspaper chain invited me to Washington, D.C., all expenses paid, for a visit to their corporate headquarters. I sat in at an editorial board meeting without ever being told that the questions I was being asked would soon become a part of their editorial page.

I was introduced to their Black representative for equal opportunity, their Hispanic rep for equal opportunity, and their woman rep for equal opportunity. When I asked if they would consider having an Indian rep for equal opportunity they looked at me as if I had asked if their chairman of the board was a Communist. "We don't give preferential treatment to anyone because of their race or color," one high level manager told me with a straight face.

Eventually, I was offered a job as editorial page editor of a midsized daily newspaper in a community made up primarily of people with Scandinavian and Germanic ancestry. I see nothing wrong with this except that I attempted employment with this large newspaper chain because they had several newspapers way out west in Indian country and since I considered the coverage of Indian issues to be my main field of expertise, I assumed I would be utilized for this purpose. You know what they say about "assuming."

This particular newspaper chain is looked upon by much of the Indian population it serves out west as a "redneck" chain and it is an image I hoped they would be willing to change for the sake of the newspaper group. As a matter of fact, one of the newspapers in this group had just lost a lawsuit to an Indian tribe for violating its sacred religious ceremonies.

When I called the personnel director and told her I would not be interested in the job offered and suggested that I could better be utilized in one of their far western newspapers, a stony silence followed. "Well, you'll be hearing from us," was her response, uttered in a very cold voice.

I immediately called her supervisor, divulged what had just occurred, and said that I was sure I would never hear from this particular personnel director again. Of course, I was right. I had committed the unpardonable sin of suggesting that I had an independent mind.

It is my contention that seminars should be held to educate those newspaper executives about Indians and the complexities of covering news stories emanating from the Indian reservations. Educating the personnel directors should also be mandatory.

Mary Kay Blake, director of recruitment/placement for the Gannett Newspaper Group, made a comment in the January issue of the in-house news organ, the *Gannetteer*, that is so typical of this suffocating ignorance that it should be used as an example for all personnel directors charged with hiring minorities.

Blake was asked, "During an interview with a prospective employee, which characteristics impress you? Which turn you off? She itemized the things that impressed her, and then proceeded to nibble on her stylish shoes with this: "These things don't impress me: mumbled or yes-no answers; an inability to sustain eye contact . . ."

I stopped right there. Doesn't Ms. Blake know that there are many Indian tribes in this country who teach their children that direct eye contact is impolite, nay even disrespectful?

When interviewing an Indian from one of these tribes, would that individual be eliminated from job consideration because of a cultural trait? According to Mary Kay Blake . . . yes.

What all of this has done is convince me that Indians joining the mainstream press do not change the media but instead end up being corrupted by it. They do not, and cannot . . . change the media's perception of Indians because that change must start at the top.

The people at the top are too busy patting themselves on the back for being impartial to be impartial. Ignorance is bliss has never had more meaning. Ours has become a world of McPapers, McEditors, and McSoundbites.

From: Giago, Tim. "Bringing an End to Stereotyping in Mainstream Media Must Start at the Top." *Lakota Times*, February 20, 1990.

A BONA FIDE
RELIGIOUS CEREMONY

Woody Kipp

Woody Kipp, a South Piegan (Blackfeet from Montana), graduated in journalism from the University of Montana in 1991. In the April 5, 1990, edition of a now-defunct newspaper from Stand Off, Alberta, Canada, he writes about non-Indians' ignorance about Native American spirituality.

Here's how it happened. I had been asked to give a presentation concerning the Native American view of Sacred Lands during the University of Montana–based Badger Chapter's annual confab concerning wilderness preservation. This was in the latter part of October 1988.

Also on the panel was the distinguished Canadian Native American spiritual leader Joe Crow Shoe. Joe is a North Piegan. I am a South Piegan. Our band, which is one of the principal divisions of the Blackfoot Confederacy, was split by the creation of the Forty-ninth Parallel which divides the United States from Canada. They ended up as Canucks and we ended up as Yankees. Through the stroke of the imperialist pen, our nation was torn asunder.

After the panel, which was composed of individuals from various tribes who knew something about their people's attachment to their respective homelands, Crow Shoe invited members of the audience to participate in a Sacred Pipe ceremony.

Joe Crow Shoe is an elder who is often called upon to officiate at ceremonial gatherings in the Blackfeet Nation, has traveled extensively in North America and Europe, and is Keeper of the Sacred Thunder Pipe Bundle, which was given to the Blackfeet eons ago in vision quest. It was given by the Thunder Beings. The bundle is opened at the sound of the first thunder in the springtime.

Approximately twenty-five of us were sitting in a circle on the floor while Crow Shoe readied his ceremonial pipe. Blackfeet ceremonial smoking is not hallucinogenic. Before a pipe can be touched, it must first be purified with incenses we use to purify ourselves and our ceremonial items before a ceremony. Sage was burning. Suddenly the back door of the room flew open and a woman who works in the UC stood in the doorway, her mouth

267

hanging open, her eyes wide in disbelief. She could have asked what we were doing. She didn't.

The smell of the purification herb, the sage, had apparently attracted her. When she opened the door and saw all these people sitting around on the floor, it boggled her mind. Had she come all the way into the room, she would have seen the ceremonial items laid out before Crow Shoe—the long black stone ceremonial pipe, the intricately beaded pipe bag, the large abalone shell from the ocean in which the sage was burned.

But instead of coming into the room, she stood halfway through the door and blurted: "This is is going to stop." Casting a baleful glare at all in the room taking part in what she believed to be a huge pot party, she continued, "This is going to stop right now. I'm calling security." And away she went, walking the walk of the wrathfully indignant.

It happened so suddenly. She was gone before anyone could collect their senses. A non-Indian woman who attends native ceremonies finally rushed after the woman. From where we sat we could hear the flurried exchange through the door.

"This is a religious ceremony," the woman was told.

"Don't tell me," she said. "I grew up in the seventies. I know what pot smells like."

And on and on until she was finally convinced she had barged in on a bona fide religious ceremony. Here, one must remember the old Indian adage: "Don't criticize your neighbor until you have walked a mile in his moccasins."

So, I guess if I didn't know any better and stumbled upon this gathering, the mistake is understandable. Thusly: Boy, look at that, here us good white folk are trying to make a living and look at these people, sitting around in the middle of the afternoon smoking pot—in the UC, no less. Cheeky. Audacious.

It was ignorance of other people's ways of life. In this case, ways that were being practiced long before her ancestors ever stepped ashore onto this Turtle Island that is North America.

As natives, we've grown used to it. We've had a lot of time to get used to it—since 1492 when that first load of people came sailing across the high seas in their wooden tubs singing "We Shall Overcome."

In 1978, the Congress of the United States of America passed a law, the American Indian Religious Freedom Act. After only 486 years, they gave us the legal right to pray to God.

Damnant quod non intelligunt.

From: Kipp, Woody. "Viewpoint: Because of Ignorance." *Kanai News*, April 5, 1990.

K-MART'S WEEKEND SPECIAL: INDIAN SPIRITUALITY

Trudie Lamb-Richmond

Trudie Lamb-Richmond, a Schaghticoke woman, is Director of Education at the Institute for American Indian Studies in Washington, Connecticut. In an editorial written in 1993, she decries commercialization of Indian beliefs.

Native cultures and native people have been a curiosity and cause for stereotyping and misunderstanding for several hundred years. Periodically, waves of interest about Indians flood the country. Some people want to be Indian, others collect Indian items, and still others hold Indian weddings. But of even more serious concern is the growing numbers of "plastic medicine men" performing ceremonies and conducting sweats.

Now everyone is a shaman.

Perhaps native cultures need to be placed on the endangered species list along with our animal and plant relatives and be protected against destruction, exploitation, and assimilation.

Among native people there needs to be a reaffirmation of traditional values; a respect for traditional ways of the medicine societies. Native traditions teach respect for the natural world, that all creation is sacred. As our ceremonies and medicine societies evolved, certain symbols and objects became an integral part of ceremonies. They serve as reminders and are themselves considered sacred.

How can our ceremonies, our religious rituals, be protected when sweat lodges, pipe ceremonies, or cornhusk dolls wearing false face masks are as readily accessible as K-Mart specials? Or when elements of native cultures are taken out of context and sold as objects of curiosity?

What is a sacred object? When is a sacred object not a sacred object?

Native cultures are diverse and there is no single answer. The Plains people have their pipe ceremony and the Sun Dance. The Diné (Navajo) medicine man will "destroy" his sandpainting after a healing ceremony.

The Hopi people carve their Kachina dolls to represent the spirit world. However, the Hopi also say that when the dolls are not consecrated, they may be presented to the public for sale, either for economic reasons or to educate and promote understanding. The Zuni have declared that their

ceremonies are no longer open to the public because of the frequent disrespect that is shown. . . . .

It is clear that native nations handle sacred objects and ceremonies differently. But, it must be emphasized, it is the medicine societies and the
traditional societies that make the determinations. Some groups who once
permitted inclusion now realize that if they do not protect their ceremonies
they will be lost.

At one time native ceremonies were banned by the American government. Now they are being exploited. We have been Americanized,
Christianized, scrutinized, and factionalized. How much more can our cultures take?

Yet how can we be taken seriously when elements of our religions are sold
as crafts and non-Indians pay to participate in ceremonies? How can we
teach respect for the drum when it is sold as an end table or used as a coffee
table to receive nicks and cigarette burns?

While some native people are struggling to obtain legislation to protect
our ancestors' remains and religious freedom, other native people are con-
fusing our white brothers and sisters by "selling" our spirituality to them.

If there isn't a debate about this going on in Indian Country, there needs
to be. For decades others have either claimed or acted as if they owned and
controlled our past, our history. Now we are taking control and our views are
being heard. Now there are discussions about museum ethics and repatria-
tion. Some museums and historical societies have returned ancestral remains
to be reinterred. But there is still an enormous imbalance.

There are too many native people who do not know or understand their
own culture; young people who have lived away from their traditions. At the
same time not all native people are traditional. Some have joined other
faiths. Nevertheless, everyone should respect the teachings of the medicine
societies and the cumulative spiritual wisdom of the elders.

But as long as people—Indian and non-Indian alike—conduct income-
producing ceremonies and sweat lodges, as long as crafts-people market our
sacred objects, we will have this dilemma.

If it is unfortunate while other groups are advocating inclusiveness, native
people need to be exclusive.

But our spirituality is not for sale.

From: Lamb-Richmond, Trudie. "K-Mart's Weekend Special: Indian Spirituality." *The Eagle*,
11, no. 2 (Spring 1993): 13.

HER REMARK OFFENDED ME

Amera Ignacio

Amera Ignacio, a Ute-Wampanoag student from Gay Head, Massachu-
setts, wrote the following essay in 1993 for a freshman English class at
Martha's Vineyard Regional High School. In this piece, she expresses the
pride she takes in her cultural traditions, which motivated her to protest
a teacher's remarks about Indians.

My name is Amera Ignacio and I wrote this essay to tell you why I am so special. I think I am special because I am Native American. I am very special because I have a heritage to be proud about. For a very long time the Native American people of Martha's Vineyard did not have what we have now, like the different cultural programs. For example, the boys and girls who sing and dance. When I dance I always feel special because I am showing not only the Native Americans, but people of all nationalities what we can do and how to dance. Native Americans danced all over this country before Columbus arrived.

I think I am special because I think very deeply about the problems of my people. I do not look at people for their color and I do not look at the way they live. If we can talk to each other and share our problems, then that is good. If I can talk to a person then we can get along. Some of the older Wampanoag people brought their children up to think white was better. Their children had to try to be white.

If you are proud of who you are and take time to learn your heritage, you will not take stupid remarks and let it slide. In my Eighth Grade year, we got a new teacher and we were doing some exercise and she said, 'everybody jump around and howl like Indians.' I sat down. It was important to me that she knew how much her remark had offended me so after class I approached her and told her that it really had offended me. All she said was that was how she was brought up. Doing this was very hard for me, and it took a lot of courage and that is how I know that being brave is something special about me.

I think I am special because I am my own person. When my mind is made up about something I do not change, and I never let people talk for me. . . .

From: Ignacio, Amera. "Why I Am So Special."

HOLLYWOOD HAS
NOT CHANGED

Beverly Singer

Beverly Singer, a Santa Clara Pueblo woman from New Mexico who resides in New York City, has taught Native American studies in several colleges and is an artist and independent filmmaker. Her recent video He Wo Un Peh: Recovery in Native America, *was shown at the Vienna International Film Festival in October 1994. Ms. Singer, who is a research associate at Columbia University School of Social Work, co-edited* Rising Voices: Writings of Young Native Americans. *In the following excerpt from a piece published in the December 1994 issue of* The Independent: Film and Video Monthly *she briefly describes a film by Hopi filmmaker Victor Masayesva, Jr., that zeros in on Hollywood stereotypes of American Indians.*

I*magining Indians* (1992) by Hopi filmmaker Victor Masayesva, Jr., addresses the manifestation of the "Indian" as a cultural non-entity in popular culture. Through interviews with Native American actors, it becomes clear that Hollywood has not changed its perception of "Indians," but holds the same attitudes as when it first began employing them in early westerns. In addition to showing how Hollywood has appropriated Native culture into stereotypical images, *Imagining Indians* depicts how the impact of commerce upon Native communities has led to a slow disintegration of values and respect for Native lifeways.

The residue left by Hollywood filmmakers when they entered Masayesva's community is demonstrated through verité footage in which Hopi elders voice their opposition to the filming of *Dark Wind* on Hopi soil. Their discussion (conducted in Hopi with English subtitles) concerns the sacredness of the area where the producers wish to film. Despite the elders' opposition, elected Hopi leaders permit the filming after a financial agreement is reached.

Masayesva's aesthetic treatment of and sensitivity toward Hopi life are woven into the film through the director's use of transitions. After the interview segments with Lakotas regarding their participation in *Dances with Wolves*, for instance, we see an approaching afternoon thunderstorm that stretches across Hopi territory, suggesting the filmmakers' return home. In another transition, rustling leaves form a mirage of sea waves through which female "fancy shawl dancers" emerge at a powwow. This occurs as a woman's voice speaks about the loss in meaning when the practice of trading goods and services was replaced by a cash economy.

Imagining Indians raises ethical questions about the importance of cultural integrity and how, within our communities, we need to protect the things we say are important to us: elders, land, ceremonial art forms, and life itself.

From: Singer, Beverly. "Replaying the Native Experience." *The Independent Film & Video Monthly*, a publication of the Foundation for Independent Video and Film. vol. 17, no. 10 (December 1994): 22–24.

SELECTED RESOURCES

NATIVE AMERICAN JOURNALS

Akwe:kon Journal (formerly
Northeast Indian Quarterly)
American Indian Program
300 Caldwell Hall
Ithaca, NY 14853
- Covers economic development,
  agriculture, community health,
  arts, land rights, education, environmental issues, oral history,
  poetry, book reviews

*American Indian Culture and
Research Journal*
American Indian Studies Center
University of California at
Los Angeles
3220 Campbell Hall
Los Angeles, CA 90024
- Historical and contemporary
  American Indian life and
  culture; book reviews

American Indian Quarterly
University of Oklahoma
Department of Anthropology
Dale Hall Tower/Room 521
455 W. Lindsey
Norman, OK 73019-0535
- Historical and contemporary
  American Indian life and
  culture; book reviews

Honor Digest
2647 N. Stowell Avenue
Milwaukee, WI 53211
- Covers treaty rights, issues in
  sovereignty and religious freedom, discrimination and stereotyping in popular culture

Explorations in Ethnic Studies
National Association for Ethnic
Studies, Inc.
Department of English
Arizona State University
Tempe, AZ 85287-0302
- Covers cultural life of ethnic
  peoples

Medium Rare
1433 East Franklin Avenue,
Suite 11
Minneapolis, MN 55404
- Covers issues relating to Native
  American journalism

Native Peoples
P.O. Box 36820
Phoenix, AZ 85067-6820
- Covers arts and culture

News from Native California
P.O. Box 9145
Berkeley, CA 94709
- Covers native arts, culture,
  language, history, and language
  in California

NARF Legal Review
1506 Broadway
Boulder, CO 80302
- Covers sovereignty of tribes, legal issues and legislation, court decisions

Studies in American Indian Literature
Box 112
University of Richmond
Richmond, VA 23173
- Covers all aspects of oral and written Native American literature, and live and recorded performances of verbal art

Tribal College
P.O. Box 898
Chestertown, MD 21620
- Covers American Indian higher education and curriculum and activities of 31 tribal colleges in North America

Turtle Quarterly
25 Rainbow Mall
Niagara Falls, NY 14303
- Covers arts and culture; contemporary issues

Wicazo Sa Review
Association for American Indian Research
3755 Blake Court North
Rapid City, SD 57701-4716
- Scholarly essays about Native American studies

Winds of Change
AISES Publishing
1630 30th Street/Suite 301
Boulder, CO 80301

- Covers science and mathematics education; environmental issues

NATIVE AMERICAN NEWSPAPERS

The Circle (monthly)
Published by the Minneapolis American Indian Center
1530 E. Franklin Avenue
Minneapolis, MN 55404

Indian Country Today (weekly)
Box 2180
Rapid City, SD 57709

News from Indian Country (twice monthly)
Rt. 2, Box 2900-A
Hayward, WI 54843

SELECTED LIBRARIES WITH LARGE COLLECTIONS

Alaska Native Language Center
University of Alaska
Fairbanks, AK 99775

Center for Great Plains Studies
University of Nebraska
1213 Oldfather Hall
Lincoln, NE 68588-0314

Heard Museum Library
22 E. Monte Vista Road
Phoenix, AZ 85004

Institute of American Indian Arts Library/Native American Videotapes Archives
Learning Resource Center
College of Santa Fe

Alexis Hall, St. Michael's Drive
Santa Fe, NM 87501

Library of Congress
1st and Independence Ave., S.E.
Washington, DC 20540

Milwaukee Public Museum Library
600 N. Wells Street
Milwaukee, WI 53233

Museum of the American Indian Library
Huntington Free Library
9 Westchester Square
Bronx, NY 10461

National Anthropological Archives/Smithsonian Institution
Natural History Building
1st and Constitution Ave., N.W.
Washington, DC 20560

National Archives and Records Administration
8th and Pennsylvania Ave., N.W.
Washington, DC 20408

National Indian Education Association Library
1819 H Street, N.W., Suite 800
Washington, DC 20006

National Indian Law Library
Native American Rights Fund
1522 Broadway
Boulder, CO 80302-6296

Newberry Library
60 West Walton
Chicago, IL 60610

New York Public Library
42nd Street and Fifth Avenue
New York, NY 10018

Western History Collection
Division of Manuscripts and Library

University of Oklahoma
401 West Brooks Street
Norman, OK 73069

NATIVE AMERICAN PERIODICAL ARCHIVES

American Native Press Archives
Stabler Hall 502
2801 South University Avenue
Little Rock, AR 72204

• Contains over 1000 periodical titles published by American Indians and Alaska Natives

State Historical Society of Wisconsin
816 State Street
Madison, Wisconsin 53706

• Contains largest collection of Native American newspapers in the world

STATE HISTORICAL SOCIETY ARCHIVAL COLLECTIONS

Some historical societies have special Indian archives. The Oklahoma Historical Society in Oklahoma City, has an Indian Archives Division housing many original documents relating to a number of tribes. The Colorado Historical Society has materials from the Rosebud Indian Agency. The Idaho State Historical Society has Nez Percé and Shoshone literature. The Minnesota Historical Sociey has special collections on Ojibwe and Dakota tribes. Check with other state historical societies to see if they have Indian archival collections.

ORAL HISTORY COLLECTIONS

The Duke Oral History Project was begun at several places across the United States in the 1960s and 1970s. Regional interviews were conducted at the Universities of Oklahoma, South Dakota, New Mexico, Utah, and Florida. Some tribes have begun their own oral history projects. For example, in Oklahoma, the Kiowa, the Citizen Band Potawatomi, the Creek, the Western Oklahoma Delaware, the Fort Sill Apache, and the Chickasaw Nation have all begun taping people on audio or video.

TRIBAL COLLEGES

Some tribally controlled community colleges, including the following, have collections of manuscript materials that may be available for research purposes.

Bay Mills Community College
Route 1, Box 315-A
Brimley, MI 49715

Blackfeet Community College
Box 819
Browning, MT 59417

Cheyenne River Community College
P.O. Box 220
Eagle Butte, SD 57625

College of the Menominee Nation
P.O. Box 1179
Keshena, WI 54135

Crownpoint Institute of Technology
P.O. Box 849
Crownpoint, NM 87313

D.Q. University
P.O. Box 409
Davis, CA 95617

Dull Knife Memorial College
P.O. Box 98
Lame Deer, MT 59043

Fond du Lac Community College
2101 14th Street
Cloquet, MN 55720

Fort Belknap Community College
P.O. Box 159
Harlem, MT 59526

Fort Berthold Community College
P.O. Box 490
New Town, ND 58763

Fort Peck Community College
P.O. Box 398
Poplar, MT 59255-0398

Haskell Indian Nations University
155 Indian Avenue
Lawrence, KS 66046

Lac Courte Oreilles Ojibwa Community College
R.R. 2, Box 2357
Hayward, WI 54843

Leech Lake Community College
Route 3, Box 100
Cass Lake, MN 56633

Little Big Horn Community College
Box 370, Crow Center
Crow Agency, MT 59022

Little Hoop Community College
P.O. Box 269
Fort Totten, ND 58335

Lummi College of Fisheries
P.O. Box 11
Lummi Island, WA 98262

Navajo Community College
Tsaile Rural Post Office
Tsaile, AZ 86556

Nebraska Indian Community College
P.O. Box 752
Winnebago, NE 68071

Northwest Indian College
2522 Kwina Road
Bellingham, WA 98226

Oglala Sioux Community College
P.O. Box 490
Kyle, SD 57752

Red Crow College
P.O. Box 1258
Cardston, Alberta
Tok-Oko, Canada

Salish-Kootenai Community College
P.O. Box 117
Pablo, MT 59855

Saskatchewan Indian Federated College
127 College West
University of Regina
Regina, Saskatchewan
Canada S4S OA2

Sinte Gleska University
P.O. Box 490
Rosebud, SD 57570

Sisseton-Wahpeton Community College
Old Agency, P.O. Box 689
Sisseton, SD 57262

Southwest Indian Polytechnic Institute
Box 10146
Albuquerque, NM 87184

Standing Rock College
HC 1, Box 4
Fort Yates, ND 58538

Stone Child Community College
Rocky Boy Route, Box 1082
Box Elder, MT 59521

Turtle Mountain Community College
P.O. Box 340
Belcourt, ND 58316

United Tribes Technical College
3315 University Drive
Bismarck, ND 58501

ACKNOWLEDGMENTS

Permission to reprint copyrighted material is gratefully acknowledged. Every reasonable effort to trace copyright holders of materials appearing in this book has been made. Information that will enable the publisher to correct any error or omission will be welcomed. Errors brought to our attention will be corrected in subsequent printings.

FAMILY

"Hidatsa Kinship": Originally published as "Wa-Hee-Nee: An Indian Girl's Story Told by Herself (to Gilbert L. Wilson)" in *North Dakota History: Journal of the Northern Plains* 38, nos. 1 and 2 (Winter/Spring 1971). Reprinted by permission of the State Historical Society of North Dakota.

"Playing Family": From Grenville Goodwin, Social Organization of the Western Apache. Copyright © 1942 by the Department of Anthropology, University of Chicago Press. Reprinted by permission of the Department of Anthropology, University of Chicago.

"Without the Family We Are Nothing": From B.W. and E.G. Aginsky, *Deep Valley*. Stein and Day. Copyright © 1967 by Burt W. and Ethel G. Aginsky.

"Kinship Was the All-important Matter": Reprinted from Ella Deloria, *Speaking of Indians*. Copyright © by the University of South Dakota Press. Reprinted by permission of the University of South Dakota Press.

"*Tiospayes:* Lakota Relatives": From Vivian One Feather, Copyright © 1972 by Black Hills State University. Reprinted by permission of Black Hills State University.

"Hopi Clans": From Emory Sekaquaptewa, "Preserving the Good Things of Hopi Life" in *Plural Society in the Southwest.* Copyright © 1972 by the Trustees of the Weatherhead Foundation. Reprinted by permission of the Trustees of the Weatherhead Foundation.

"Traditional Indian Family Values": From Arthur L. McDonald, "Why Do Indian Students Drop Out of School?" in *The Schooling of Native America* (1978), 81–83. Copyright © 1978 by the American Association of Colleges for Teacher Education. Reprinted by permission of the American Association of Colleges for Teacher Education.

"Family Is a Matter of Clan Membership": From Paula Gunn Allen, *The Sacred Hoop*. Copyright © 1986, 1992 by Paula Gunn Allen. Reprinted by permission of Beacon Press.

"I Was Taught by My Mother": This excerpt is reprinted with permission of the publisher from David Neel, *Our Chiefs and Elders: Words and Photographs of Native Leaders* (Vancouver: UBC Press, 1992). Copyright © 1992 by the University of British Columbia Press. All rights reserved.

"There Is Strength in the Family": From Ed Edmo, "Finding the Best of Two Worlds." Copyright © by Ed Edmo. Reprinted courtesy of Ed Edmo, Northwest Indian Child Welfare Association.

"We Went to Live with Grandma": From Ardith Morrow, "My Grandmother" in *Speaking of Ourselves,* September 1990. Reprinted by permission of the Minnesota Chippewa Tribe.

LAND AND ITS RESOURCES

"Water Is as Precious as Food": From Leo W. Simmons, *Sun Chief: Autobiography of a Hopi Indian.* Copyright © 1963 by Yale University Press. Reprinted by permission of the publisher.

"Corn: The Staff of Life": From *Me and Mine: The Life Story of Helen Sekaquaptewa* as told to Louise Udall. Copyright © 1969 by the University of Arizona Press. Reprinted by permission of the University of Arizona Press.

"The Pueblos Rely on Deer": Excerpted from Sylvester M. Morey and Olivia L. Gilliam, editors, *Respect for Life*, copyright © 1974 by The Myrin Institute, New York, 1974. Reprinted by permission of the publisher.

"Whale Hunting Season": From Helen Slwooko Carius, *Sevukakmet: Ways of Life on St. Lawrence Island*. Copyright © 1979 by Alaska Pacific University Press. Reprinted by permission of Alaska Pacific University Press.

"Fire and Water": Reprinted from *Indian Water Policy in a Changing Environment* (Oakland, Calif. 1982), Copyright © 1982 by the American Indian Training Program, Inc. Reprinted by permission of the publisher, American Indian Lawyer Training Program, Inc.

"My People Never Killed a Tree Unnecessarily": From Dorothy Haegert, *Children of the First People* (Tillicum/Arsenal Pulp, 1983). Copyright © 1983 by Dorothy Haegert. Reprinted by permission of Tillicum/Arsenal Pulp.

"They're Taught Not to Waste Anything": From Moses Cruikshank, *The Life I've Been Living* . Copyright © 1986 by the University of Alaska Press. Reprinted by permission of the University of Alaska Press.

"Spirituality and the Environment": This excerpt is reprinted with permission of the publisher from David Neel, *Our Chiefs and Elders: Words and Photographs of Native Leaders* (Vancouver: UBC Press, 1992). Copyright © 1992 by the University of British Columbia Press. All rights reserved.

"Water Is the Giver of Life": Reprinted from *Oregon Humanities: A Journal of Ideas and Information* (Winter 1990), 8–10. Copyright © 1990 by the Oregon Council for the Humanities. Used with permission by the Oregon Council for the Humanities.

"Ensoulment of Nature": From Gregory A. Cajete, "Land and Education." Copyright © 1993 by Gregory A. Cajete. Reprinted by permission of Dr. Gregory Cajete, Santa Clara Pueblo.

LANGUAGE

"In Our Language There Is No Profanity": From *In the Days of Victorio: Recollections of a Warm Springs Apache*, edited by Eve Ball. Copyright © 1970 by the University of Arizona Press. Reprinted by permission of the University of Arizona Press.

"Teaching His Language Back to His Tribe": From Dorothy Haegert, *Children of the First People* (Tillicum/Arsenal Pulp, 1983). Copyright © 1983 by Dorothy Haegert. Reprinted by permission of Tillicum/Arsenal Pulp.

"The Origin of Sign Language": Approximately 2.5 pages from Percy Bullchild, *The Sun Came Down*. Copyright © 1985 by Percy Bullchild. Reprinted by permission of HarperCollins Publishers, Inc.

"Language Is Life": Reprinted from Laura Coltelli, *Winged Words: American Indian Writers Speak* by permission of the University of Nebraska Press. Copyright © 1990 by the University of Nebraska Press.

"The Power and Beauty of Language": From N. Scott Momaday, "Personal Reflections." Copyright © by N. Scott Momaday. Reprinted by permission of N. Scott Momaday.

"Ögwehöwe:ka:? Languages": From *Ögwehöwe:ka:?: Native Languages for Communication, New York State Syllabus*. Reprinted with permission of the University of the State of New York.

"The Spoken Word Is Revered": From Anna Lee Walters, *Talking Indian: Reflections on Survival and Writing* (Ithaca, New York: Firebrand Books). Copyright © 1992 by Anna Lee Walters. Reprinted by permission of Firebrand Books.

"My Algonquin Vocabulary": From Deborah Decontie, "My Viewpoint on Native Languages." Copyright © by Deborah Decontie. Reprinted by permission of Deborah Decontie.

"We Must Encourage the Use of Our Language": From Lydia Whirlwind Soldier, "Survival and Restoration: Lessons from the Boarding School." Copyright © by Lydia Whirlwind Soldier. Reprinted by permission of Lydia Whirlwind Soldier and *Tribal College*.

NATIVE EDUCATION

TRADITIONAL STORYTELLING

"Uncle and Aunt, Tell Us Stories": Excerpt from Morris E. Opler, *Apache Odyssey: A Journey Between Two Worlds.* Copyright © 1969 by Holt, Rinehart and Winston, Inc. Reprinted by permission of the publisher.

"Cheyenne Stories": From John Stands in Timber with Margot Liberty and Robert M. Utley, *Cheyenne Memories.* Copyright © 1967 by Yale University Press. Reprinted by permission of the publisher.

"Stories Have a Life of Their Own": Reprinted from *Journal of Ethnic Studies* 13 (Winter 1986), with the permission of Western Washington University.

"Stories Were Told in the Wintertime": From Margaret B. Blackman, *Sadie Brower Neakok: An Iñupiaq Woman.* Copyright © 1989 by the University of Washington Press. Reprinted with permission of the University of Washington Press.

"Now, You Tell a Story!": From Robin K. Wright, *A Time of Gathering: Native Heritage in Washington State.* Copyright © 1991 by the Burke Museum and University of Washington Press. Reprinted with permission of the University of Washington Press.

"Retelling Navajo Stories": From Luci Tapahonso, "Singing in Navajo, Writing in English." Copyright © by Luci Tapahonso. Reprinted by permission of Luci Tapahonso and *Culturefront.*

"Coyote Stories": From Janet Campbell Hale, *Bloodlines: Odyssey of a Native Daughter.* Copyright © 1993 by Janet Campbell Hale. Reprinted by permission of Random House, Inc.

"Her Stories Taught Us a Lesson": From Wilma Mankiller and Michael Wallis, *Mankiller: A Chief and her People.* Copyright © 1993 by Wilma Mankiller. Reprinted by permission of St. Martin's Press Inc., New York, New York.

TRADITIONS

"The Council-Tent Is Our Congress": From Sarah Winnemucca Hopkins, *Life Among the Piutes: Their Wrongs and Claims.* Copyright © 1969 by Sierra Media, Inc. Reprinted by permission from Chalfant Press, Inc.

"Rules of Polite Behavior": From Luther Standing Bear, *Land of the Spotted Eagle.* Reprinted by permission of Jeff Standing Bear.

"The Assiniboines' Twelve-Moon Calendar": From James Larpenteur Long, *The Assiniboines: From the Accounts of the Old Ones Told to First Boy (James Larpenteur Long),* edited by Michael Stephen Kennedy. Copyright © 1961 by the University of Oklahoma Press. Reprinted by permission of the University of Oklahoma Press.

"We Counted Time by Sleeps": From Carl Sweezy, *The Arapaho Way: A Memoir of Indian Boyhood,* edited by Althea Bass. Copyright © 1966 by Althea Bass. Reprinted by permission of Crown Publishers, Inc.

"Eskimo Moon Names": From *I, Nuligak,* edited by Maurice Metayer. Reprinted with permission of Stoddart Publishing Co., Limited, Don Mills, Ontario, Canada.

"Tattooing and Nose Piercing": From Florence C. Shipek, *Delfina Cuero: Her Autobiography. An Account of Her Last Years and Her Ethnobotanic Contributions.* Menlo Park, California: Ballena Press, 1991. Reprinted by permission of Florence C. Shipek.

"They Give Away": From "Myrtle Lincoln" in the Duke Indian Oral History Collections. Reprinted by permission of the Western History Collections, University of Oklahoma Libraries.

"Avoiding In-Laws": From Kathy Weist, *Belle Highwalking: The Narrative of a Northern Cheyenne Woman.* Copyright © 1979 by the Montana Council for Indian Education. Reprinted by permission of the Montana Council for Indian Education.

"Male and Female Relatives": From John (Fire) Lame Deer and Richard Erdoes, *Lame Deer: Seeker of Visions.* Copyright © 1972 by John Fire/Lame Deer and Richard Erdoes. Reprinted by permission of Simon & Schuster, Inc.

"The Museum of the Plains White Person": From Rayna Green, "After Feast Speech: Contemporary Indian Humor." Reprinted by permission of Rayna Green.

"We Were a Sharing People": Excerpted from Ignatia Broker, *Night Flying Woman: An Ojibway Narrative.* Copyright © 1983 by the Minnesota Historical Society. Reprinted by permission of the Minnesota Historical Society.

"Potlatches": From *Walter Northway,* a publication of the Alaska Native Language Center, University of Alaska, Fairbanks, 1987. Reprinted by permission of the University of Alaska Press.

"Traditional Indian Sports": From J. B. Oxendine, *American Indian Sports Heritage* (Champaign, IL: Human Kinetics Publishers), xix, 3–6, 9. Copyright © 1988 by Joseph B. Oxendine. Reprinted by permission of the publisher.

"Contemporary Potlatches": From Mark Tucker, "Potlatches Are an Integral Part of Culture." Copyright © by Mark Tucker. Reprinted by permission of Mark Tucker.

"Indian Humor": From Joseph Medicine Crow, *From the Heart Of Crow Country*. Copyright © 1991 by Joseph Medicine Crow. Reprinted by permission of Crown Publishers, Inc.

"Powwows": From Arlene Hirschfelder and Martha Kreipe de Montaño, *Native American Almanac: A Portrait of Native America Today*. Copyright © 1993 by Prentice Hall General Reference. Reprinted by permission of Macmillan General Reference.

WORSHIP

"Puberty Fast": From Leonard Bloomfield, *Menomini Texts*. Reprinted by permission of the American Ethnological Society.

"Spiritual Training": Reprinted from *Mourning Dove: A Salishan Autobiography*, edited by Jay Miller, by permission of the University of Nebraska Press. Copyright © 1990 by the University of Nebraska Press.

"Bread Dance": From *Civilization and the Story of the Absentee Shawnee*, as Told to Florence Drake by Thomas Wildcat Alford. Copyright © 1936, 1979 by the University of Oklahoma Press. Reprinted by permission of the University of Oklahoma Press.

"*Lonewis* (Crying Dance)": From Frank F. Latta, "Yoimut's Story of the Lonewis" in *The Handbook of Yokuts Indians*, 1977 edition. Reprinted by permission of Monna Olson.

"*Dine'e* Rituals": From Irene Stewart, *A Voice in Her Tribe: A Navajo Woman's Own Story*. Copyright © by Ballena Press. Reprinted by permission of Ballena Press, Menlo Park, California.

"Crow Sun Dance": From *To Be An Indian: An Oral History*, edited by Joseph H. Cash & Herbert Hoover (reprint, St. Paul: Minnesota Historical Society, Borealis Books, 1995), 39–44. Reprinted by permission of Herbert T. Hoover.

"Medicine Man": From John (Fire) Lame Deer and Richard Erdoes, *Lame Deer: Seeker of Visions*. Copyright © 1972 by John Fire/Lame Deer and Richard Erdoes. Reprinted by permission of Simon & Schuster,Inc.

"The First Salmon Ceremony": From Fay G. Cohen, *Treaties on Trial: The Continuing Controversy Over Northwest Indian Fishing Rights*. Copyright © 1986 by the University of Washington Press. Reprinted with permission of the University of Washington Press.

"Baskets Are Like Jewels": From Julian Lang, "The Basket and World Renewal." Copyright © 1991 by Julian Lang. Reprinted by permission of Julian Lang, Karuk tribal scholar and artist. Reprinted from *Parabola, The Magazine of Myth and Tradition* 16, no. 3 (Fall 1991).

"Sweat Lodge Ceremony": From Linda Hogan, "All My Relations." Copyright © 1992 by Linda Hogan. Reprinted by permission of Linda Hogan. Reprinted from *Parabola, The Magazine of Myth and Tradition* 17, no. 1 (Spring 1992).

"Indian Healing Arts": From Joseph Medicine Crow, *From the Heart of Crow Country*. Copyright © 1991 by Joseph Medicine Crow. Reprinted by permission of Crown Publishers, Inc.

"The Pueblos Have No Word for 'Religion'": From Joe S. Sando, *Pueblo Nations: Eight Centuries of Pueblo Indian History* (Santa Fe, New Mexico: Clear Light Publishers). Copyright © 1992 by Joe S. Sando. Reprinted by permission of Clear Light Publishers.

DISCRIMINATION

"They Told Us That Indian Ways Were Bad": From Edwin Embree, *Indians of the Americas: Historical Pageant*. Copyright © 1993 by Edwin R. Embree, Copyright renewed © 1967 by Kate C. Embree. Used by permission of Houghton Mifflin Co.

"Too Many Scientists, Not Enough Chiefs": From Howard Rock, "Too Many Scientists, Not Enough Chiefs." Reprinted by permission of *Tundra Times*.

RECOMMENDED READINGS

GENERAL

Abbott, Lawrence, ed. *I Stand in the Center of the Good: Interviews with Contemporary Native American Artists.* Lincoln: Univesity of Nebraska Press, 1994.

Bruchac, Joseph, ed. *Survival This Way: Interviews with American Indian Poets.* Tucson: University of Arizona Press, 1987.

Brumble, H. David, III. *American Indian Autobiography.* Berkeley: University of California Press, 1988.

———. *An Annotated Bibliography of American Indian and Eskimo Autobiographies.* Lincoln: University of Nebraska Press, 1981.

Coltelli, Laura. *Winged Words: American Indian Writers Speak.* Lincoln: University of Nebraska Press, 1990.

Katz, Jane, ed. *Messengers of the Wind: Native American Women Tell Their Life Stories.* New York: Ballantine, 1995.

Krupat, Arnold. *Native American Autobiography: An Anthology.* Madison, Wisconsin: University of Wisconsin Press, 1994.

Nabokov, Peter, ed. *Native American Testimony: A Chronicle of Indian-White Relations from Prophecy to the Present.* New York: Viking, 1991.

Riley, Patricia, ed. *Growing Up Native American: An Anthology.* New York: William Morrow and Co., 1993.

Swann, Brian and Arnold Krupat. *I Tell You Now: Autobiographical Essays by Native American Writers.* Lincoln: University of Nebraska Press, 1987.

SELECTED AUTOBIOGRAPHIES

Alford, Thomas Wildcat [Shawnee]. *Civilization, as Told to Florence Drake.* Norman: University of Oklahoma Press, 1936.

Apess, William [Pequot]. *On Our Own Ground: The Complete Writings of William Apess, a Pequot.* Edited by Barry O'Connell. Amherst: University of Massachusetts Press, 1992. (*A Son of the Forest*, 1829, and other writings discussed).

Bennett, Kay (Kaibah) [Navajo]. *Kaibah: Recollections of a Navajo Girlhood.* Los Angeles: Westernlore Press, 1964.

Betzinez, Jason [Apache]. *I Fought with Geronimo.* Harrisburg, Pennsylvania: The Stackpole Co., 1959.

Black Elk [Oglala Sioux]. *Black Elk Speaks: Being the Life Story of a Holy Man of the Oglala Sioux*, as told to John Neihardt. Lincoln: University of Nebraska Press, 1932. (Reprinted).

Black Hawk [Sac]. *Black Hawk, an Autobiography.* Edited by Donald Jackson. Urbana: University of Illinois Press, 1955. Earlier editions: *Life of Ma-ka-tai-me-she-kia-kiak, or Black Hawk* (1833, 1834, 1836, 1842, 1847, 1916, 1932).

Blowsnake, Sam (pseudonym: Crashing Thunder) [Winnebago]. *The Autobiography of a Winnebago Indian.* Edited by Paul Radin. New York: Dover Publications, 1963.

Bullchild, Percy [Blackfeet]. *The Sun Came Down: The History of the World as My Blackfeet Elders Told It.* New York: Harper and Row, 1985.

Campbell, Maria [Metis]. *Halfbreed.* Toronto: McClelland and Stewart– Bantam, Ltd., 1973. (Reprinted)

Carius, Helen Slwooko [Eskimo]. *Sevukakmet: Ways of Life on St. Lawrence Island.* Anchorage: Alaska Pacific University Press, 1979.

Chona, Maria [Papago]. *The Autobiography of a Papago Woman.* Edited by Ruth Underhill. Menasha, Wisconsin: American Anthropological Association Memoirs, vol. 46, 1936. (Reprinted)

Cody, Iron Eyes [Cherokee]. *Iron Eyes Cody: My Life as a Hollywood Indian*. Edited by Collin Perry. New York: Everest House, 1982.

Copway, George (Kah-ge-ga-gah-bowh) [Ojibway]. *The Life, History, and Travels of Kah-ge-ga-gah-bowh*. Albany: Weed and Parsons, 1847. Several later editions. Also titled *Recollections of a Forest Life* (1850).

Crow Dog, Mary. *Lakota Woman*. With Richard Erdoes. New York: Grove Weidenfeld, 1990. (*Ohitika Woman*, sequel)

Cruikshank, Julie, in collaboration with Angela Sidney, Kitty Smith, and Annie Ned [Athabascan/Tlingit]. *Life Lived Like a Story: Life Stories of Three Yukon Native Elders*. Lincoln: University of Nebraska Press, 1990.

Cuero, Delfina [Diegueno]. *The Autobiography of Delfina Cuero*. Edited by Florence Shipek. Los Angeles: Dawson's Book Shop, 1968.

Davidson, Florence Edenshaw [Haida]. *During My Time: Florence Edenshaw Davidson, a Haida Woman*. Edited by Margaret B. Blackman. Seattle: University of Washington Press, 1982.

Delorme, Eugene Chief: *The Life History of Eugene Delorme, Imprisoned Santee Sioux*. Lincoln: University of Nebraska Press, 1994.

Dudley, Joseph Iron Eyes [Sioux]. *Choteau Creek: A Sioux Remembrance*. Lincoln: University of Nebraska Press, 1992.

Eastman, Charles [Santee Dakota]. *Indian Boyhood*. Boston: Little Brown and Co., 1902. (Reprinted)

Eastman, Charles Alexander [Santee Dakota]. *From the Deep Woods to Civilization: Chapters in the Autobiography of an Indian*. 1916. (Reprinted)

Geronimo [Apache]. *Geronimo's Story of His Life*. Told to S. M. Barrett. New York: Duffield and Co., 1906. (Reprinted)

Goodbird [Hidatsa]. *Goodbird the Indian: His Story, Told by Himself to Gilbert L. Wilson*. New York: Fleming H. Revell Co., 1914. (Reprinted)

Herbert, Belle [Athabascan]. *Shandaa: In My Lifetime*. Anchorage: University of Alaska Press, 1982.

Highwalking, Belle [Northern Cheyenne]. *Belle Highwalking: The Narrative of a Northern Cheyenne Woman*. Edited by Katherine M. Weist. Billings, Montana: Montana Council for Indian Education, 1979.

Hopkins, Sarah Winnemucca [Paiute]. *Life Among the Piutes: Their Wrongs and Claims*. New York: G. P. Putnam's Sons, 1883. (Reprinted)

Hungry Wolf, Beverly [Blackfeet]. *The Ways of My Grandmothers*. New York: William Morrow and Co., 1980.

Johnson, Broderick, ed. *Stories of Traditional Navajo Life and Culture, by Twenty-two Navajo Men and Women*. Tsaile, Arizona: Navajo Community College Press, 1977.

Johnston, Basil [Ojibway]. *Ojibway Heritage*. Lincoln: University of Nebraska Press, 1990.

Kakaianak, Nathan [Eskimo]. *Eskimo Boyhood: An Autobiography in Psychosocial Perspective*. Edited by Charles C. Hughes. Lexington: University of Kentucky Press, 1974.

Kaywaykla, James [Apache]. *In the Days of Victorio: Recollections of a Warm Springs Apache*. Edited by Eve Ball. Tucson: University of Arizona Press, 1970.

Kegg, Maude (Naawakamigookwe) [Chippewa]. *Gabekanaansing/At the End of the Trail: Memories of Chippewa Childhood in Minnesota, with Texts in Ojibwa and English*. Edited by John Nichols. Greely, Colorado: University of Northern Colorado Museum of Anthropology, 1978.

LaFlesche, Francis [Omaha]. *The Middle Five: Indian Schoolboys of the Omaha Tribe*. Madison: University of Wisconsin Press, 1963.

Lame Deer, John (Fire) [Lakota] and Richard Erdoes. *Lame Deer: Seeker of Visions*. New York: Simon and Schuster, 1972.

Left Handed [Navajo]. *Son of Old Man Hat. A Navaho Autobiography*. Edited by Walter Dyk. New York: Harcourt Brace, 1938. (Reprinted)

Long, James Larpenteur (First Boy) [Assiniboine]. *The Assiniboines: From the Accounts of the Old Ones, Told to First Boy*. Norman: University of Oklahoma Press, 1961.

Lowry, Annie [Paiute]. *Karnee: A Paiute Narrative*. Edited by Lalla Scott. Reno: University of Nevada Press, 1966.

MacDonald, Peter. *The Last Warrior and the Navajo Nation*. With Ted Schwarz. New York: Orion Press, 1993.

Mankiller, Wilma [Cherokee]. *Mankiller: A Chief and Her People*. With Michael Wallis. New York: St. Martin's, 1993.

Maxidiwiac [Hidatsa]. *Wa-Hee-Nee: An Indian Girl's Story, Told by Herself.* St. Paul, Minnesota: Webb Publishing, 1921. (Reprinted)

McCarthy, James [Papago]. *A Papago Traveler: The Memories of James McCarthy.* Edited by John G. Westover. Tucson: University of Arizona Press, 1985.

Medicine Crow, Joseph [Crow]. *From the Heart of the Crow Country: The Crow Indians' Own Stories.* New York: Orion, 1992.

Mitchell, Emerson Blackhorse [Navajo]. *Miracle Hill: The Story of a Navajo Boy.* Edited by T. D. Allen. Norman: University of Oklahoma Press, 1967.

Mitchell, Frank [Navajo]. *Navajo Blessingway Singer: The Autobiography of Frank Mitchell, 1881–1967.* Edited by Charlotte J. Frisbie and David P. McAllester. Tucson: University of Arizona Press, 1978.

Modesto, Ruby [Cahuilla] and Guy Mount. *Not for Innocent Ears: Spiritual Traditions of a Cahuilla Medicine Woman.* Angelus Oaks, California: Sweetlight Books, 1980.

Moises, Rosalio [Yaqui]. *The Tall Candle: The Personal Chronicle of a Yaqui Indian.* Edited by Jane Holden Kelley and William Curry Holden. Lincoln: University of Nebraska Press, 1971.

Momaday, N. Scott [Kiowa]. *The Names.* New York: Harper and Row, 1976.

———. *The Way to Rainy Mountain.* New York: Ballantine Books, 1969. (Reprinted)

Mountain Wolf Woman [Winnebago]. *Mountain Wolf Woman, Sister of Crashing Thunder: The Autobiography of a Winnebago Indian.* Edited by Nancy O. Lurie. Ann Arbor: University of Michigan Press, 1961. (Reprinted)

Mourning Dove (Christine Quintasket). *Mourning Dove: A Salishan Autobiography.* Edited by Jay Miller. Lincoln: University of Nebraska Press, 1990.

Neakok, Sadie Brower. *Sadie Brower Neakok An Iñupiaq Woman.* Edited by Margaret B. Blackman. Seattle: University of Washington Press, 1989.

Nequaptewa, Edmund [Hopi]. *Born a Chief: The Nineteenth-Century Hopi Boyhood of Edmund Nequaptewa.* Edited by David Seaman. Tucson: University of Arizona Press, 1993.

Nowell, Charles James [Kwakiutl]. *Smoke from Their Fires: The Life of a Kwakiutl Chief.* Edited by Clellan S. Ford. Hamden, Connecticut: Archon Books, 1941. (Reprinted)

Nuligak [Eskimo]. *I, Nuligak.* Edited by Maurice Metayer. Toronto: Peter Martin Associates, 1966.

Panquin, Ron [Chippewa]. *Not First in Nobody's Heart: The Life Story of a Contemporary Chippewa.* Ames: Iowa State University Press, 1992

Pitseolak [Eskimo]. *Pitseolak: Pictures Out of My Life.* Edited by Dorothy Eber. Montreal: Oxford University Press, 1971.

Pitseolak, Peter [Eskimo]. *People from Our Side: A Life Story with Photographs and Oral Biography.* Edited by Dorothy Eber. Edmonton, Alberta: Hurtig Publishers, 1975.

Plenty-Coups [Crow]. *American: The Life Story of a Great Indian.* Edited by Frank B. Linderman. New York: John Day Co., 1930. (Reprinted as *Plenty-Coups, Chief of the Crows*)

Pretty-Shield [Crow]. *Red Mother.* Edited by Frank B. Linderman. New York: John Day Co., 1932. (Reprinted as *Pretty-Shield: Medicine Woman of the Crows*)

Qoyawayma, Polingaysi (Elizabeth Q. White) [Hopi]. *No Turning Back: A True Account of a Hopi Girl's Struggle to Bridge the Gap between the World of Her People and the World of the White Man.* Edited by Vada Carlson. Albuquerque: University of New Mexico Press, 1964.

Rickard, Clinton [Tuscarora]. *Fighting Tuscarora: The Autobiography of Chief Clinton Rickard.* Edited by Barbara Graymont. Syracuse: Syracuse University Press, 1973.

Rogers, John (Chief Snow Cloud) [Chippewa]. *Red World: Memories of a Chippewa Boyhood.* Norman: University of Oklahoma Press, 1974.

Sanapia [Comanche]. *Sanapia, Comanche Medicine Woman.* Edited by David E. Jones. New York: Holt, Rinehart and Winston, 1972.

Sekaquaptewa, Helen [Hopi]. *Me and Mine: The Life Story of Helen Sekaquaptewa.* Edited by Louise Udall. Tucson: University of Arizona Press, 1969.

Senungetuk, Joseph E. [Eskimo]. *Give or Take a Century: An Eskimo Chronicle.* San Francisco: Indian Historian Press, 1971.

Sewid, James [Kwakiutl]. *Guests Never Leave Hungry: The Autobiography of James Sewid, a Kwakiutl Indian.* Edited by James P. Spradley. New Haven: Yale University Press, 1969.

Shaw, Anna Moore [Pima]. *A Pima Past*. Tucson: University of Arizona Press, 1974.

Silko, Leslie [Laguna Pueblo]. *Storyteller*. New York: Seaver Books, 1981.

Standing Bear, Luther [Lakota]. *Land of the Spotted Eagle*. New York: Houghton Mifflin, 1933. (Reprinted)

———. *My Indian Boyhood*. New York: Houghton Mifflin, 1931. (Reprinted)

Stands in Timber, John [Cheyenne]. *Cheyenne Memories*. Edited by Margot Liberty. Lincoln: University of Nebraska Press, 1967. (Reprinted)

Swan, Madonna [Lakota]. *Madonna Swan: A Lakota Woman's Story*. Told to Mark St. Pierre. Norman: University of Oklahoma Press, 1991.

Sweezy, Carl [Arapaho]. *The Arapaho Way: A Memoir of an Indian Boyhood*. Edited by Althea Bass. New York: Clarkson N. Potter, 1966.

Talayesva, Don (Sun Chief) [Hopi]. *Sun Chief: The Autobiography of a Hopi Indian*. Edited by Leo W. Simmons. New Haven: Yale University Press, 1942. (Reprinted)

Thompson, Lucy (Che-na-wah Weitch-ah-wah) [Yurok]. *To the American Indian: Reminiscenses of a Yurok Woman*. 1916. (Reprinted)

Two Leggings [Crow]. *Two Leggings: The Making of a Crow Warrior*. Edited by Peter Nabokov. New York: Thomas Y. Crowell Co., 1967. (Reprinted)

Walters, Anna Lee [Pawnee/Otoe]. *Talking Indian: Reflections on Survival and Writing*. Ithaca, New York: Firebrand Books, 1992.

Webb, George [Pima]. *A Pima Remembers*. Tucson: University of Arizona Press, 1959.

Whitewolf, Jim (pseudonym) [Kiowa]. *Jim Whitewolf: The Life of a Kiowa Apache Indian*. Edited by Charles S. Brant. New York: Dover Publications, 1969.

Wooden Leg [Cheyenne]. *Wooden Leg: A Warrior Who Fought Custer*. Edited by Thomas B. Marquis. Lincoln: University of Nebraska Press, 1931. (Reprinted)

Yava, Albert [Tewa-Hopi]. *Big Falling Snow: A Tewa-Hopi Indian's Life and Times and the History and Traditions of His People*. Edited by Harold Courlander. New York: Crown Publishers, 1978.

Yellowtail, Thomas [Crow]. *Yellowtail, Crow Medicine Man and Sun Dance Chief: An Autobiography*. Norman: University of Oklahoma Press, 1991.

Zitkala-Sa (Gertrude Bonnin) [Sioux]. *American Indian Stories*. Glorieta, New Mexico: Rio Grande Press, 1976. (Reprint of *Atlantic Monthly* articles from 1900–1902)

Zuni People. *The Zunis: Self-Portrayals*. Albuquerque: University of New Mexico Press, 1972.

INDEX

Page numbers in italics refer to illustrations